Career Planning

AGS PUBLISHING

by
Thomas F. Harrington
and
Spencer G. Niles
with Garbette A. M. Garraway

AGS Publishing
Circle Pines, Minnesota 55014-1796
800-328-2560

About the Authors

Thomas F. Harrington, Ph.D.

Thomas F. Harrington holds a Ph.D. in counseling from Purdue University and teaches vocational psychology and career counseling courses in the Department of Counseling and Applied Educational Psychology at Northeastern University in Boston. In 2004 he received the National Career Development Association's highest honor, The Eminent Career Award. He has edited or co-edited several books and is the co-author of the award winning *Harrington-O'Shea Career Decision-Making System*. He has served as President of the Association for Assessment in Counseling, a division of the American Counseling Association, and the Massachusetts Personnel and Guidance Association. He is a frequent speaker at regional, national, and international career development conferences.

Spencer G. Niles, Ed.D., LPC, NCC

Spencer G. Niles holds a Doctor of Education in Counselor Education from Penn State University and is currently Professor-in-Charge of the Counselor Education Program there. He has served as President of the National Career Development Association, President of the Pennsylvania Association of Counselor Education and Supervision, President of the Virginia Career Development Association, and editor of *The Career Development Quarterly*. In 2003, he received the American Counseling Association (ACA) David Brooks Distinguished Mentor Award and in 2004 he received the ACA Extended Research Award. He has been a visiting scholar at several international universities and is the author or co-author of over 75 publications. He has delivered over 75 presentations at international, national and regional conferences.

Garbette A. M. Garraway

Garbette A. M. Garraway holds master's degrees in English Education from Simon Fraser University, and Counseling Psychology from the University of British Columbia. He is currently a doctoral student in Counselor Education at Penn State University. He has worked as a teacher and a counselor in the public school system for 14 years. He has been a co-presenter at the National Career Development Association conference.

Photo credits for this textbook can be found on page 324.

The publisher wishes to thank the following educators for their helpful comments during the review process for *Career Planning*. Their assistance has been invaluable.

Kathy Bedre, Counselor, Flour Bluff High School, Corpus Christi, TX; **Larry Greer,** Special Day Class Teacher, Loara High School, Anaheim, CA; **Mary Hartfield,** Special Education Instructor in MIMS program, Marion Park Alternative School, Meridian, MS; **Debora J. Hartzell,** Lead Teacher for Special Education, Columbia and Lakeside High Schools, Atlanta, GA; **Karen Larimer,** Transition Coordinator, Keystone Area Education Agency, Elkader, IA; **Susan Loving,** Transition Specialist, Utah State Office of Education, Salt Lake City, UT; **Carole Mottar,** Coordinator, Renaissance Academy, River Falls, WI; **Ann C. Moore,** Transition Specialist, Spartanburg County School District Number 7, Spartanburg, SC; **Cindi A. Nixon,** Director, Special Services, Richland School District Two, Columbia, SC; **Karen M. Owens,** Special Education Teacher, Bruce High School, Bruce, MS; **Richard D. Scott,** Guidance Specialist, Maryland State Department of Education, Baltimore, MD; **Cecilia E. Williams,** ESE Teacher, Gaither High School, Tampa, FL; **Judy S. Wright,** Language Arts Instructor/Curriculum Director, Carlisle Community School, Carlisle, IA.

Publisher's Project Staff

Vice President of Curriculum and Publisher: Sari Follansbee; Director, Curriculum Development: Teri Mathews; Managing Editor: Julie Maas; Senior Editor: Jody Peterson; Development Assistant: Bev Johnson; Director, Creative Services: Nancy Condon; Production Coordinator/Designer: Katie Sonmor; Project Coordinator/Designer: Carol Bowling; Senior Project Coordinator: Barb Drewlo; Purchasing Agent: Mary Kaye Kuzma; Curriculum Product Manager: Brian Holl

© 2006 AGS Publishing
4201 Woodland Road
Circle Pines, MN 55014-1796
800-328-2560 • www.agsnet.com

Printed in the United States of America

ISBN 0-7854-4031-3

Product Number 94210

A 0 9 8 7 6 5 4 3 2 1

Contents

Career Profiles

Communication Connections

Gender and Careers

The Economy

On the Job

Get Involved

Portfolio Activities

Technology Notes

Writing Practice

Figures

Tables

How to Use This Book: A Study Guide

Welcome to *Career Planning*. Everyone needs to develop skills that will help them choose and plan for a career. Whether you are going on to a job or to a postsecondary school after high school, career planning skills will help you prepare for your future.

As you read the chapters and lessons in this book, you will learn skills that will help you assess yourself, make career decisions, and plan for your future. You will learn about many career opportunities in different industries. You will practice writing a résumé, preparing for interviews, and gathering references. You will also learn conflict resolution, self-advocacy, and time-management skills. In addition to making a career plan, you will learn about living a productive life outside of work.

How to Study

These tips can help you study more effectively:

◆ Plan a regular time to study.

◆ Choose a quiet place where you will not be distracted. Find a desk or table in a spot that has good lighting.

◆ Gather all the books, pencils, and paper you need to complete your assignments.

◆ Decide on a goal. For example, "I will finish reading and take notes on Chapter 1, Lesson 1, by 8:00."

◆ Take a five- or ten-minute break every hour to stay alert.

◆ If you start to feel sleepy, take a break and get some fresh air.

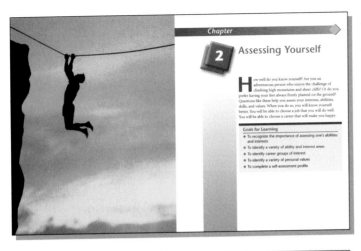

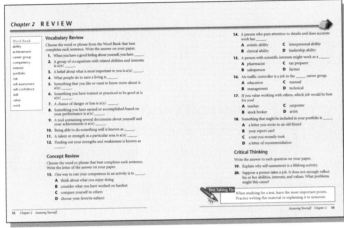

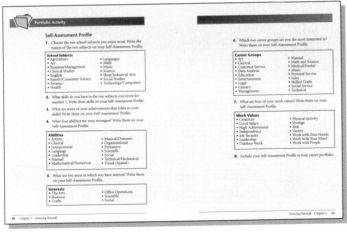

Before Beginning Each Chapter

◆ Read the chapter title and study the photograph. What does the photo say to you about the chapter title?

◆ Read the opening paragraphs.

◆ Study the Goals for Learning. The chapter review and tests will ask questions related to these goals.

◆ Look at the Chapter Review. The questions cover the most important information in the chapter.

◆ Look at the Portfolio Activity. Each chapter has an activity that will give you a chance to practice an important career planning skill.

Note the Features

Career Tips—Short, easy-to-use tips about career-related topics

Career Profiles—Up-close, high-interest looks at specific careers or jobs.

Communication Connection—Communication skills related to chapter or lesson content

The Economy—Aspects of the U.S. or the global economy that relate to careers

Gender and Careers—Aspects related to gender roles, gender stereotyping, and gender equality in the workplace

Get Involved—Civics, Community, or Volunteer activities that provide an opportunity to learn interpersonal and job skills

On the Job—Skills used in the workplace that are important for any career

Technology Notes—Uses of current technology related to the chapter or lesson topic

Think Positive—Examples of how a positive attitude can affect career success

Writing Practice—Writing tasks related to chapter or lesson content

Before Beginning Each Lesson

Read the lesson title and restate it in the form of a question. For example, write: *What is the importance of work?*

Look over the entire lesson, noting…

- ◆ photographs
- ◆ charts
- ◆ tables
- ◆ bold words
- ◆ vocabulary words
- ◆ headings
- ◆ lesson review questions

As You Read the Lesson

- ◆ Read the major headings.
- ◆ Read the paragraphs that follow the headings.
- ◆ Before moving on to the next heading, make sure you understand what you read. If you do not, reread the section or ask for help.

Using the Bold Words

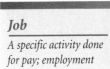

Job

A specific activity done for pay; employment

Knowing the meaning of all the boxed words in the narrow column will help you understand what you read.

These words appear in **bold type** the first time they appear in the text and are often defined in the paragraph.

The **job,** or work you choose to do for pay, will affect how you spend most of your time as an adult.

All of the words in the narrow column are also defined in the **glossary**.

Job (job) A specific activity done for pay; employment (p. 3)

Definitions of Occupational Titles

The titles of specific occupations are used throughout this textbook. They appear in tables and charts as well as in the text. All the occupational titles that appear in the book are defined in the **appendix.**

computer systems analyst studies and solves problems related to computer systems and software; finds ways to use computer systems better (Ch. 2, 4)

Word Study Tips

◆ Start a vocabulary file with index cards to use for review.

◆ Write one term on the front of each card. Write the chapter number, lesson number, and definition on the back.

◆ You can use these cards as flash cards by yourself or with a study partner to test your knowledge.

Occupation

Chapter 1, Lesson 1

A group of similar

or related jobs or

job skills

What to Do with a Word You Do Not Know

When you come to a word you do not know, ask yourself:

◆ Is the word a compound word?

◆ Can you find two words within the word? This could help you understand the meaning. For example: *salesperson*.

◆ Does the word have a prefix at the beginning?

◆ For example: *improper*. The prefix *im-* means "not," so this word refers to something that is not proper.

◆ Does the word have a suffix at the end?
For example: *variable, -able*. This means "able to vary."

◆ Can you identify the root word? Can you sound it out in parts? For example: *un known*

◆ Are there any clues in the sentence that will help you understand the word?

Look for the word in the margin box, glossary, appendix, or dictionary. If you are still having trouble with a word, ask for help.

Taking Notes in Class

As you read, you will be learning many new facts and ideas. Your notes will be useful and will help you remember when preparing for class discussions and studying for tests.

◆ Write the main ideas and supporting details.

◆ Use your own words.

◆ Keep your notes brief. You many want to set up some abbreviations to speed up your note-taking. For example: with = w/, United States = US, dollars = $, etc.

◆ Make notes on your worksheets or in your Student Workbook. Use them to study.

◆ Use the same method all the time. Then when you study for a test, you will know where to find the information you need to review.

Some students prefer taking notes on index cards.

Some students write down key ideas in a notebook

Using the Lesson Reviews

◆ Answer the questions for each lesson.

◆ Review the lesson content before moving on.

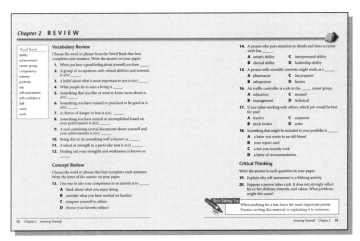

Using the Chapter Reviews

◆ Answer the questions under Vocabulary Review.

◆ Study the words and definitions. Say them aloud to help you remember them.

◆ Answer the questions under Concept Review.

◆ Use complete sentences to answer the questions under Critical Thinking.

Preparing for Tests

◆ Complete the Lesson Reviews and Chapter Reviews. Make up similar questions to practice what you have learned. You may want to do this with a classmate and share your questions.

◆ Review your answers to Lesson Reviews and Chapter Reviews.

◆ Test yourself on vocabulary words and key ideas.

◆ Read the Test-Taking Tips at the end of each chapter.

1

What Is a Career?

People work for a lot of reasons. Most people need to earn money to live. People also choose to work to use skills they enjoy, to express themselves creatively, and to help people. How you choose to make your living as an adult will have a great impact on the kind of life you will lead. It will affect how much money you make and how you spend most of your time. Your job will affect how much freedom you have to be creative. It will also affect what kind of training or education you will need. It could also determine where you will live. Choosing and preparing for a career that you will enjoy may not be a piece of cake. However, the rewards of doing work that suits your interests, talents, and goals will be great. In this chapter, we will look at what work is, why it is important, and how it is impacted by the economy.

Goals for Learning

◆ To define work

◆ To describe how the work you do affects many parts of your life

◆ To recognize work stereotypes

◆ To identify formal and informal workplaces

◆ To explain how the business cycle influences the job market

Work

What people do or how they spend their time to earn a living

The word **work** seems like a simple word, but what does it mean? If you look it up in a dictionary, you can see it has many different meanings. Work could mean the effort needed to get something done: "It takes a lot of *work* to build a bridge." It could mean something that someone has created: "That painting is one of the artist's greatest pieces of *work*." Work could also mean that something performs or operates as it should: "I changed the batteries, but I could not get my flashlight to *work*." In this lesson, the word *work* refers to how people spend their time to earn a living.

Why Is Work Important?

If work refers to how people spend their time to earn a living, what is the importance of work in your life? You might not know how to answer that question yet. First, think about examples of work you might see in your day-to-day life. You might see adults going to work or hear them talking about work. You see people at work whenever you turn on the television. On your way to school, you might see workers repairing roads or bus drivers driving to school.

A janitor is one example of a worker you might see at school.

> **Job**
> *A specific activity done for pay; employment*

At school, you see teachers, janitors, cafeteria workers, and office workers. There are also many workers you don't see. Workers build the school buses you ride, grow the food you eat, and repair the computers you use. Work is all around us! When you think about the many examples of work in your daily life, you can see that work is very important.

So why is work important to you? Well, the **job,** or work you choose to do for pay, will affect how you spend most of your time as an adult. Full-time workers in the United States spend between 40 and 50 hours per week at work. The type of work you choose to do will affect many parts of your life:

- How many years of school you will need to prepare for a job
- Who you spend your time with each week
- How much money and time you will have available for fun activities
- Where you will live
- How you will have to dress each work day

Look at these examples to see how different jobs compare.

Oceanographer
- Studies oceans and things in oceans
- Lives near the ocean
- Spends a lot of time on a boat
- Dresses in casual clothing

Accountant
- Keeps track of money and spending for a business
- Can work/live anywhere
- Spends a lot of time in an office
- Dresses in more formal clothing

Ski Instructor
- Teaches people to ski
- Lives where there is cold weather and snow or mountains
- Spends a lot of time outdoors
- Dresses for the weather, in outdoor clothing
- May need to find other work during the summer months

Because adults spend a lot of their time working, they arrange their lives according to the work they do. So, it makes sense that you should choose to work in an **occupation** that you enjoy. An occupation is a group of similar or related jobs or job skills. When you choose to work in an occupation you enjoy, you will likely be happier with your life. However, if you work in an occupation that you do not like, then your life might be less enjoyable. The occupation you choose is important if you want to live a more enjoyable life.

What Are the Reasons People Work?

Most people will say that work is important to them. However, they give different reasons for working. At first, you might think that everyone works for money. People want and need to be paid for the work they do. Money may not be the most important reason people work, however. For example, people who want to help others might work for less money if they can help other people in their job. Teachers, counselors, and ministers often view helping others as the most important part of their work. People who like to work with their hands might be mechanics or construction workers.

Career Profile

Park Ranger

Would you like to spend your days looking out over the Grand Canyon? Or watching storks in the swamps of the Florida Everglades? Or looking at the huge carvings of Washington, Lincoln, Jefferson, and Roosevelt at Mount Rushmore? Some lucky employees of the National Park Service have national parks as their workplaces. Park rangers do a variety of jobs. Some help visitors and make sure they care for our national parks. Others help care for forests or wildlife. Many states also employ park rangers. For example, Dan is a ranger at Governor Nelson State Park near Madison, Wisconsin. He spends his days observing and helping visitors to the park. One day he may issue a ticket to campers who disobey rules. Another day, he may give first aid to an injured lake swimmer. Not all park rangers have the great outdoors as their workplace. Some work in historic buildings. Still others do research or office work. The job market for park rangers is competitive, but it offers a wide variety of jobs and job locations.

Career Tip

To learn about careers, talk to people with interesting jobs. Ask about their training, typical day, and workplace.

These people enjoy fixing or building things. This makes their work meaningful to them. Artists, musicians, and actors express themselves creatively. They feel this is the most important part of the work they do. It is important to understand what makes work meaningful to you.

You have seen how work is important to people for different reasons. People who live in countries other than the United States also have different reasons for working. In some countries, people work to survive. They spend time hunting for food, growing crops, preparing meals, and caring for children. In other countries, people may be expected to do the same work as their parents. In some countries, parents choose the work that their children will do when they grow up. In many countries, including the United States, people choose a type of work because of its **prestige.** Prestige is how important people think something is. The meaning of work is different for different people.

These workers in China are harvesting rice.

What Are Work Stereotypes?

You may have noticed that when adults first meet each other, they often ask "What do you do?" People want to know what type of work others do. Then, they expect to know what kind of person someone is. For example, you meet a doctor. You might think that he or she is smart, rich, and hard working. You probably think he or she cares about the health of others. Maybe you meet a grade-school teacher. You might think he or she is kind, caring, and interested in helping others learn. Your ideas in both cases are based on work **stereotypes.** A stereotype is a general belief that many people have about an activity or group of people. For example, a general belief that many people have about basketball players is that "all basketball players are tall." This may be a true statement for many basketball players, but it is not true for all basketball players. In fact, some basketball players who were not very tall were great players. You must be very careful when using stereotypes because they are not always true.

Gender and Careers

One kind of work stereotype is gender stereotyping. For example, "Construction is a male field" or "Nursing is a job for women." At one time, there was some truth to gender stereotypes like these. Few women worked as carpenters or road builders. Few men went to nursing school. But today, almost every career is open to both men and women. Men have jobs in fields based on caring for others, such as child care and senior care. Women have jobs in fields where only men used to work, such as engineering and the military. Avoid thinking of an occupation as a "man's job" or a "woman's job." Also, avoid gender stereotypes when you observe jobs and the people who do them.

It is also important to be careful about drawing conclusions about jobs based on what you see on TV. Characters might act in ways that are based on work stereotypes. You might think you would like certain jobs based on what you see on TV and in the movies. However, these TV and movie images of what a job is like are not usually correct.

As you plan for your future, you need to understand the things you enjoy doing. You should know what things are important to you. This will help you to choose jobs and find the occupation that is right for you. This book will help you choose and plan for a **career.** Your career is the job path that you prepare for and follow throughout your lifetime.

Lesson 1 Review Write your answers to these questions on a sheet of paper.

1. What is the difference between a job and an occupation? Give an example of each.

2. What are some reasons people have for choosing a particular occupation?

3. What is an example of a work stereotype that you know of? Why should you be careful about using work stereotypes?

Technology Note

The Internet is an excellent resource for finding out more about specific careers. Suppose you are interested in the field of marine biology. You would like to know about some careers in this field. You can use a search engine to look up Web sites on marine biology careers. Start with the key words "marine biology careers." The search engine will lead you to a variety of articles about careers in the field. You can find out about several different careers. Some might be familiar to you, like "oceanographer." Others might be unfamiliar, such as "marine mammal trainer" and "whale biologist." Researching careers on the Internet is a good way to learn about different career paths. Your research will also help you avoid work stereotypes.

Workplace

Where work is done

You have learned ways in which work is important. You know that work is a major part of your life. It is also important to understand the **workplace**. A workplace is where work is done. Each job has a specific workplace. A construction worker has a different workplace than a schoolteacher. An accountant has a different workplace than a mechanic.

How Are Workplaces Different?

Workplaces have their own "cultures," or ways of dressing, behaving, and interacting. They can be formal or informal. In a formal workplace, you would have to wear a suit or a dress. You would not be able to joke and laugh with your coworkers. Your boss would expect you to be at your job on time. You would have to follow rules as you do your work. The military is an example of a formal workplace. Workers must be in uniform and salute officers. They have to follow a set schedule each day. The rules are strongly enforced.

A park ranger works outdoors and wears a uniform.

Communication Connection

Did you know that the way you dress is a form of communication? The clothes you wear send a message to people. A t-shirt and shorts say "time to relax." Wearing neat, tailored clothes shows respect for a job and for coworkers. Dressing properly for your job is key in any workplace.

In an informal workplace, you can wear more casual clothing. You can be more relaxed when dealing with your boss and coworkers. Work hours are often more flexible in an informal workplace. For example, college professors work in an informal workplace. They often can dress casually. They can usually schedule their own hours. For the most part, they are in charge of their own work. Look at the workplaces of these four jobs to see how they compare.

Job	Workplace
Zookeeper	outdoors, working with animals
Architect	indoors, working with computers and drawing equipment
Park Ranger	outdoors, taking care of land or animals
Teacher	indoors, working in a classroom with others

Each workplace is different. The workplace depends on the work being done. It also depends on what the workers in a job are like.

Writing Practice

What would your ideal workplace be like? Would it be an office with formally dressed workers? Would it be outdoors where the dress code is to be comfortable? Write a description of the kind of workplace you would like. Describe the surroundings, dress code, time flexibility, and interaction with coworkers.

Answering the phone is an important part of many jobs. Your voice may be the first impression a person gets of your company. How you answer the phone depends on the kinds of calls your company deals with. Also, formal workplaces have different phone styles than informal workplaces. Answering the phone in a clear, pleasant voice is appropriate for any workplace.

The military has a formal workplace.

Think about what jobs you might want. It is helpful to know what kind of a workplace you would like. Keep in mind that workplaces can be different even within the same job. For example, one university may be an informal workplace while another may be more formal. You need to understand the workplaces for the different jobs in which you may be interested. You need to find a job that fits who you are. This will help you to feel comfortable in your workplace.

Learning facts about workplaces in general is relatively easy. For example, it is easy to see that most park rangers work outdoors and wear uniforms. Learning about a specific workplace, however, takes more work. When you go on a job interview or talk to workers, you can get more detailed information about a workplace. You will learn more about interviews in Chapter 8.

How Does the Economy Affect Work?

Economy

State of business of an area or country, including how resources are used for goods and services

Job security

An understanding that workers will not lose their jobs

Interest rate

A percentage of money charged for borrowing money

Business cycle

The pattern of ups and downs in production and need, supply and demand, in the economy

In addition to understanding the workplace, you need to know how the **economy** affects work. The economy is the state of business of an area or country, including how resources are used for goods and services. Perhaps the most important thing to know is how the economy can impact **job security.** Job security is an understanding that workers will not lose their jobs. For example, one part of the economy deals with **interest rates.** These rates reflect the cost of borrowing money. If interest rates are low, it costs less to borrow money. If interest rates are high, it costs more to borrow money.

With high interest rates, people may not be able to buy certain things. When interest rates are low, more people can afford to buy a home. When more people are buying homes, the need to build more homes increases. So, more homes are built. Then, more people are able to find work as carpenters, plumbers, and painters. There are also more jobs in banks, where people borrow money to build homes. When more people are finding jobs, then more people are able to buy things. Then, more people are needed to work in places like department stores, grocery stores, and car dealerships. This pattern is called the **business cycle.**

Get Involved

Young people looking for jobs have a challenge. Most do not have much work experience. One excellent way to get work experience is to volunteer. High school students can volunteer in their communities after school and on weekends. In the summer, they can volunteer full time. For example, many young people volunteer at Boys and Girls Harbor each summer. This is a summer camp on Long Island, New York. It is for children from Harlem in New York City. Teens from all over the country volunteer their services. They work and play with children. They help maintain the camp with painting and repair projects. Volunteer service says a lot about a potential employee. One volunteer said, "I not only helped out others but I also learned about myself."

The Business Cycle

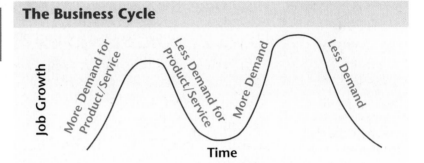

What Affects the Business Cycle?

Many things can affect the business cycle. Events like September 11, 2001, can have a big impact on the economy. The cost of oil and other products we buy from other countries can affect the economy. The cost of products we sell can also cause ups and downs in the business cycle.

Certain jobs are more by influenced by changes in the business cycle than others. Jobs related to homebuilding are good examples of jobs that are influenced by the business cycle. When the business cycle is positive (interest rates are low and it costs less to borrow money), there are more work opportunities. When the business cycle is not as positive (interest rates are high and it costs more to borrow money), more people are out of work. When people are out of work or do not have a job, they are **unemployed.**

It is important for workers to know if their jobs are influenced by the business cycle. Workers will need to plan for the times when they are unemployed. Ways to plan for this include saving money and identifying other jobs that can be done when regular employment is not available.

What Are Other Causes of Unemployment?

There are other reasons besides changes in the business cycle that people experience unemployment. For example, the demand for some jobs can decrease because of new inventions and technology. Today, jobs related to designing, building, and repairing typewriters are not in demand. They have been replaced with jobs related to the computer. In these situations, people who are unemployed often need to identify new jobs. They often need more education or training to get the new job they want.

Career Tip

Looking for a career that interests you?

Find out about a company on the Internet or at the library. Ask companies for brochures.

People can also be unemployed when their jobs are influenced by the change in season or the weather. For example, people who work as ski instructors must find other work to do in the summer months. Lifeguards in cold climates must find other work to do in the winter months. Some teachers need to find work to do in the summer to earn more money. It is usually easy to know if you are interested in a job that is affected by seasonal unemployment. Workers can plan for seasonal unemployment. They can save money. They can also find other jobs to do when they are not working their main jobs.

There are many things that are important to know about how the economy affects work. When workers know whether a job they are interested in is likely to be influenced by unemployment, they can plan for it when it happens.

Lesson 2 Review Write your answers to these questions on a sheet of paper.

1. What are some differences between a formal workplace and an informal workplace?
2. What are three ways to get more detailed information about a workplace?
3. What effect does the economy have on job security?
4. What effects do low interest rates have on the economy?
5. Jobs related to typewriters are not in demand today because of new technology. Describe another job with little demand today because of new inventions or technology.

The Economy

Unemployment is often related to a certain industry or region. For example, most Americans were working and making money during the 1920s. But many shoe and clothing factories in New England closed down. So unemployment was high in that region. In the 1970s, the steel industry faced challenges. There was less demand for steel, so many plants closed. Workers in steel factories in Indiana, Ohio, and Pennsylvania became unemployed. In the late 1980s, the oil industry in Texas and Louisiana had economic problems. Many oil industry employees in these states became unemployed. In the late 1990s, many Internet companies went out of business. Many of these companies were based in the "Silicon Valley" region of Northern California. This became an area of high unemployment.

Setting Goals

As you know, choosing a job affects many parts of your life. To choose a career path, you need to decide what you hope to achieve. You need to think about achievements in different aspects of your life.

Most people have both short-term goals and long-term goals. A short-term goal is one that you can reach in the near future. A long-term goal is one that can be reached in the more distant future.

For example, your short-term goal related to money may be to save enough money for a car. Your long-term goal related to money may be to buy a house in the next 15 years.

You may be unsure about the career path you will follow. Still, you can set job-related goals. Perhaps you know that you would like to be a manager by the time you are 25. Maybe you would like to own your own shop or business by the time you are 30.

Write one or more sentences to answer each question on page 15. Add the activity to your career portfolio.

One of your goals might be to travel to a different country.

1. What short-term goal have you achieved recently?

2. What long-term goal have you achieved in the past?

3. What are your short-term educational goals?

4. What are your long-term educational goals?

5. What are your short-term goals related to money?

6. What are your long-term goals related to money?

7. What short-term goals do you have for sports, travel, and other fun activities?

8. What long-term goals do you have for sports, travel, and other fun activities?

9. Where would you like to live in 5 years?

10. Where would you like to live in 15 years?

11. What kind of job would you like to have in 5 years?

12. What kind of job would you like to have in 15 years?

Chapter 1 REVIEW

Word Bank

business cycle

career

economy

job

job security

occupation

prestige

stereotype

unemployed

work

workplace

Vocabulary Review

Choose the word or phrase from the Word Bank that best completes each sentence. Write the answer on your paper.

1. A general belief held by many people about a certain activity or group of people is a(n) _____.

2. The state of business and use of resources in an area is the _____.

3. A group of similar or related jobs or job skills is known as a(n) _____.

4. Some people choose a type of work based on how important most people think it is, or its _____.

5. The pattern of ups and downs in supply and demand in the economy is known as the _____.

6. To be out of work is to be _____.

7. The way people spend their time earning a living is known as _____.

8. A formal or informal area where work is done is the _____.

9. The job path a person follows throughout a lifetime is a(n) _____.

10. The work you choose to do for pay is called a(n) _____.

11. An understanding that workers will not lose their jobs is _____.

Concept Review

Choose the word or phrase that best completes each sentence. Write the letter of the answer on your paper.

12. A week of work for full-time workers in the United States consists of _____.

    A 25 to 30 hours   **C** 40 to 50 hours

    B 30 to 40 hours   **D** 50 or more hours

13. The most important reason to work is _____.

    A money   **C** helping others

    B prestige   **D** different for each person

14. Being a ski instructor is an example of a job which _____.

 A does not require special clothing **C** involves a formal workplace

 B affects where a person lives **D** has great job security

15. An example of a work stereotype is that _____.

 A news reporters are very nosy **C** lawyers went to law school

 B accountants work with numbers **D** veterinarians treat animals

16. A bank where workers follow a strict schedule is an example of _____.

 A an informal workplace **C** a casual workplace

 B an unstructured workplace **D** a formal workplace

17. An example of a job affected most by the business cycle is that of _____.

 A an emergency-room nurse **C** an elementary school teacher

 B a carpenter working on new homes **D** a dentist

Critical Thinking

Write the answer to each question on your paper.

18. Why is it important for a person to carefully choose an occupation?

19. What advantages do American workers have over workers in many other countries?

20. Suppose you are interested in working in a casual, flexible workplace. What are three jobs you might like?

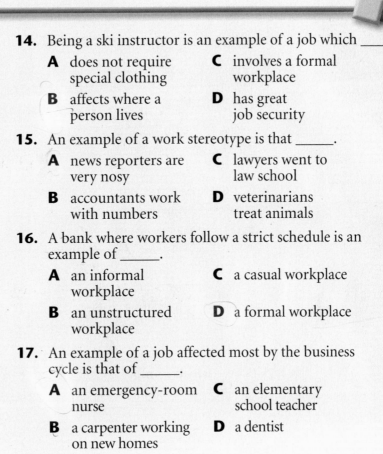

Test-Taking Tip

When studying for a test, work with a partner to write your own test questions. Then answer each other's questions. Check your answers.

2 Assessing Yourself

How well do you know yourself? Are you an adventurous person who enjoys the challenge of climbing high mountains and sheer cliffs? Or do you prefer having your feet always firmly planted on the ground? Questions like these help you assess your interests, abilities, skills, and values. When you do so, you will know yourself better. You will be able to choose a job that you will do well. You will be able to choose a career that will make you happy.

Goals for Learning

◆ To recognize the importance of assessing one's abilities and interests

◆ To identify a variety of ability and interest areas

◆ To identify career groups of interest

◆ To identify a variety of personal values

◆ To complete a self-assessment profile

In this lesson, you will use **self-assessment** to find out what you have liked learning in school. You can use this knowledge in many ways. You may be required to tell an admissions counselor or an employer what you are good at. Or, you may need to write a personal essay for an application. You should be able to describe your school experience and what your plans are for the future. To do this, you need to know what **skills** you have. A skill is something you can do because you have practiced or trained. You also need to know in which skills you have developed **competency.** When you have competency in something, you are able to do it well.

What Are Your Favorite School Subjects?

To investigate your skills and competencies, start by choosing what school subjects you like the most. Look at the school subjects listed here. Choose the two you like the best. For help, look at the list of possible class titles under each school subject.

Agriculture
animal science
farming
forestry
horticulture
landscaping

Art
drawing
fashion design
graphic design
interior decorating
painting
sculpture

Business and Management
accounting
business administration
management
marketing
sales

Clerical Studies
office practices
spreadsheets and databases
typing
word processing

English
communications
creative writing
essay writing
journalism
literature
public speaking

Family/Consumer Science
child care
cooking and food service
cosmetology (beauty care)
sewing

Finance
accounting
business law
economics

Health
health
physical education
recreational studies

Languages
Chinese
French
German
Italian
Japanese
Russian
Spanish

Math
algebra
basic math
calculus
geometry
pre-algebra
statistics

Music
band
choir
dance
drama
orchestra

Science
biology
chemistry
computer science
earth science
environmental science
geology
physical science
physics

Shop/Industrial Arts
automotive
carpentry
machine shop
metal working
plumbing
printing
woodworking

Social Studies
civics
government
history
political science
psychology
social work
sociology

Technology/Computers
computer-aided design (CAD)
computer programming
computer technology
drafting
engineering
electronics

What Skills Do You Have?

Now that you have chosen your favorite subjects, you need to choose some specific skills you learned in a course. This step may be more difficult than the first step. Think about why you chose the subjects you did. What skills do you have in those areas? For example, if you chose art as a favorite subject, you might have the following skills:

- sketching
- drawing portraits
- drawing cartoons
- etching on glass
- editing music or film
- painting
- making pottery

This student shows her skill of using a pottery wheel.

What Are Some of Your Achievements?

You could also think about some of your **achievements.** An achievement is something you have earned or done successfully based on your performance. For example, an achievement might be that a photograph you took won a prize at an art show. Knowing your achievements can show your competence—how good you are at performing an activity. You can rate your competence two ways. One way is to look at your grades over time. Let's say your grades show that you are better in math than in English. You would rate yourself as good in math. Another way is to compare yourself with others. You can use grades or feedback from teachers, coaches, and parents to do this. If you feel that others are better than you at a certain activity, you might rate yourself as average.

Lesson 1 Review Write your answers to these questions on a sheet of paper.

1. Why is self-assessment important?

2. List the two school subjects you like the most.

3. What is the difference between skill and competency?

4. List two skills you have and an achievement in each.

5. How would you rate yourself in the area you chose as your favorite subject? Why did you rate yourself the way you did?

Writing Practice

What was your most enjoyable learning experience? Recall a class or an after-school activity you especially liked. For example, you might remember a speech class in which you did well. Or you might recall a cooking or tennis class. Write a journal entry. Describe the experience. Explain why you enjoyed it.

Ability

A talent; something a
person is able to do well

Self-confidence

Feeling good about
oneself

An **ability** is something a person can do well. You know best
what things you are good at. These are your abilities. People
have different abilities. Some people do certain things better
than others. Things you do well are your strengths. Things you
have a hard time doing are your weaknesses. Everyone has
strengths and weaknesses. In this lesson, you will learn about
the 14 major work-related abilities.

How you feel about your ability to do an activity affects how you
perform that activity. For example, if you feel you talk differently
than others, you might not think you are a good communicator.
You might not feel comfortable talking to people. So, you may
not want to work in a job that requires you to talk to a lot of
people. Or, you might be good at fixing computers. Knowing
and believing that you are skilled with computers can help your
self-confidence. Feeling good about yourself can help you to
succeed. It can also help you find an occupation.

Now read about the 14 abilities on the next few pages. See what
occupations are listed for each ability area. Think about what
three or four abilities you believe are your strongest. These
abilities are your strengths.

A photographer has artistic ability.

Artistic

People who have this ability understand artistic ideas. They may use their skills to draw, paint, sculpt, or take photographs. They may also use their artistic ability to decorate, design, or create products. Artistic ability is important in these careers:

- art director
- cartoonist
- commercial designer
- engraver
- fashion designer
- industrial designer
- interior designer
- photographic developer
- professional photographer
- sketch artist

Clerical

People who have clerical ability pay attention to details. They do accurate work. They often use their eyes, hands, and fingers at the same time. They might enter figures in books and forms, or operate calculators, computers, and other office machines. Here are some clerical careers:

- bookkeeping clerk
- cashier
- data entry keyer
- medical records technician
- secretary
- teller
- police dispatcher
- postal service clerk

Interpersonal

People with this ability can communicate well. They are understanding, friendly, adaptable, and polite in many different situations. Most employers would agree that this is an important ability in any career. Careers that require interpersonal ability include the following:

- bank manager
- customer service representative
- elementary school teacher
- flight attendant
- home health aide
- human resources assistant
- police officer
- retail salesperson

Language

People who have this ability can use spelling, grammar, and punctuation correctly. They are skilled at writing letters, manuals, reports, proposals, or stories. They can speak clearly. They can also understand and respond to feedback. They know what questions to ask and when to ask them. Being able to communicate well through speaking and writing is a basic skill needed in any career. Language ability is very important in these careers:

- editor
- paralegal
- receptionist
- reporter
- sales manager
- secretary
- social worker
- special education teacher
- translator

A leader sets good examples for others.

Leadership

People who have leadership ability are able to get others to work together. They also have the ability to share thoughts, feelings, and ideas in order to explain a position. Leaders must be able to react quickly in emergencies. They may make choices that involve money or the safety of other people. The ability to lead is important in these careers:

- administrative assistant
- executive secretary
- educational administrator
- food service manager
- lawyer
- property or real estate manager
- surgeon

Manual

People with manual ability are skilled in the use of their hands, fingers, and eyes. They use these skills to operate equipment, adjust controls, use hand tools, or to build products. They can read and follow directions well. Careers in which manual ability is important may involve outdoor work. The jobs often require physical strength. Examples of these careers include the following:

- animal caretaker
- bus driver
- carpenter
- firefighter
- forest and conservation worker
- highway maintenance worker
- landscaper
- machine operator
- painter
- product assembler

Mathematical/Numerical

People who have mathematical and numerical ability are very good at solving problems in business, technology, or science. They use math skills to solve these problems. They are also able to express mathematical ideas aloud and in writing. Today's employers value mathematical and numerical ability in many careers. Here are some examples:

- accountant
- bookkeeping clerk
- cashier
- computer programmer
- computer software engineer
- financial analyst
- information systems manager
- mathematician
- medical assistant
- optometrist
- pharmacist
- teller

Musical/Dramatic

People who have musical ability have a keen ear for musical sounds. They might play instruments, sing or teach, or direct instrumental or vocal music. People with dramatic ability are skilled at acting. They interpret roles and express ideas and emotions through gestures and facial expressions. They may also produce, direct, or perform in plays. Careers that use musical and/or dramatic ability include the following:

- choral director
- dancer
- drama teacher
- music arranger
- musician
- radio/TV/movie producer
- singer

Organizational

Individuals with organizational ability know how to plan. They make sure the most important task is done first and on time. They can organize, process, and maintain records and information in a orderly way. Most employers expect employees to be well organized. Careers in which organizational ability is important include these:

- air traffic controller
- computer systems analyst
- medical and health services manager
- nurse
- operations research analyst
- police dispatcher
- tax preparer
- travel agent

A police dispatcher must be organized.

Persuasive

Persuasive people can influence others by sharing their own views and opinions. They can convince people to do things. They can get people to agree with certain ideas. Persuasive people are able to talk to others using clear language. They are good at selling things. These are some careers in which the ability to be persuasive is important for success:

- construction manager
- lawyer
- marketing manager
- psychiatrist
- retail salesperson
- secondary school teacher

Scientific

Individuals who have this ability are good at research, logic, or scientific thinking. They use their skills to solve problems. They might apply their skills in the medical sciences, life sciences, or natural sciences. They may diagnose or treat human and animal injuries and illnesses. Often they base their conclusions on information that can be measured or proven. Scientific ability is important for success in many careers. Here are some examples:

- agricultural inspector
- athletic trainer
- biologist
- dental assistant
- dietician
- electrical engineer
- licensed nurse practitioner
- physical therapist
- veterinarian

Social

People with social ability use logical thinking and special skills to counsel others. These people may help others identify and solve personal problems. People with social ability work well with others. Individuals who have this ability may gather and study information about other people. They may also work one-on-one or with groups of people. Careers requiring good social skills include the following:

- educational, vocational, or school counselor
- home health aide
- nurse
- psychiatric aide
- recreational worker
- social worker
- sociologist

Visual (Spatial)

People with visual or spatial ability can visualize what objects would look like from a different angle or point of view. They can see differences in size and shape. They understand how things fit together or come apart. Visual or spatial ability is important for success in many careers. Some of these careers include the following:

- carpenter
- dentist
- fashion designer
- graphic designer
- interior designer
- landscaping and groundskeeping worker
- mechanical drafter
- surveyor

Technical/Mechanical

Individuals with this ability understand technical and mechanical language. They understand how to set up and operate machines such as vending machines. They can also determine how to use or fix various machines. Many careers require technical/mechanical ability, including these:

- airplane pilot
- automotive master mechanic
- computer service technician
- electrician
- electronic equipment installer and repairer
- heating and air-conditioning mechanic

How Can You Develop Your Abilities?

To develop your abilities, you need to get involved in activities. You need to get experience. If you have never had a chance to play an instrument or to sing, how would you know your musical ability? Self-assessment can help you see what abilities you have. It can also show you in which areas you want to get more experience. It is helpful to know what abilities a job requires. You can then find out more about how you can develop that ability. For example, if you want to become an engineer, you might be more willing to learn about math and physics.

A landscaper has visual ability.

Activities outside of school can also give you information about your abilities. For example, if you play a sport, you might learn whether you are a good leader. Do you want to be the captain of the team? Do you enjoy leading or being in charge of others? Feedback from others can be helpful. They can give you specific information on how well you are performing a task. You can also find out if you need to work on certain skills in order to get better at them.

Lesson 2 Review Write your answers to these questions on a sheet of paper.

1. What is an ability?

2. What are your four strongest abilities?

3. How can your self-confidence affect your abilities?

4. What school subjects, out-of-school activities, part-time work, or volunteer activities can help you improve in an ability area? Have you done any of these yet?

The Economy

A current issue related to the U.S. economy is offshore outsourcing. In offshore outsourcing, American companies give work to employees in other countries. They hire the employees to do some specific jobs. For example, a computer company may hire workers in India. They pay the employees to help customers who call the company. The American companies save money because employees in India will work for less. But the American companies lay off the American workers who had done the job. Some people feel that this type of outsourcing leads to more unemployment for Americans. Others believe that it helps American companies make more money. They say that strong companies help the American economy. Lawmakers are currently debating the issue of offshore outsourcing.

Interest

Something you like, want to know more about, or want to see or do

Career group

Occupations with related abilities, interests, and education requirements

Interests are things that you like or want to know more about. If you know your interests, you can more easily plan a career. For many people, interests are things that they can do well. But you might have an interest in something that you cannot do well. In this way, interests are different from abilities. It can be easier to assess your abilities in an area you like or have interest in.

By exploring your interests, you can discover what school or work plans might be the best for you. This lesson will show you two ways to find out your interests. One way is to choose which of the six interest areas are the most important to you. Another way is to use **career groups.** A career group includes several related occupations.

What Are Your Interests?

Look at the six interest areas on pages 33 and 34. Interests can show you details about yourself. See what occupations are listed under each interest area. You will probably have interests in several areas. Think about two interest areas that best describe you and your interests.

Technology Note

You can find career profiles on the Internet. Type key words such as "Career Profiles" on a search engine. You will find many Web sites about careers. In fact, you will probably be surprised at how many different careers exist. The sites provide some or all of the following facts:

- Pay
- Education and training needed
- Job descriptions
- Future demand
- Related careers

The Arts

People interested in the arts enjoy music, painting, writing, and entertaining others. They are creative and independent. They enjoy visiting museums, going to the theater, and reading books. Here are some jobs related to the arts:

- actor/actress
- artist
- editor
- fashion designer
- musician
- photographer
- radio/TV announcer
- reporter

Business

People with business interests are leaders. They are good at selling things. They can also easily get people to think the way they do. They enjoy coming up with new ideas. People interested in business might work at these jobs:

- bank manager
- business executive
- lawyer
- salesperson

Crafts

People with interests in crafts like to work with tools and build things. They enjoy seeing the results of their work. They are interested in mechanical activities. They like work that requires physical strength. Jobs related to crafts include the following:

- animal caretaker
- auto mechanic
- construction equipment operator
- cook
- electrician
- farmer
- truck driver

Office Operations

These people work with words and numbers. They like jobs in which they know exactly what to do. They are well organized. Here are some jobs in the office operations area:

- accountant
- bank teller
- computer operator
- medical records technician
- secretary
- tax preparer

Career Tip
When talking to
others about finding
a job, share your
career goals
with them.

Scientific

People with scientific interests believe math and science are important. They are curious and creative. They study a lot and often work by themselves. They enjoy thinking about ideas. Scientific jobs include the following:

- architect
- biologist
- computer scientist
- economist
- forester
- mechanical engineer
- medical lab technician
- pharmacist
- physician
- veterinarian

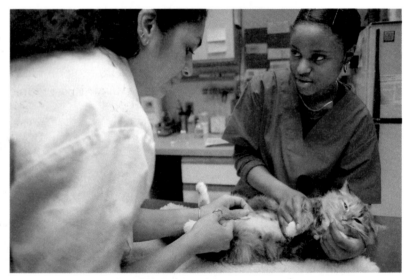

A veterinarian may have scientific and social interests.

Social

Social people enjoy helping others. They like to provide services for others. Social people get along well with others. They have good communication skills. People with social interests might have one of these jobs:

- clinical psychologist
- counselor
- nurse
- police officer/sheriff
- recreation worker
- school administrator
- social worker
- teacher

It is important to know what your interests are. Counselors, college admissions officers, and employers will ask what you are interested in. You can use the words from the six interest areas to answer their questions.

What Career Groups Interest You?

You are now ready to explore the career groups. A career group includes related occupations. The occupations in each group are related by abilities, interests, and educational requirements. Read the occupations under all 18 groups listed on the next two pages.

Art

- art teacher
- artist
- fashion designer
- floral designer
- graphic designer
- interior designer
- photographer

Clerical

- cashier
- court reporter
- hotel/motel clerk
- medical records technician
- police dispatcher
- receptionist
- secretary
- word processor

Customer Service

- hair stylist
- flight attendant
- park ranger
- police officer
- security guard
- taxi driver
- waiter/waitress

Data Analysis

- accountant
- auditor
- bookkeeping clerk
- computer operator
- financial analyst
- payroll clerk
- real estate appraiser

Education

- college administrator
- college professor
- elementary school teacher
- preschool teacher
- school administrator
- secondary school teacher

Entertainment

- actor/actress
- advertising manager
- comedian
- model
- producer
- radio/TV announcer
- radio/TV program assistant
- stage director

Legal

- customs inspector
- FBI agent
- insurance claims adjuster
- judge
- lawyer
- legal assistant
- police detective
- private investigator

Literary

- editor
- novelist
- playwright
- poet
- reporter
- technical writer
- translator

Management

- bank manager
- business executive
- farm manager
- hotel/motel manager
- office manager
- restaurant manager
- store manager

Manual

- animal caretaker
- construction laborer
- food preparation worker
- landscaper
- machine operator
- product assembler
- truck driver

Math and Science

- architect
- biologist
- chemist
- computer programmer
- database administrator
- engineer
- physicist
- Web site developer

Medical/Dental

- chiropractor
- dental hygienist
- dentist
- family practitioner
- optometrist
- pharmacist
- physical therapist
- veterinarian

Music

- choreographer
- composer
- conductor
- dancer
- music teacher
- musician
- producer
- singer

Personal Service

- child care worker
- coach
- emergency medical technician
- home health aide
- recreation leader
- vocational teacher

Skilled Crafts

- auto technician/ mechanic
- carpenter
- cook
- desktop publishing specialist
- electrician
- farmer
- electronics repairer
- military service

Social Service

- clergy
- clinical psychologist
- counselor
- dental hygienist
- nurse
- social worker
- sociologist

Sales

- auto salesperson
- buyer
- financial planner
- insurance agent
- real estate agent
- retail sales worker
- travel agent

Technical

- air traffic controller
- airline pilot
- computer support specialist
- diagnostic medical sonographer
- drafter
- medical technician
- surveyor
- technical illustrator

Career Tip
Talk to family members, friends, and other people you know about their jobs. Find out where they work and if they like their jobs.

Now choose the two career groups you like the most. What occupations appeal to you from those two groups? If you do not know what workers in an occupation do, ask your teacher or counselor or look it up in your school's career center. Here is an example of how your interests can help you learn what jobs you might like:

> Marcos likes people. He always likes to meet new people. He enjoys talking to them and finding out about them. Marcos also has an after-school job. He takes care of two children who live next door to him. He really likes helping them play and learn.

Marcos sees that he has social interest. He might want to think about a career as a teacher or child-care provider. He would probably be most happy in an occupation where he works with people every day. You will find out how you can get more information about an occupation in Chapter 3.

Lesson 3 Review Write your answers to these questions on a sheet of paper.

1. What is an interest?

2. List the two interest areas you like the most.

3. What is the difference between an interest and an ability?

4. What is a career group?

5. List the two career groups you like the most.

Career Profile

Nurse Practitioner

Nursing is a career for which there continues to be great demand. One nursing job that is growing in popularity is nurse practitioner. A nurse practitioner is a Registered Nurse who has two to three years additional training. This training allows the nurse practitioner to take on added responsibilities. A nurse practitioner is supervised by a doctor. Doctors often have nurse practitioners take medical histories and treat routine problems. A nurse practitioner may order lab tests and prescribe some medicines. Nurse practitioners work for hospitals and private medical practices. They also work in nursing homes, women's clinics, and even the Peace Corps. Students in Nurse Practitioner programs usually must be Registered Nurses. The programs award a master's degree or a certificate.

Value

What is important to a person

You have assessed your abilities and interests. Now you will look at your personal needs. To do this, think about what things are important to you. These are your **values.** Values are beliefs that get stronger or change with experience. Your values are personal. They are related to how you think and act. Here are some common personal values.

Helping Others	Community	Environmentalism
Improving the quality of the lives of others	Taking an active part in community events	Conserving or restoring the environment
Family	**Leisure**	**Personal Growth**
Raising a family or caring for aged parents	Having time and money for fun activities	Working on self-improvement
Personal Satisfaction	**Spirituality**	
Achieving a comfortable way of life	Doing things that follow one's personal beliefs	

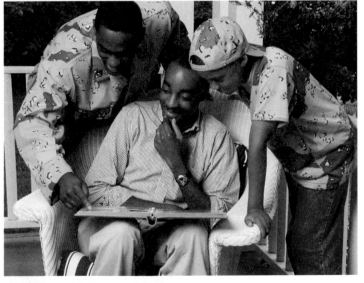

Many of your values come from your family.

Work value

Something people want to get out of a job or that brings them job satisfaction

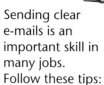

What Are Your Values?

Think about what your values are. Ask yourself, "What things are important to me?" You first learn your values from your family and your community. Most of you have met or will meet people who have ideas that are different from yours. As you continue your education or enter the workforce, you will meet even more people. Many of these people will have experiences and values that are different from yours. As you get older, you might change your values or accept the values of others.

What Are Your Work Values?

In this lesson, you will explore your **work values.** Work values are related to personal values, but may be different. (In Chapter 3, you will further explore the differences between work and personal values.) Look at the 14 work values below and on page 40. Read their definitions. Then choose the four values that are most important to you.

Creativity	Good Salary
Having a job in which you can use your imagination	Being paid well for your work

High Achievement	Independence
Being able to do things of importance or succeed on a job that is difficult	Doing work that lets you be your own boss, and doing the job the way you want to without someone watching over you

Job Security	Leadership
Having a steady job from which you are unlikely to be fired	Directing the work of others and making choices affecting others

Outdoor Work	Physical Activity
Working outside most of the time	Doing work that calls for moving about and using physical strength

Prestige

Having a job in which you are respected and feel important

Risk

Working in a job that involves danger or requires you to take risks

Variety

Doing many different and interesting things

Work with Your Hands

Having a job in which you can use your hands, machines, or tools to make or repair things

Work with Your Mind

Doing work that requires a high level of thinking and mental ability

Work with People

Working in close contact with people and being able to comfort and help others

How Do Your Values Affect Your Career?

Now that you have chosen your four strongest work values, think about how these values can affect your career choices. For example, if you value taking **risks**, you might get a job as a stock broker, one who invests money in order to make more money. Or you might choose a job that involves adventure or requires you to work outdoors, such as a river rafting guide. You would feel successful in these jobs because you are achieving something you value—taking risks. By looking at your values, you can get an idea of what plans you might make for your future.

Lesson 4 Review Write your answers to these questions on a sheet of paper.

1. What are three of your personal values?

2. What are three of your work values?

3. How do your personal values differ from your work values?

4. How can your values change?

5. How can your values affect your career choice?

Get Involved

Have you ever thought about working in a zoo? Zookeepers, veterinarians, and zoo administrators all spend their workdays among animals. Many zoos have volunteer programs for young people. For example, the National Zoo in Washington, D.C. has a summer program for teens. Volunteers do several different jobs. Some work in the kids' zoo or the kids' farm. They greet kids who come to see the animals. They help them enjoy the activities. Other volunteers welcome visitors at the doors to special exhibits. Still other volunteers help the zoo's gardeners. They learn about the zoo's plants and help keep the zoo beautiful. Zoos in other areas of the country also offer volunteer opportunities. Zoo volunteers get to help their community. They also get to learn more about some exciting occupations.

You have now identified several things about yourself. You have named the things that you can do best and the things you like most. You have identified what you have learned and enjoyed in school. You have also determined what values are most important to you. Now you will see how your school experience, abilities, values, and interests may match possible career areas. If you know what careers would be a good fit for you, you can increase your chances of enjoying your work.

The following examples of Self-Assessment Profiles will show you two ways to use this information. One way is to search for connections between abilities and interest areas and school subjects you like. Another way is to examine the connections between your abilities, interests, values, and education to find a possible career path. These connections can point to ways that encourage you to succeed. After reading each profile, you can complete and study your own profile.

Jamie is a junior in high school. She plays on the soccer team. She works part-time as a helper for her father who is an electrician. Her father owns his business. He says Jamie will get the business after he retires. Jamie is not sure if she wants to be an electrician. She has also thought about a career as a police officer. However, she cannot apply to be a police officer until she is 21 years old. Jamie has also thought about going to college. She would like to study criminal justice. This would help prepare her to be a police officer. When she graduates from college, she would be old enough to apply for a job as a police officer.

Jamie's Self-Assessment Profile

1. School Subjects

Math
Science

2. Skills

good at algebra
good with numbers
able to solve problems
good reasoning ability

3. Achievements

highest score on math test
math league team trophy
science fair award
As and Bs in science classes

4. Abilities

Manual
Technical/ Mechanical
Interpersonal
Social

5. Interests

Social
Crafts

6. Preferred Career Groups

First Choice: Customer Service
Second Choice: Skilled Crafts

7. Work Values

Work with Your Mind	Work with Your Hands	Outdoor Work	Variety

Use the information in the Self-Assessment Profile as a map. A map can help you get where you want to go. For example, you can start by looking at the area in which Jamie has some work experience—Skilled Crafts—her second Preferred Career Group. Jamie likes the school subjects of Math and Science. These subjects would help prepare her for one of her career choices—to be an electrician. What skills do electricians need? They need math for measuring, and scientific knowledge to understand theories. School, then, is a good place for Jamie to begin to prepare for a career as an electrician.

Jamie rated herself as strong in the manual and technical/mechanical abilities. These abilities also match her best-liked school subjects. Her technical/mechanical abilities show that she can figure out or fix a problem. Solving problems is useful in math or science classes.

Gender and Careers

Many jobs have traditionally been held by mostly men or mostly women. But, there are no occupations that are for men only or for women only. As long as a person has the knowledge, skills, and physical characteristics required for a job, either a male or female can do it. You can enter any field of study or job you wish.

Before the 1960s, many businesses paid men higher salaries than they paid women. This was because men had traditionally provided the main source of income for their families. As more and more women entered the workforce, people found this salary gap unfair. In 1963, Congress passed the Equal Pay Act. It said women must receive the same pay as men for the same job. Over the years, the gap between men's pay and women's pay has narrowed. However, in 2002, women were paid only 77 cents for every dollar men earned. One problem is deciding when two jobs are equivalent. Also, some jobs, such as clerical jobs, still pay less than other jobs. These are often jobs that women have traditionally held. Today men and women are both working to close the gender pay gap.

Jamie can satisfy all her work values by doing the work of an electrician. This career would require her to use her mind and her hands on the job. No matter where she lives, in a large city or a small town, her skills would always be needed. She could work outdoors or indoors. She could do different tasks for variety.

Jamie had a hard time deciding what her best interests were. She wrote down both Crafts and Social interests. She was not sure about the Crafts area because not many females are working there. But, she knows that she gets along well with men in other trades during her summer job. She enjoys the good pay she receives for her work. She makes more money than some of her friends who have other summer jobs. But Jamie finally picked Social interest over Crafts.

Jamie sees two sides to her personality. She gets along well with people. She would like to help others. But she does not see herself as a teacher, nurse, or social worker. Instead, she knows that she likes to see results from her work right away. She likes that she can use tools and fix things. It makes her feel independent.

What does Jamie's Self-Assessment Profile show that relates to police work? The values of Work with Your Mind, Outdoor Work, and Variety match with police work. Social and Interpersonal abilities and Social interest also fit with police work.

When Jamie chose her two Preferred Career Groups, she picked Customer Service and Skilled Crafts. Customer Service includes police officer. Skilled Crafts includes electrician. Jamie knows she needs more information about law enforcement. She wants to talk with police officers. She wants to know how to get experience in the field. She also understands that choosing a career takes time, information, and careful choices.

Now let's look at another example. You will read about Derrick. His interests, abilities, and values are different from Jamie's. It is helpful for you to see how different students fill out a Self-Assessment Profile. Think about yourself and how you would fill out your own profile as you read about Derrick.

Derrick is in ninth grade. He is a good student and an athlete. His mom always talks to Derrick about going to college when he graduates from high school.

Look at Derrick's Self-Assessment Profile. There are no clear-cut connections between his best-liked subjects, abilities, and interests. This will make it hard for him to choose what he should study in his sophomore year. He wants to study computers.

Derrick's first Preferred Career Group is Math and Science because he likes computers. This matches one of his best-liked school subjects, Technology. It also matches his Scientific ability. But these choices do not match the things he says he is interested in—Business or Social. He did not pick values consistent with careers in math, science, and law. For example, he did not select High Achievement, which is needed to succeed in a job that is difficult. He also did not choose Work with Your Mind.

If Derrick wants to combine his interest in business with his interest in computers, he could explore the career opportunities in information technologies, management information systems, and database administration. However, Derrick must research what these careers involve. He should find out the courses and skills he needs to fulfill his plans.

Derrick's Self-Assessment Profile

1. School Subjects

Technology
English

2. Skills

creating Web pages
programming computers
good at persuading people
good leader

3. Achievements

designed Web page for high school
spelling bee award
accepted into Honors English class
short stories printed in school paper

4. Abilities

Persuasive
Language
Scientific
Social

5. Interests

Business
Social

6. Preferred Career Groups

First Choice: Math and Science
Second Choice: Legal

7. Work Values

Good Salary	Job Security	Independence	Physical Activity

Derrick's second choice of Career Group is Legal. One of his best-liked school subjects, English, is a very important skill for law. He has to have a strong reading ability. Management courses are also important. In these courses, Derrick could study contracts and labor relations. Derrick could use his Language, Social, and Persuasive abilities in the practice of law. Attorneys, or lawyers, can earn a good income. Business is an interest that includes legal studies.

Derrick described himself as a leader. He said he is a good communicator. He can persuade people to his point of view. Law appears to be a good career direction for Derrick. But he needs to find more information about the legal field. He will learn that he must finish four years of college before he can apply to law school. He will be in law school for at least three more years. Derrick will also need to think about how he will be able to pay for his education. Getting accepted into law school is competitive and difficult. Finding legal jobs is also very competitive. Knowing what steps he needs to take to start a law career can make it easier for Derrick to plan.

Career Profile

Electrician

Electricians work with electrical wiring and equipment. Some electricians work on wiring inside homes or buildings. Others might repair street lights or outside electric wires. Electricians are good at working with their hands. They are able to find out what the problem is and then decide how to repair it. They may have to climb ladders to work on equipment. They often have to build or fix electronic parts. Sometimes, electricians need to do special tasks during a power failure like drive vehicles, operate flood lights, or set up emergency flares. Electricians need to have a license. They must do their work according to government rules and regulations. Most electricians go to vocational schools and earn either two-year or four-year degrees. They also need to get on-the-job experience or training. Jobs for electricians are expected to grow at an average rate.

What Is a Portfolio?

A **portfolio** is a tool you can use as you explore career choices and develop a career plan. Your portfolio can be a folder or electronic device that contains these things:

- evidence of planning
- skills
- competencies
- achievements
- letters of recommendation
- a résumé
- references
- jobs held
- activities performed
- writing samples

A portfolio shows your school and career progress. It also shows that you have done self-assessment. An early step for you to begin your portfolio is to include your Self-Assessment Profile. You will complete this in the Portfolio Activity on pages 50 and 51. You will update and continue to add to your portfolio as you work through this book.

Lesson 5 Review Write your answers to these questions on a sheet of paper.

1. How can a portfolio help you choose a career?

2. What are three things you might include in your portfolio?

Self-Assessment Profile

1. Choose the two school subjects you enjoy most. Write the names of the two subjects on your Self-Assessment Profile.

School Subjects
- Agriculture
- Art
- Business/Management
- Clerical Studies
- English
- Family/Consumer Science
- Finance
- Health
- Languages
- Math
- Music
- Science
- Shop/Industrial Arts
- Social Studies
- Technology/Computers

---

2. What skills do you have in the two subjects you wrote for number 1? Write these skills on your Self-Assessment Profile.

3. What are some of your achievements that relate to your skills? Write them on your Self-Assessment Profile.

4. What four abilities are your strongest? Write them on your Self-Assessment Profile.

Abilities
- Artistic
- Clerical
- Interpersonal
- Language
- Leadership
- Manual
- Mathematical/Numerical
- Musical/Dramatic
- Organizational
- Persuasive
- Scientific
- Social
- Technical/Mechanical
- Visual (Spatial)

---

5. What are two areas in which you have interest? Write them on your Self-Assessment Profile.

Interests
- The Arts
- Business
- Crafts
- Office Operations
- Scientific
- Social

---

6. Which two career groups are you the most interested in? Write them on your Self-Assessment Profile.

Career Groups
- Art
- Clerical
- Customer Service
- Data Analysis
- Education
- Entertainment
- Legal
- Literary
- Management

- Manual
- Math and Science
- Medical/Dental
- Music
- Personal Service
- Sales
- Skilled Crafts
- Social Service
- Technical

---

7. What are four of your work values? Write them on your Self-Assessment Profile.

Work Values
- Creativity
- Good Salary
- High Achievement
- Independence
- Job Security
- Leadership
- Outdoor Work

- Physical Activity
- Prestige
- Risk
- Variety
- Work with Your Hands
- Work with Your Mind
- Work with People

---

8. Include your Self-Assessment Profile in your career portfolio.

Chapter 2   R E V I E W

Word Bank

- ability
- achievement
- career group
- competency
- interest
- portfolio
- risk
- self-assessment
- self-confidence
- skill
- value
- work

Vocabulary Review

Choose the word or phrase from the Word Bank that best completes each sentence. Write the answer on your paper.

1. When you have a good feeling about yourself, you have _____.

2. A group of occupations with related abilities and interests is a(n) _____.

3. A belief about what is most important to you is a(n) _____.

4. What people do to earn a living is _____.

5. Something that you like or want to know more about is a(n) _____.

6. Something you have trained or practiced to be good at is a(n) _____.

7. A chance of danger or loss is a(n) _____.

8. Something you have earned or accomplished based on your performance is a(n) _____.

9. A tool containing several documents about yourself and your achievements is a(n) _____.

10. Being able to do something well is known as _____.

11. A talent or strength in a particular area is a(n) _____.

12. Finding out your strengths and weaknesses is known as _____.

Concept Review

Choose the word or phrase that best completes each sentence. Write the letter of the answer on your paper.

13. One way to rate your competence in an activity is to _____.

    A think about what you enjoy doing

    B consider what you have worked on hardest

    C compare yourself to others

    D choose your favorite subject

14. A person who pays attention to details and does accurate work has _____.

    A artistic ability   **C** interpersonal ability

    B clerical ability   **D** leadership ability

15. A person with scientific interests might work as a _____.

    A pharmacist   **C** tax preparer

    B salesperson   **D** farmer

16. Air traffic controller is a job in the _____ career group.

    A education   **C** manual

    B management   **D** technical

17. If you value working with others, which job would be best for you?

    A teacher   **C** carpenter

    B stock broker   **D** artist

18. Something that might be included in your portfolio is _____.

    A a letter you wrote to an old friend

    B your report card

    C a test you recently took

    D a letter of recommendation

Critical Thinking

Write the answer to each question on your paper.

19. Explain why self-assessment is a lifelong activity.

20. Suppose a person takes a job. It does not strongly reflect his or her abilities, interests, and values. What problems might this cause?

Test-Taking Tip

When studying for a test, learn the most important points. Practice writing this material or explaining it to someone.

3

Careers and Decision Making

Would you choose a dentist or buy a car without first researching your options? Then why would you choose a career without doing just as much research? The Internet, libraries, books, and newspapers are some sources of career information. This chapter will help you use these resources wisely. It will help you make decisions and set goals related to your career.

Goals for Learning

◆ To identify the best sources for information about careers

◆ To define and practice the five steps in making a decision

Wage
A set amount of money earned per hour of work

This lesson will show you how to find and use information about occupations. Remember that an occupation is a group of similar or related jobs or job skills. The job market is always changing. How do you find the most current information about an occupation? What occupations are growing? What knowledge and skills do jobs in these fields require? What is the **wage** for a job? To answer these questions, you need to do research. There are many good reasons to research occupational information:

1. Before a job interview, you will know what an employer might want you to be able to do on the job.

2. You will know what skills and knowledge you need for an occupation.

3. When you plan for college you will know what programs or classes you need for your career.

How Can I Find Career Information?

Two resources you can use to find career information are CDMCareerZone and the *Occupational Outlook Handbook* (OOH). Both are based on information from the U.S. Department of Labor. CDMCareerZone is a Web site that describes nearly 1,000 occupations. The OOH is a book. It is available in most libraries. You might also find it in guidance offices and career centers. Both of these resources include the knowledge, skills, and personal characteristics needed for specific jobs.

You can use a computer to research careers.

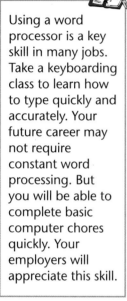
As you explore these resources, you will notice that the information you will study does not say whether a job is for men or women. Remember that there is no occupation that is for only men or only women. CDMCareerZone and the OOH both follow **wage equity**—men and women doing the same job earn the same amount of money.

What Information Can I Find on CDMCareerZone?

At the CDMCareerZone Web site, you can enter the name of an occupation you want to explore. When you enter an occupation, the first piece of information you will see is a short job description. After the description, you can read about the following:

- Interests
- Tasks/Job Duties
- Skills
- Knowledge
- Education/Training Needed

- School Programs
- Wages
- Job Outlook
- Similar Jobs
- Locations of Job Openings

On CDMCareerZone, you can print out a copy of a summary called an occupational brief. Figure 3.1 on page 58 is an example of this summary for cashiers. At the end of the brief, you can choose to see all of the occupations within the CareerZone system. By looking at the list, you can choose another job to explore. You can also view videos for more than 300 occupations.

Technology Note

Go to the CDMCareerZone Web site (www.cdmcareerzone.com). Enter one of the occupations you identified in Chapter 2. If you do not know the name of an occupation or how to spell it, click on the Go button. This will give you a list of all the CareerZone occupations. Read the information about the occupation you chose. Now, use the information to answer these questions: Do I think I would like doing this kind of work? How much money do these workers earn? Do I want to spend that much money and time preparing to enter this career? Are there similar occupations that require less investment of time and money?

Figure 3.1

A CDMCareerZone Occupational Brief for:

Cashiers

Job Description

Receive and disburse money in establishments other than financial institutions. Usually involves use of electronic scanners, cash registers, or related equipment. Often involved in processing credit or debit card transactions and validating checks.

Interests

Office Operations - High Scorers on the Office Operations scale usually:

- prefer jobs with clearly defined duties
- like to work with words and numbers
- are orderly and systematic
- value financial success and status

Typical jobs: bank teller, secretary, accountant, insurance clerk, computer operator, budget analyst

Tasks

1. Answers questions and provides information to customers.

2. Bags, boxes, or wraps merchandise.

3. Cashes checks.

4. Compiles and maintains non-monetary reports and records.

5. Computes and records totals of transactions.

6. Keeps periodic balance sheet of amount and number of transactions.

7. Learns prices, stocks shelves, marks prices, weighs items, issues trading stamps, and redeems food stamps and coupons.

8. Monitors checkout stations, issues and removes cash as needed, and assigns workers to reduce customer delay.

9. Operates cash register or electronic scanner.

10. Receives sales slip, cash, check, voucher, or charge payments and issues receipts, refunds, credits, or change due to customer.

CDM CareerZone ©2003 Harrington-O'Shea

Figure 3.1. *Occupational Brief for Cashiers*

You can find job openings for the occupation you have researched. Use the drop-down menu to find job openings by state. The job openings listed are from America's Job Bank. You will find the job title, company or organization name, and city or town. Sometimes you may read that there are no jobs available. This may not be true. It may mean only that the jobs are not listed with America's Job Bank.

What Information Is in the Occupational Outlook Handbook?

The *Occupational Outlook Handbook* (OOH) describes in detail more than 200 occupations in which about 128 million people work. That is 88 percent of all jobs in the United States! The handbook also explains other jobs in less detail. In the OOH, you can learn in what jobs 95 percent of the people in the United States work. The handbook is reprinted every two years to keep the information up-to-date.

In the OOH, information is usually organized in groups of related occupations. These groups allow you to see similar or related jobs you may not have known about. These are the groups in the OOH:

- Management, business, and financial occupations
- Professional occupations
- Service occupations
- Sales occupations
- Office and administrative support occupations
- Farming, fishing, and forestry occupations
- Construction trades
- Installation, maintenance, and repair occupations
- Production occupations
- Transportation and material moving occupations
- Armed Forces

The Economy

You are probably familiar with the minimum wage. This is an hourly wage set by the government. It is the smallest amount that a company can legally pay its employees. Many young people earn the minimum wage for part-time jobs in stores and restaurants. However, it is difficult for parents to support a family on minimum wages. The living wage enables a worker to support a family. Many American cities have enacted living wage regulations. The amount of a living wage is different in each place. In Milwaukee, Wisconsin, it is considered to be about one dollar more per hour than the minimum wage. In Santa Cruz, California, it is about ten dollars per hour above the minimum wage.

Occupations are described under different headings. First go to the heading you are most interested in. Then, you can choose to research other information. Here are the different heading topics:

1. Nature of the Work
2. Working Conditions
3. Employment
4. Related Occupations
5. Training and Advancement
6. Earnings
7. Outlook
8. Sources of Additional Information

Figure 3.2

OUTLOOK   [About this section]   ▲ **Back to Top**

Employment of hotel, motel, and resort desk clerks is expected to **grow faster than the average** for all occupations through 2012, as more hotels, motels, and other lodging establishments are built and occupancy rates rise. Job opportunities for hotel and motel desk clerks also will result from a need to replace workers, because many of these clerks either transfer to other occupations that offer better pay and advancement opportunities or simply leave the workforce altogether. Opportunities for part-time work should continue to be plentiful, with front desks often staffed 24 hours a day, 7 days a week.

Employment of hotel and motel desk clerks should benefit from an increase in business and leisure travel. Shifts in preferences away from long vacations and toward long weekends and other, more frequent, shorter trips also should boost demand for these workers, because such stays increase the number of nights spent in hotels. The expansion of budget and extended-stay hotels relative to larger, luxury establishments reflects a change in the composition of the hotel and motel industry. As employment shifts from luxury hotels to those extended-stay establishments offering larger rooms with kitchenettes and laundry services, the proportion of hotel desk clerks should increase in relation to staff such as waiters and waitresses and recreation workers. Desk clerks are able to handle more of the guest's needs in these establishments, answering the main switchboard, providing business services, and coordinating services such as dry cleaning or grocery shopping.

New technologies automating check-in and checkout procedures now allow some guests to bypass the front desk in many larger establishments, reducing staffing needs. As some of the more traditional duties are automated, however, many desk clerks are assuming a wider range of responsibilities.

Employment of desk clerks is sensitive to cyclical swings in the economy. During recessions, vacation and business travel declines, and hotels and motels need fewer clerks. Similarly, employment is affected by seasonal fluctuations in tourism and travel.

Bureau of Labor Statistics

Figure 3.2. *Job Outlook for Hospitality Careers*

The OOH presents information differently than the CDMCareerZone Web site. The OOH provides complete career information in one book. You can use the book's index to find the page for an occupation you are researching. Look at the example in Figure 3.2 on page 60. Under Outlook, you can see that there are many opportunities for part-time work for Hotel/Motel Desk Clerks. Hotels and motels usually have someone working at the front desk 24 hours a day, seven days a week. These clerks might work late evening or early morning shifts or weekends. Employment can be seasonal. This is important information to have if you are considering this job.

Jobs as hotel desk clerks are growing faster than the average for all occupations.

Technology Note

The Internet is an excellent resource for job hunting. But job listings found online may not always be up-to-date. Before applying for a specific job, send an e-mail or make a phone call to the company. Make sure the job is still available.

Career Tip

Many schools have Career Resources Centers. Does your school have one? Do you know where it is? Find out and make use of this resource!

What Are Some School and Community Resources?

Most schools have many other career information resources. Books, computer programs, and videos may be available for career planning. Many colleges and postsecondary schools have catalogs and videos for students who are interested in those schools.

Community groups and businesses may also offer career resources. A business might send a guest speaker to a school. Or, a business or group might give tours. Many companies have opportunities to "shadow" or join a worker for a day. The Armed Forces also have programs to explore military careers.

These students learn about jobs on a tour of a television show set.

Where is the first place you look when job hunting? About 85 percent of job hunters use the newspaper's classified ads. However, only 20 percent of jobs are actually found through these ads. The Internet and networking are more effective.

You have now learned several ways to find career information. Remember that gathering this information will help you set a goal and make good choices as you plan for your future.

Lesson 1 Review Write your answers to these questions on a sheet of paper.

1. Why is it important to research information about occupations?

2. What are some resources in your school or community you can use to find career information?

3. Research an occupation using CDMCareerZone or the OOH. Write a brief description of the occupation.

4. What is wage equity? What are your feelings about wage equity?

Get Involved

Have you ever considered working in a medical field? One way to learn more about health-related careers is by volunteering in a hospital. Many community hospitals have volunteer programs for teens. Teen volunteers do a variety of jobs. They may help organize charts or answer telephones. They may help customers in gift shops. They may entertain children. Some volunteers may interact with patients. They may make beds, deliver food trays, or transport patients. Volunteering at a hospital gives you a close-up look at medical professionals. It also helps your community and adds to the work experience on your résumé.

Decision

A choice to take action

Goal

A plan, an intention, or aim; something that a person wants to get or reach

Decisions are choices people make. You can show that you are independent and responsible by the choices you make. Adults and employers value people who are able to make responsible decisions. This lesson will focus only on making career decisions. Career decision making is about planning for your future. It will help you know exactly what you need to do in order to get what you want. Here are the five decision-making steps:

1. Set Goals

2. Make Priorities

3. Explore the Options

4. Assess the Risks

5. Make a Plan

Decision making takes time. Give yourself enough time to make good choices. Do not rush any of the steps. If you feel pressured or worried about your decisions, talk to a teacher, parent, or career counselor. It is important to make good decisions and these people can help you to do that.

Communication Connection

Talking to others about your career goals can be helpful. You may have a close friend who can help you see how well a specific career might suit you. Parents, guardians, and teachers, however, often know much about careers from personal experience. Try talking to them about your career goals.

Step 1: Set Goals

Setting **goals** is the first step in decision-making. A goal is something you want to get or reach. To plan your career, you need to state your career goals. By setting goals, you are starting a plan of action. Think about what you want to get, do, or be in the future.

Try to set realistic goals. A goal might not be right for you if it does not match up with your grades, test scores, or personality. Sometimes, other people can see that a goal is not right for you more easily than you can. Ask parents, guardians, friends, teachers, or people you work with if they think your goals are appropriate. These people know you well. They might tell you that they believe you cannot reach a goal you have chosen. They might be able to help you set other goals. A teacher or counselor might ask you to talk with them about your decision-making process.

Step 2: Make Priorities

Next, you need to make **priorities.** A priority is something that you feel is more important than something else. When you make priorities, you choose what goals you will try to achieve first. Often, the first things you will do are those that are the easiest. When it is easy to get a successful result, you are more likely to continue. More difficult goals may take more time, more learning, or more experience.

Courage and determination are values that can help you reach your goals.

You can also put your goals in order of priority by looking at your values. Remember that values are things that bring you satisfaction. Recall the work values you identified in Chapter 2. These values reflect what is important to you—your priorities. For example, you might value outdoor work. You might decide that looking for a summer job at a camp or park will be your first priority. You may find that your work values do not always match your personal values. When that happens, think about how the conflict between these two will affect your work and non-work life.

Values can change as you get older or form relationships with people who have backgrounds different from yours. Values are important, but interests influence you more when you are younger. As you grow older, values play a larger role in your life. You might change your priorities as your values change. No matter how you decide to make priorities, you are setting up a plan to follow. As you do this, share your ideas and plans with others. They can often help you find ways to achieve a goal.

Step 3: Explore the Options

Once you have decided what goals you will try to achieve first, you need to explore the **options** related to each goal. Options are choices you have. You need to have at least two choices to make a decision. In this step, you move closer to one of your goals by selecting one of the options.

By looking at the options in detail, you may find that you have not chosen a good goal. You can always change a goal or choose a new one. For example, you may have chosen a goal based on some advice from your brother or sister. Maybe your friends have influenced you to choose a certain job because it is a job that they like. After assessing your abilities, you should come to your own conclusion about what you like to do and how well you do it. To set a new goal, simply go back to Step 1. The process should move more quickly the second time because you have already done a lot of the work. You may even need to return to Step 1 more than once. It is very important that you set goals that are right for you. Exploring your options can help you choose good goals.

Step 4: Assess the Risks

When you make decisions and explore your options, you need to think about the possible outcomes of your choices. A decision may have a positive or a negative outcome. A positive outcome is one that you would like to happen. A negative outcome is one you do not want to happen. When you make a decision, think about the risk—the chance of a negative outcome. The likelihood of either a positive or a negative outcome is called **probability**.

Writing Practice

Do you think you are a risk taker when it comes to facing challenges? Think about risks you have taken in the following areas: learning, athletics, and friendships. Write a journal entry about a risk you have taken. Explain why you took it and how it turned out. Then discuss whether you are willing to take risks that come with choosing a career.

Keep a positive, open mind in considering careers. Children sometimes make remarks like "I don't like broccoli." They have probably never tried it! Don't make negative generalizations like "I would not like to be an engineer." Instead, research many different careers, including engineering, with an open mind. Like a child who finally tries broccoli, you might find you like it!

Probability has the following ranges:

No risk: The outcome is known and certain. For example, if you flip a coin, it will land on either heads or tails. This outcome is certain. There can be no other outcomes.

Risky: The outcome has a specified probability. For example, you spin a spinner with 4 different colors: blue, red, yellow, and green. There is a 1 in 4 probability that the color will be red.

Uncertain: The chances of the outcome happening are unknown. For example, you are going to choose one marble out of a bag of marbles. If you choose a red marble, you win a prize. However, you do not know how many marbles are in the bag. You also do not know what colors the marbles are. You have no way of knowing if you will choose a red marble. The outcome is uncertain and you cannot tell how likely it is to happen.

Career Profile

Interior Designer

Do you love creating a wonderful room out of gleaming woods, beautiful fabrics, and unique accessories? Then you have probably considered an interior designing career. Interior designers do many tasks that are less glamorous than putting pretty rooms together. They must often deal with building codes and technical features such as lighting and plumbing. Interior designers need more than just artistic talent. They must communicate well with many different types of people, including clients, architects, and contractors. They need good management skills in order to complete projects on schedule.

The two main fields for interior designers are residential design and commercial design. A residential designer works with homeowners. Some specialize in kitchen or bathroom design. A commercial designer may design offices, restaurants, health-care facilities, or other businesses. Some interior designers have associates degrees from two-year colleges. Some colleges offer four- or five-year interior design degrees. Today many employers look for designers with these degrees. Interior design is a growing field, but it is also a competitive one.

You cannot totally control probabilities, but you can assess risks. To do this, you determine the probability (high, medium, or low) that the outcome you want will happen.

Read these examples of how Marinda and Tyler assessed the risks involved in their decisions.

Developing your abilities involves taking risks.

Marinda is deciding whether to try out for the varsity soccer team this year. She played on the junior varsity soccer team last year. She was voted the most valuable player. She scored the most goals of anyone on the team. She knows that more people will try out for the varsity team than there are spots available. She considers the probability of making the team high based on her abilities and past performance. She considers her risk to be low. Marinda decides to try out for the team.

Tyler wants to apply to an internship program at a large company. Each year, thousands of students apply, but only one is chosen. The competition for the internship is very high. Tyler considers the probability that he will be the one chosen to be low. However, he really wants the internship so he takes the risk and applies for it.

Some people will take many chances. Other people simply are not risk takers. Developing your talents always involves some kind of risk. Taking a risk depends on the situation and personal **motivation**. Motivation is what drives a person to act or to seek a goal. Motivation can be an inner desire. It can also be encouragement from others. In Tyler's case, he was motivated to apply for the internship because he had a strong inner desire to get it.

Step 5: Make a Plan

The final step is to write down what you need to do and when you need to do it. This sounds simple. However, it is very important to have a plan in place. This helps you put the earlier steps into action and achieve your goals.

Some of the steps on the way to your goals may be simple. Perhaps all that you need to do to sign up for a class you want is to check off a box on a class registration form. Great!

However, you might need to include a personal essay as part of an application. You will need to make a plan so you can accomplish this step on time. Then, you have to wait for a decision on whether you were accepted. What other things can you accomplish while you are waiting? You need to have a plan in place so you can keep moving toward your goal. If you wait too long to achieve a goal, you will be less motivated. Having a plan will keep you on track.

Gender and Careers

Some careers, such as law and medicine, were once considered "men's" careers. In the last 25 years, many more women have entered these careers. One career which has had a striking change in gender is veterinary medicine. In the 1960s, only five percent of veterinary students were women. By 2005, the majority of students in veterinary schools will be women. In 2002, there were 24,356 women veterinarians. There were 33,461 men veterinarians. One reason for the change is that being a veterinarian has become less difficult physically. In the past, most vets worked on farm animals. So physical strength was required. Today, many vets work only with pets. Veterinarians must take demanding courses in college plus about four additional years of study.

Lesson 2 Review Write your answers to these questions on a sheet of paper.

1. Why is decision making important?

2. What are the five decision-making steps?

3. What is one big decision you have made in the last few months? How did you make that decision?

4. Why is making decisions often difficult?

Practicing Decision-Making Steps

In this activity, you will practice the five decision-making steps you learned in Lesson 2. Your responses will become part of your portfolio.

Step 1: Set Goals

What are your career goals? Ask yourself, "What would I really want to do or be in five years?" Use the information that you discovered in Chapter 2 about your abilities, interests, and personal characteristics. Consider the occupation you researched in Lesson 1 of this chapter. What fields of study do you like? What career areas require a college education? On a separate sheet of paper, or on Portfolio Activity 3, write at least two of your career goals.

Step 2: Make Priorities

In Chapter 2 you identified the work values that are most important to you. Review the values you selected. Below each goal you wrote in Step 1, write how that goal will help you fulfill any of your highest values. Remember to keep your personal values separate from your work values. If you cannot connect your goals and values, you may need to modify your goals or re-assess your values.

Step 3: Explore the Options

Once you have prioritized your goals, you should examine the choices you will need to make. To do this, write down any two areas of study or jobs you are considering. Use the information you studied in previous lessons to rate each of your two choices with the ratings below. For each choice, answer these questions. Write your answer under the choice.

1. How well do your abilities match those required by the major, field of study, or job? Excellent match, good match, or poor match?

2. How well do your interests match those activities that the major, field of study, or job will involve? Excellent match, good match, or poor match?

3. How well do your values match the values of people in the occupations in this major, field of study, or job? Excellent match, good match, or no match?

4. How do your personal characteristics fit with people who enter occupations from this major, field of study, or job? Excellent fit, good fit, or poor fit?

5. Is the salary acceptable to you? Yes or no?

6. Would you be willing to get additional schooling or more education? Yes, no, or not sure?

7. Would you be willing to move to find employment? Yes, no, or not sure? Would you be willing to move to go to school in this major, field of study, or job? Yes, no, or not sure?

8. What is the job outlook for careers in this major, field of study, or job? Excellent, good, or poor?

9. Will you be qualified for the employment you want when you finish your education? Yes or no?

10. How much do you like the field in which the occupation is? Very much, somewhat, or not at all?

Now that you have answered these questions, you can identify the areas that are keeping you from making a decision. By exploring your options, you can weigh the positives and negatives of possible decisions.

Step 4: Assess the Risks

Which of the options you listed in Step 3 involves more risk than the other(s)? Write down the risk.

Step 5: Make a Plan

Look at the table below. You can use this table as a guide to plan your future.

Career Action Plan

Goal	Action Step (what needs to be done)	Resources or People to Contact	Date to Be Completed

Chapter 3   R E V I E W

Vocabulary Review

Choose the word or phrase from the Word Bank that best completes each sentence. Write the answer on your paper.

1. A choice is a(n) _____.

2. The set amount of money a person makes per hour of work is a(n) _____.

3. A choice that helps people take control of their lives is a(n) _____.

4. The likelihood that an event will happen is called _____.

5. An intention or something a person wants to reach is a(n) _____.

6. When a person has an inner drive or encouragement from others to act on a goal, the person has _____.

7. Something that a person feels is most important is a(n) _____.

Concept Review

Choose the word or phrase that best completes each sentence. Write the letter of the answer on your paper.

8. A source that describes in detail 88 percent of all the jobs in the United States is the _____.

   A CDMCareerZone   C OOH

   B Career Resource   D newspaper classified ads
      Center

9. When you determine the probability that a certain outcome will occur, you are _____.

   A making a decision   C making a plan

   B taking a risk   D assessing risks

10. Men and women earning the same amount for doing the same job is called _____.

A wage equity   **C** a job description

B an occupational brief   **D** probability

11. One thing about careers found in CDMCareerZone but not in the OOH is _____.

A earnings   **C** job outlook

B training required   **D** current job openings

12. The first step in making a decision is _____.

A setting priorities   **C** setting goals

B assessing risks   **D** making a plan

Critical Thinking

Write the answer to each question on your paper.

13. Suppose a friend says he does not need to use a resource such as CDMCareerZone. His reason is that he has already chosen a career. What might you tell him about other reasons to use the resources?

14. Is it a good idea to talk to others about your career goals? Explain why or why not.

15. Suppose a person decides to pursue acting. She knows there is a risk she will not get acting jobs or make much money. Do you think taking the risk is a good idea or not? Explain.

Test-Taking Tip

It is easier to learn new vocabulary words if you use them often. Make them part of your speaking and writing in other discussions and subject areas.

4

Career Clusters and the Major Industries

How are the cars of the future designed? People who design cars have computer knowledge. They are also familiar with the automotive industry. Car designers are creative. They think about what the customer will want in the next generation of cars. In their jobs, they use all of these skills. No matter what job you are interested in, you should know how your skills and interests match a particular career field. Every field includes a range of people with a variety of strengths and skills. In this chapter, you will begin to look more closely at specific career clusters. You will learn the types of work that are done in each field. You will learn about the workers and the workplaces for each field. You will learn what skill areas are the best fit for certain occupations. As you read about the wide range of career paths available today, you may just find one that matches your talents, skills, and interests.

Goals for Learning

◆ To identify the major career clusters

◆ To examine the jobs, wages, and outlooks in the major career clusters

◆ To understand the jobs of workers in major industries

◆ To identify occupations to explore in more detail

What Are the Career Clusters?

Industry

A large-scale business or service area that provides a product or service

The U.S. government collects detailed information on about 1,100 occupations. In order to look at an occupation more easily, these occupations are grouped into similar career areas. These groups are called clusters. The clusters show related occupations. The occupations in each cluster require similar preparation, draw upon similar worker skills, and have similar workplaces. Occupations in a cluster can range from entry-level opportunities to professional, technical, and management positions. The 16 lessons that follow are the U.S. Department of Education career clusters. These clusters include the occupations where 97 percent of the workers are expected to be employed in 2012.

How Can I Learn About Occupations?

By exploring each career cluster, you can learn about occupations that you may like. You can discover, examine, and research the activities that a worker in a certain **industry** does. An industry is a large-scale business or service area that provides a product or service. You can learn the knowledge and skills that workers need in order to be employed in industries you are interested in.

How Many People Work in Each Industry?

As you read about different industries, you will learn that not all industries are the same size. Some industries will have more employment opportunities than others. Some industries have occupations that are not located in every region of the country. These things may affect your career choice. You may need to move in order to work in a certain occupation. Table 4.1 on page 77 shows the amount of people by percent expected to be employed in each of the major industries in 2012.

You can see from Table 4.1 that 6.4 percent of the workers in 2012 will be self-employed. These workers are not employed by someone else. They work for themselves. The greatest opportunities for self-employment will be in arts, design media, entertainment, sports, mathematical, and computer occupations.

Table 4.1

Industry	Percent
Agriculture, Forestry, and Fishing	1.2
Construction	4.7
Education and Health Services	12.9
Finance, Insurance, and Real Estate	5.3
Government	14.5
Information	2.5
Leisure and Hospitality	8.5
Manufacturing	9.2
Mining	0.3
Other Services	4.3
Professional and Business Services	12.6
Self-Employed	6.4
Transportation, Communication, and Utilities	3.4
Wholesale and Retail Trade	14.2
Total	**100.0**

Source: Bureau of Labor Statistics

Table 4.1 *Projected Number of Employed Persons by 2012 by Major Industry Area in the United States in Percents*

Table 4.2

Occupational Group	Percent Growth
Construction and extraction	15.0
Farming, fishing, and forestry	3.3
Installation, maintenance, and repair	13.6
Management, business, and financial	15.4
Office and administrative support	6.8
Production	3.2
Professional	23.3
Sales	12.9
Service	20.1
Transportation and material moving	13.1

Source: Bureau of Labor Statistics

Table 4.2 *Growth in Percent of the Major Occupational Groups from 2002 to 2012*

Apprenticeship

On-the-job training to learn the skills required for a job

Career ladders

Related jobs that allow advancement to a higher-level job through experience, education, and training

Career Tip

Not all regions of the country pay the same wages for doing the same occupation.

What Occupational Group Will Grow the Most?

As you learned in Chapter 1, another thing that may affect your career choice is the economy. When the economy changes, different employment opportunities arise. For example, by the year 2012 the government predicts that employment in mining will decrease. The largest growth in employment will occur in educational and health, and professional and business services.

As the economy changes, workers need to be aware of which career areas will grow and be in demand. It is also good information to have when you are planning your career. Look at Table 4.2 on page 77. It shows the predicted growth in percent of the major occupational groups from 2002 to 2012.

You can see in Table 4.2 that some occupations will increase faster than others. For example, the professional and service areas will have the most new jobs. Occupational groups in farming, fishing, and forestry and those in production will experience the fewest number of new jobs.

How Do I Prepare for the Job I Want?

The different jobs in the occupational groups in Table 4.2 require different kinds of educational preparation and training. In the rest of this chapter you will learn the education and training level required for several occupations. This information will help you decide what school subjects to take and what your plans for the future will be. You will need to decide whether to attend college or vocational school, start military training, or start on-the-job training. On-the-job training is also often called an **apprenticeship.** In an apprenticeship program, you learn from an experienced worker. Eventually, you do the job yourself.

Some jobs require little or no training and education. Other jobs require four years of college or more. You might begin in a job that does not require a lot of training. Then, if you learn more skills or get more education, you can advance to a higher-level job. Jobs that are related in this way are called **career ladders.** The more new skills, job duties, and education you get, the higher you can move on the ladder.

Look at the chart below of the average weekly earnings for full-time workers with different education and training levels for the year 2002. You can see that getting more education and training results in higher pay.

Education/Training	Average Weekly Earnings
Less than high school	$409
High school	$562
Some college, no degree	$644
Associate's degree (2 years of college), educational	$673
Associate's degree (2 years of college), vocational	$711
Bachelor's degree (4 years of college)	$996
Master's degree or higher (more than 4 years of college)	$1,273

Source: Horrigon, Michael. (February 2004). Employment projections to 2012: Concepts and context. *The Monthly Labor Review.* p. 21.

More than 20 percent of the workers referenced in Tables 4.1 and 4.2 have attended and graduated from a college. Another 8 percent went to a community college or postsecondary school. The information in this chapter will help you plan to meet your career goal.

In Chapters 2 and 3, you stated activities in which you have an interest. You identified the school subjects you like and the skills in which you have competence. You also identified your abilities and strengths and determined what work values are important to you. School subjects, abilities, and values that relate to each cluster are given in the next lesson. As you read about each cluster, you can refer to this information.

Lesson 1 Review Write your answers to these questions on a sheet of paper.

1. What is an industry?

2. How many workers in 2012 are expected to be self-employed?

3. Which fields will have the most new jobs from 2002 to 2012? Which fields will have the fewest?

4. People with a bachelor's degree or more education earn more money than other workers. Why do you think this is so?

Agriculture

Farming; producing crops and raising livestock

Natural resources

Minerals and other things found in nature

Key to Education and Training Needed

1—Entry Level training a few days up to 2 months with an experienced worker

2—On-the-Job Training 2 to 6 months of training with an experienced worker

3—Apprenticeship training 6 months up to 5 years with an experienced worker

4—Technical/ Vocational Program completion of program lasting usually 1 to 4 years

5—College 4-year degree or advanced degree completed

This cluster includes two main areas: **agriculture** and **natural resources.** Agriculture deals with plants, animals, and food production. Natural resources involves the mining of resources beneath the earth. These industries are the oldest in the world. They help us meet our basic needs for food, shelter, and heat.

The Agriculture Workplace

The workplaces for most agricultural jobs are where conditions are best. For example, oranges are grown in Florida and California. The weather, soil conditions, and length of the growing season are good for growing oranges there. Different parts of the country are known for the agricultural products they provide. For example, the Midwest is known for corn, wheat, and soybeans. The South is known for cotton and rice.

Agriculture Workers

Farmers are agricultural workers. They till the soil, plant seed, and care for and harvest their produce. Landscapers and gardeners may water and trim trees. Some workers pick fruits and nuts and pack them for shipping. Ranchers breed and care for animals. Inspectors and graders make sure food is safe to eat before it is sold.

Sample Agriculture Occupations

Animal Scientist	5
Farm and Ranch Manager	3, 4, or 5
Farmworkers, Farm and Ranch Animals	1
Landscaping and Groundskeeping Worker	1
Plant Scientist	5
Veterinarian Technologist and Technician	4

The number after each occupation shows the minimum education and training needed for that occupation. See the key on the left.

Forestry

Another part of the agricultural cluster is forestry. Wood from trees is used to make products like furniture and paper. Forestry workers include machine and tractor operators who drag the logs from the forests. Sorters separate logs to grade them for type of wood and quality. Loggers load the logs onto trucks for sawmills or papermaking plants. Some forest workers raise trees on tree farms to use for special events, or to plant around the outside of homes.

Sample Forestry Occupations

Faller	1
Forest and Conservation Worker	2
Forester	5
Log Grader and Scaler	3
Logger	1

(See the key on page 80.)

Fishing

Workers in the fishing industry harvest fish and shellfish. A large amount of fish, such as catfish and salmon, is raised on fish farms. Workers usually fish for only one kind of fish, such as lobsters, oysters, shrimp, or tuna. Fishing is hard work. Nets and other equipment need to be repaired often. Boats can be very expensive to buy and operate.

Sample Fishing Occupations

Fisher	1
Ship and Boat Captain	3 or 4

(See the key on page 80.)

Mining

Removing minerals
from the earth

Extraction

The pumping of oil and
natural gas from
underground

Workers in agriculture value working on their own. They do not have to work in office jobs for a set amount of hours. People in this cluster like to do things and see results. They are skilled at working with their hands. They enjoy a variety of tasks in their jobs. They also value status within their community, outside work, and the opportunity for high achievement. They have crafts interests. This is one of the interest areas you learned about in Chapter 2.

Agriculture and the Environment

Farming, forestry, and fishing can affect the land, water, and air. The government has laws to protect the environment. The agriculture industry must follow these laws. Workers make sure chemicals do not pollute lakes and rivers. They replant seedlings to create new forests. They are careful not to overfish the oceans. The government teaches farmers and other agricultural workers how to protect the environment.

The Natural Resources Workplace

The natural resources industry employs the smallest number of people of the major industries. Natural resources occupations include jobs related to **mining** and **extraction.** Mining is the removal of minerals from the ground, including coal and iron. Coal provides heat. Iron is used to make steel. Steel is used to make buildings, bridges, and automobiles. Extraction is the pumping of oil and natural gas from underground. People use oil or gas to power their cars, light and heat their homes, and operate factories.

Mining is done where there are mineral deposits. Geologists find out where the deposits are by using scientific equipment. Before mining begins, geologists and petroleum engineers estimate the cost of mining and extracting these minerals or fuels. Then the actual removal can begin. The removal may include drilling or blasting. The minerals are then moved to storage areas. Extracted oil and gas is collected, pumped, and transported in pipes.

Natural Resources Workers

Workers in this career cluster work outside almost all the time. The weather can be very hot, cold, wet, or windy. Workers are still expected do their jobs no matter what the weather. The main interest of people in this cluster is crafts. Workers should be strong. They should be able to work well with their hands. Well and core drill operators run the drills. Petroleum engineers design oil pipes. Surveyors and civil engineers draw the maps of the mineral deposits. Mining engineers need management skills. They need to monitor airflow, drainage, water, communications, power supplies, and transportation systems. Like agriculture workers, natural resources workers value independent work, a variety of job tasks, status, and high achievement. People in this industry observe what is happening. They have good memory for detail. They seek facts in order to make judgments.

Sample Natural Resources Occupations	
Civil Drafter	4
Construction Equipment Operator	3
Continuous Mining Machine Operator	2
Derrick Operator, oil and gas	2
Explosive Worker and Blaster	2
Geologist	5
Metal-Refining Furnace Operator	2
Mining and Geological Engineer	5
Mobile Heavy Equipment Mechanic	3
Petroleum Engineer	5
Pump Operator	2
Rotary Drill Operator, small oil and gas	3
Roustabout, oil and gas	2
Well and Core Drill Operator	3

(See the key on page 80.)

Agriculture, Food, and Natural Resources Outlook

Most workers in this industry are farm workers and laborers. Employment in these areas will grow more slowly than other occupations. Employment in the forestry and fishing industries is expected to decline. The parts of the agricultural industry that will expand are farm labor contractors, agricultural managers, and horticultural service workers. Landscapers and nursery workers will also see more job opportunities.

Jobs in mining are expected to decrease by almost 12 percent by 2012. There will be fewer jobs available as mining machine operators and petroleum engineers. Natural resources jobs that are expected to grow include environmental scientists, gas plant operators, and explosives workers. By 2012, jobs in water and waste treatment plants are expected to increase by 16 percent.

Of all workers employed in 2012, only 3.2 percent will have jobs in the Agriculture, Food, and Natural Resources cluster. Average national wages for occupations in this cluster depend on the amount of training and education required.

Entry Level	$20,500–$21,000
On-the-Job Training/Apprenticeship	$31,000–$33,300
Technical/Vocational Program	$35,500–$37,000
College Degree	$47,500–$67,300

Lesson 2 Review Write your answers to these questions on a sheet of paper.

1. What are the oldest industries in the world? Why are they the oldest?

2. What determines the workplaces for agricultural jobs?

3. Which industry employs the smallest number of people of the major industries?

4. Workers in agriculture and natural resources fields often do hard physical work in uncomfortable weather. Do you think there are positive features that make up for this hard work? Explain.

Manufacturing involves making products. It can also be called production. Manufacturing begins with raw material. That material is made into something else. Look at the example below.

Raw Material   **Final Product**

The people who manufacture products are called **production workers.** They make many of the things we use every day, such as toothbrushes and soap. One of the largest manufacturing industries is the automobile industry. Many manufacturing workers have jobs related to making cars and trucks. Other manufacturing industries include electronics, printing, and paper products.

The manufacturing cluster also includes the utilities and telecommunication industries. The utilities industry includes power plants and nuclear reactor plants. Telecommunications includes telephones, wireless or cellular phones, the Internet, and cable.

The Workplace

A group of buildings where manufacturing happens is called a **manufacturing plant.** Different buildings are used for different things. One building may be for storage of raw materials or parts. Parts might be put together, or **assembled,** in another building.

Other buildings may be for painting, storage, or shipping. Some plants may be very large, have noisy machines, or be very hot or cold inside. Other plants may be small, quiet, or air-conditioned. Utilities and telecommunications work can take place in an office or a plant. It can also take place outdoors on power or telephone lines.

Manufacturing

Turning raw material into products people use every day

Production worker

Person who manufactures products

Manufacturing plant

A group of buildings where manufacturing happens

Assemble

To put together

Related School Subjects
General Science
Math
Shop
Technology

Related Abilities
Manual
Mathematical
Scientific
Visual (Spatial)

Related Values
Good Salary
Independence
Outdoor Work
Work with Hands

The Workers

Most manufacturing workers operate machines, such as drills, grinders, furnaces, or forklifts. Machine repairers make sure the equipment is in working order. Assembly workers put things together. They might repeat the same task over and over again. Manufacturing work often requires strength and lifting. Some workers put raw materials into machines. Other workers move materials around the plant. Workers might also package and label products. Manufacturing managers make sure their products are of high quality.

Power plant operators and dispatchers work throughout the country. Power plant operators monitor and control the working parts and machinery of the plant. Dispatchers control the flow of electricity through power lines.

Sample Manufacturing Occupations	
Aircraft Structure Assembler	3
Baker, Manufacturing	3
Cabinetmaker and Bench Carpenter	3
Electronic Assembler	2
Engine and Other Machine Assembler	3
Jeweler	3
Machinist	3
Manufacturing Optician	2
Mechanical Inspector	2 or 3
Molding and Casting Worker	2
Painting, Coating, and Decorating Worker	1
Photographic Processing Machine Operator	2
Printing Press Machine Operator	3
Stationary Engineer	3
Structural Metal Fabricator	4
Telecommunications Line Installer	3
Tool and Die Maker	3
Welders, Production	2 or 3

(See the key on page 87.)

Workers in the manufacturing cluster enjoy physical activities. They like to work with their hands. They enjoy seeing the results of their work right away. Manufacturing and production workers have crafts interests such as working with tools and repairing things. Utility workers usually have good math and science skills. They also have mechanical and technical abilities. Telecommunications workers need skills in computers. They also need to know how to relate to customers. Many of these workers must be physically strong to do their jobs.

Outlook

Some manufacturing areas will grow slightly. There will be more jobs in computer, electronic, and plastic manufacturing. Clothing manufacturing jobs will decrease. Many assembly industries will see a decrease in jobs because of **automation.** Automation is the use of machines to do jobs that used to be done by people. Automation makes it easier for plants to do more work with fewer workers. Other manufacturing jobs are being given to workers in other countries. This is called **offshore outsourcing.** It is cheaper for companies to pay these workers than it is to pay workers in the United States. This will also lead to a decrease in some manufacturing occupations.

There will be more telecommunications jobs for workers in central offices. There will also be more jobs for workers who set up new telecommunications services. This is because of the growth of the Internet, more video options, and a growth in high-speed data transmission. In the utilities industry, job growth will be less for electrical power line installers and repairers than for all occupations.

By 2012, manufacturing workers will make up 8.5 percent of all employed workers. Here are the average wages for occupations in manufacturing, based on training and education:

Entry Level	$25,400
On-the-Job Training/Apprenticeship	$26,700–$30,200
Technical/Vocational Program	$30,700
College Degree	$57,600

Lesson 3 Review Write your answers to these questions on a sheet of paper.

1. Why is manufacturing an important industry?

2. Why must many workers in the manufacturing cluster be physically strong?

3. Why are many companies in the United States using offshore outsourcing? Explain why you think offshore outsourcing is a good idea or not.

Distribute

To move or give out goods and products to buyers or customers

Logistics

Planning and operations involved in moving people and products

Freight

Goods or products transported by truck, train, boat, or airplane

Related School Subjects
Keyboarding
Math
Science
Shop
Technology

Related Abilities
Leadership
Manual
Mathematical
Scientific
Technical/Mechanical
Visual (Spatial)

Related Values
Good Salary
Independence
Physical Activity
Risk
Work with Hands
Work with Mind

This industry deals with the use of roads, waterways, and rail and air systems. The transportation industry connects the product with the customer. The purpose of transportation is to **distribute** materials and products. Transportation also involves helping people get to places they need to go. People use highways and airlines to travel across the United States. Businesses ship heavy materials by railroad or ship.

Transportation is more than driving a truck or flying a plane. Many sales and service occupations are related to the transportation industry. People prepare billing statements and sell tickets. Others collect payments for transportation services. These jobs deal with the planning and daily tasks needed to move people and products. This part of the industry is called **logistics.**

The Workplace

Truck drivers deliver **freight** from companies, warehouses, or distribution centers. Freight is goods or products that are transported. Local drivers might drive small trucks and work in only one city or town. Other truck drivers might own their own large trucks and travel from state to state. Railroad workers work on freight and passenger trains. They also work on subways. Water transportation is a relatively small industry. It takes place on coastlines, rivers, and lakes. Passenger ferries and tourist boats operate on the waterways. Barges tow freight and oil. The airline industry includes maintenance work on planes in addition to the pilots and flight crew who work on the airplane itself.

The Workers

Transportation workers include truck, taxi, and bus drivers. Some drivers might also sell products out of their trucks. These drivers may sell and deliver bread, bottled water, or laundry services. Freight truck drivers drive heavy trucks or tractor-trailers to deliver products. Drivers are paid by the number of miles they drive. In addition to drivers, dispatchers work for trucking companies. They keep track of where the company trucks are. They also let drivers know of bad weather or road conditions.

Key to Education and Training Needed

1—Entry Level

2—On-the-Job Training

3—Apprenticeship

4—Technical/ Vocational Program

5—College

Common railroad occupations are locomotive engineer (train driver), brake operator (joins and separates train cars), and conductor. Other railroad workers maintain the tracks. Most railroad workers begin as laborers. They may take a formal training program to advance to locomotive engineer or conductor later.

The water transportation industry employs captains, ship engineers, oilers, and sailors. Seamen or deckhands learn on the job. Deck and engineering officers typically are graduates of maritime academies. Maritime academies are special schools that teach about a ship's operation, travel, and business at sea.

Common airline occupations include pilots, airplane mechanics, and air traffic controllers. Flight attendants, baggage and cargo handlers, airport security personnel, and gate attendants also work in the airline industry. Pilots are usually college graduates. Most airlines require at least two years of college. Military experience is often a requirement for pilots as well. Pilots must be licensed by the Federal Aviation Administration. Air traffic controllers make sure air travel stays safe. They prepare for this job with a lot of training, testing, and schooling. Other airline jobs require less preparation and training, such as clerical occupations that involve office work.

Sample Transportation Occupations	
Airline Pilot	4
Cargo and Freight Agent	1
Locomotive Engineer	3 or 4
Railroad Conductor	3
Sailor	1 or 2
Ship's Engineer	4 or 5
Shipping, Receiving, and Traffic Clerk	1
Tractor-Trailer Truck Driver	1 or 2
Transportation Attendant (Ticket Taker)	1
Truck Driver, Light or Delivery Services	1

The number after each occupation shows the minimum education and training needed for that occupation. See the key on the left.

People who work in the transportation, distribution, and logistics career cluster have a main interest in the crafts area. Some occupations involve office operations interests and require clerical skills. Transportation workers have a range of skills. These include physical strength, the ability to handle emergencies, good eye-hand coordination, and the ability to make good judgments. Pilots and ship officers need to understand complicated equipment and the weather. People in this cluster enjoy traveling, working alone, and being paid well.

Outlook

In this cluster, the employment of drivers is expected to increase. By 2012, jobs as bus, truck, and taxi drivers will increase by 15 to 20 percent. Jobs in the airline industry are also expected to increase. There will be job growth for occupations in logistics such as laborers, truck operators, production clerks, shipping clerks, and record keepers. Railroad transportation occupations are expected to decrease by about 5 percent.

About 9.3 percent of all workers in 2012 will be employed in transportation, distribution, and logistics occupations. Average wages for these occupations depend on the amount of training and education a job requires.

Entry Level	$21,300
On-the-Job Training/Apprenticeship	$28,400–$46,900
Technical/Vocational Program	$66,000
College Degree	$50,000

Lesson 4 Review Write your answers to these questions on a sheet of paper.

1. Explain why the transportation industry is more than just driving a truck or flying a plane.

2. Name one occupation in each of the following fields: road transportation, railroads, water transportation, and airlines.

3. Experts forecast that more drivers will be employed in the future. How might this fact affect people in other industries?

The Economy

Employment is closely related to a healthy economy. Government economists use several kinds of statistics to measure how much our economy grows. A large percentage of unemployed people is a sign of a weak economy. On the other hand, adding many new jobs is a sign of a healthy, growing economy. Government economists collect facts on jobs regularly. For example, in July of 2004, 5.5 percent of the American workforce was unemployed. This figure had not changed much since December 2003. So it was not a sign of a rapidly growing economy. Thirty-two thousand new jobs were added in July of 2004. This sounds like a positive sign. However, economists hoped for even greater job growth. Job facts like these have a wide-ranging effect on the American economy.

Architecture

Planning and designing buildings or other structures

Construction

The act of building

Related School Subjects
Art
Health
Math
Science
Shop
Technology

Related Abilities
Artistic
Interpersonal
Language
Manual
Mathematical
Mechanical
Scientific

Related Values
Creativity
Good Salary
Independence
Outdoor Work
Physical Activity
Risk
Work with Hands

This cluster involves **architecture** and **construction.** Think of some famous buildings—the Egyptian pyramids, the Eiffel Tower in France, or the Opera House in Australia. What does it take to build one of these structures? Building begins with an idea. It involves planning and design. People need to pay for the building and the land it will be built on. The building plan needs to be safe and meet building codes and laws. As you can see, a lot of work goes into building. There are many occupations related to building, from planning to construction. Construction can involve many projects besides buildings, such as roads, bridges, and tunnels.

The Eiffel tower in Paris, France, is famous for its design.

The Workplace

Architects and other people who design and plan building projects may work in offices. They may also visit the building site while they are planning the project. In order to get approval for the project, workers may need to visit city government buildings or offices to get permits.

The workplace for the actual construction of a project is the job site itself. Construction involves both indoor and outdoor work at the job site.

The Workers

The construction industry employs workers with a lot of different skills. Usually, construction workers learn their craft on the job. Most workers need to have special licenses. Building inspectors check that the workers have done everything correctly. The work must meet the codes and laws of a state or city. Once a project is complete, many workers help to maintain buildings, bridges, and tunnels. Other workers make sure the structures stay safe.

When planning a building project, **developers** arrange for money to pay for building costs. Architects design the structure itself. Surveyors lay out the plans for the building site. Other workers get the needed permits. Once the actual work begins, contractors act as construction managers. They oversee all the different workers on the job site. Masons, carpenters, steelworkers, and roofers build the general building structure. Then electricians, plumbers, and sheet metal workers work on the inside. Drywall workers, plasterers, and painters, and cabinetmakers come next to finish the inside. Building a bridge or other structure also involves many different workers.

Workers in this cluster usually have interests in the crafts area. They like hands-on activities. They enjoy seeing results of their work right away. They also enjoy the variety of working at different job sites. Planners and developers have business and office operations interests. Architects have scientific and artistic interests. Most construction workers have physical strength, good depth perception, and balance. They need good math skills for measuring. An important ability construction workers need is the ability to read and follow plans. Construction workers need to understand directions and safety warnings. Construction sites can be dangerous. The more skills required for a construction job, the longer the training period is.

Sample Architecture and Construction Occupations

Occupation	
Architect	5
Boilermaker	3
Brickmason and Blockmason	3
Carpenter	3
Cement Mason	3
Contractor	3, 4, or 5
Construction Equipment Operator	3
Construction Laborer	2
Drywall Installer	2
Electrician	3
Elevator Installer	3
Glazier (installs windows)	3
Helper, Construction and Trades	1 or 2
Insulation Worker	3
Painter, Construction and Maintenance	3
Paving, Surfacing, and Tamping Equipment Operator	2
Pipefitter	3
Plasterer	3
Plumber	3
Roofer	2
Sheet Metal Worker	3
Structural Iron and Steel Worker	3
Tile and Marble Setter	3

Outlook

Employment in this cluster is expected to increase by about 15 percent by 2012. Most of the growth will be in the construction of new houses, roads, bridges, and tunnels. The construction industry expects to have 1.1 million new workers by 2012.

Architecture and construction workers will make up 5.7 percent of all employed workers by 2012. Average pay for occupations in this cluster are listed below, based on training and education.

Entry Level	$22,650
On-the-Job Training/ Apprenticeship	$31,000–$35,350
Technical/Vocational Program	$50,500
College Degree	$41,060–$67,720

Key to Education and Training Needed

1—Entry Level

2—On-the-Job Training

3—Apprenticeship

4—Technical/ Vocational Program

5—College

Lesson 5 Review Write your answers to these questions on a sheet of paper.

1. Name the different workers who contribute to the construction of a building. Why is it important for the different workers to work together?

2. Why is it important for construction workers to be good readers?

3. Describe ways in which the construction field is artistic. Describe ways in which it is based on technical knowledge.

Related School Subjects
Agriculture
Clerical Studies
English
Math
Science

Related Abilities
Clerical
Interpersonal
Language
Leadership
Manual
Mathematical
Mechanical
Organizational
Scientific
Social
Visual (Spatial)

Related Values
Creativity
Good Salary
High Achievement
Independence
Job Security
Leadership
Prestige
Variety
Work with Mind
Work with People

The Health Science career cluster includes occupations related to keeping people healthy. Workers in this field work to prevent and treat disease and illness. Common occupations in health science are doctors and nurses. Others you might not think of right away are biologists, dieticians, athletic trainers, and physical therapists.

The Workplace

Doctors, nurses, and many other health-care workers may work in hospitals, private clinics, home health agencies, schools, or public health settings. Other health-care jobs, like administrative support and clerical work, may take place in offices. Health scientists may work in laboratories or research centers. Athletic trainers might work at health clubs or gyms.

The Workers

Medicine is a major part of this career cluster. One-third of medical doctors provide primary care. A primary care doctor is your personal doctor. He or she coordinates all of your medical care, answers your questions, and works to make sure you get the kind of treatment you need. Other doctors may provide care for only certain parts of the body, like the heart or lungs. Surgeons operate to fix broken bones or remove sick parts of the body. In addition to medical doctors, other doctors focus on a variety of areas. Here are some examples.

Doctor	Specialty
Chiropractor	back
Dentist	teeth and gums
Podiatrist	feet
Optometrist	eyes
Veterinarian	animals

There are many kinds of communication among coworkers in the workplace. Most communication revolves around work, both in meetings and in one-to-one conferences. But most workplaces also include informal chats among workers. Getting to know your coworkers helps you do your job better. Just remember to save informal communication for appropriate times such as lunches and breaks.

Key to Education and Training Needed

1—Entry Level

2—On-the-Job Training

3—Apprenticeship

4—Technical/ Vocational Program

5—College

Other health-care occupations include pharmacists, physician assistants, nurses, and social workers. Jobs related to health science and research include x-ray and medical technologists, laboratory technicians, and clinical laboratory personnel.

Health care also has administrative requirements. Health care is a business. People work to make sure hospitals and doctors follow government rules. Other administrators work with insurance companies or the health insurance industry. Admitting clerks record patient information. Other workers keep medical records up to date.

Sample Health Science Occupations

Athletic Trainer	5
Chiropractor	5
Dentist	5
Dietician	5
Licensed Practical Nurse	4
Medical and Clinical Laboratory Technician	4
Medical and Clinical Laboratory Technologist	5
Medical and Health Services Manager	5
Medical Assistant	3 or 4
Medical Records and Health Information Technician	4
Optometrist	5
Pharmacist	5
Pharmacy Technician	2
Physical Therapist	5
Physician	5
Registered Nurse	4 or 5
Social Worker	5
Speech-Language Pathologist	5
Veterinarian	5

The number after each occupation shows the minimum education and training needed for that occupation. See the key on the left.

Most of the careers in this cluster require an education beyond high school. The main interest area is science. People in this career field value high achievement, variety, prestige, and helping others. It is important for workers to have good communication skills when dealing with patients and families.

Outlook

Health science occupations are expected to increase greatly by 2012. This is partly because more people are getting older in the United States. The aging population requires more health care. Jobs that will see the most growth include dental hygienists and dental assistants. There will also be more jobs for physician assistants, medical records technicians, and physical therapy aides. All of these jobs are expected to increase by more than 40 percent by 2012. No occupations in the Health Science cluster are expected to see a decrease in employment.

Workers in health science will account for 7 percent of all people employed by 2012. The average wages for health science occupations can vary greatly. Pay depends on the amount of education and training a job requires.

On-the-Job Training (Moderate-Term Preparation)	$29,100
Technical/Vocational Program	$31,300
College Degree (4 years)	$54,400
Advanced Degree (more than 4 years)	$73,600

Lesson 6 Review Write your answers to these questions on a sheet of paper.

1. Name five places where health-care workers may work.

2. Explain why health care is a business.

3. People who choose health-care fields value prestige. Explain why these fields provide prestige.

Engineering

The science of planning and building machines, tools, and transportation systems

Technology

The use of science to create new products or make old ones better

Related School Subjects
Agriculture
English
Math
Science
Technology

Related Abilities
Clerical
Language
Leadership
Manual
Mathematical
Mechanical
Organizational
Scientific
Visual (Spatial)

Related Values
Creativity
Good Salary
High Achievement
Independence
Job Security
Leadership
Prestige
Variety
Work with Hands
Work with Mind

Most of the occupations in this cluster require a basic knowledge of math and science. Some occupations directly put this knowledge to use, like **engineering.** The occupations in this cluster relate to **technology.** Technology is the use of science to create new products or make old ones better. In 2012, an estimated 50 percent of the people employed in this cluster will be in engineering and related occupations. Forty-six percent will work in life and physical science, and 4 percent in mathematical science.

Engineering

Engineering requires knowledge in science and math. Most engineers design, develop, and test products. The four major engineering fields are electrical, civil, mechanical, and industrial.

The Engineering Workplace

Engineers work in every state, including urban and rural areas. They may work for large research companies, universities, governments, or small businesses. They might work in labs, offices, or schools. Their work may require both indoor or outdoor locations.

Engineering Workers

Electrical and electronics engineers can be involved in getting power and light to homes, schools, and businesses. They may also work on telephones, computers, and electric motors—anything that is designed to use electricity.

Civil engineers design roads, buildings, airports, bridges, water treatment systems, and similar structures. As the population of the United States grows, more and larger buildings, roads, and other transportation systems are needed.

Mechanical engineers work on many different projects. They design tools and machines such as refrigerators, air conditioners, and car motors. They may prepare plans and drawings of the parts needed to create a product.

Industrial engineers try to find the best way to make a product or provide a service. They help companies make the best use of their people, machines, and raw materials. They also make sure workers stay safe.

Other engineering specialties are computer, environmental, chemical, aerospace, petroleum, mining, and biomedical.

In general, engineers pay attention to details and are organized. They need to communicate well with others. They also need good writing skills to write reports. They value and enjoy being creative and working on their own. They may have scientific or business interests.

Life and Physical Science

Life scientists work in fields related to biology, food and agriculture, forestry, and the environment. Physical scientists work in the fields of physics, space exploration, chemistry, and weather.

The Life and Physical Science Workplace

Most chemists work in industrial areas. Most physicists work either for the federal government or colleges and universities. Four in ten biological scientists work for the government. Others are employed in labs, drug companies, or schools and colleges.

Life and Physical Science Workers

Life scientists may be biologists who study genetics or small living things. They may also be food scientists who help keep food safe and healthy. Other occupations in life science are animal scientists, medical researchers, chemists, and scientists who study our use of soil and water. Biologists and life scientists are interested in science and technology. They value prestige, variety, and getting a good salary.

Physical scientists work in occupations related to nuclear energy, electronics, optics, aerospace, and medical technology. They try to find out how and why things work by studying things like electricity, heat, gravity, and the particles that make up non-living things. Scientists are required to plan, record information, and write reports. They need good writing and computer skills.

Mathematics

Mathematics deals with numbers, amounts, and symbols. Mathematics can involve the study of ideas. Or, it can involve using mathematical rules to solve problems or answer questions. Many other fields rely on mathematical knowledge.

The Mathematics Workplace

Mathematics workers may be employed in almost any field. They are often involved in scientific work in laboratories or computer-related businesses. They may also teach mathematics in schools or universities.

Mathematics Workers

Many workers use mathematical skills and knowledge. They may be engineers, computer scientists, physicists, or economists. Mathematicians have scientific interests. They may study and teach mathematics. They need to have reasoning and computer skills. Those working in this cluster value variety, prestige, and a good salary.

Key to Education and Training Needed	Science, Technology, Engineering, and Mathematics Occupations	
1—Entry Level	Anthropologist	5
	Architectural Drafter	4
2—On-the-Job Training	Biologist	5
	Chemical Engineer	5
3—Apprenticeship	Chemist	5
	Civil Engineer	5
4—Technical/ Vocational Program	Computer Hardware Engineer	5
	Economist	5
5—College	Electrical Engineer	5
	Environmental Scientist	5
	Geologist	5
	Mathematician	5
	Mechanical Engineer	5
	Science Teacher	5
	Statistician	5

(See the key on the left.)

Science, Technology, Engineering, and Mathematics Outlook

The occupations in this cluster do not form their own industry. Workers with science, technology, engineering, and mathematics jobs can work in any industry. In 2002, about one out of every three engineers worked in manufacturing. By 2012, one out of every eight engineers will work for the government. Occupations that will see the most job growth in this cluster include environmental and biomedical engineers, biochemists, biological scientists, veterinary assistants, and laboratory animal caretakers. By 2012, jobs for mining, nuclear, and petroleum engineers are expected to decrease. Jobs for mathematicians are expected to decrease slightly.

Only 1.6 percent of all workers in 2012 will have occupations in the Science, Technology, Engineering, and Mathematics cluster. Most jobs in this cluster require a lot of training and education. Average wages depend on the amount of preparation needed for a job.

Technical/Vocational Program (Long-Term Preparation)	$37,300
College Degree (4 years)	$53,700
Advanced Degree (more than 4 years)	$65,500

Lesson 7 Review Write your answers to these questions on a sheet of paper.

1. Name the four engineering fields and explain what each involves.

2. Give an example of a job in the life and physical science field and one in the mathematics field.

Writing Practice

Did you have a career goal when you were a child? Maybe you wanted to work on a ranch or fight fires. Write a journal entry. Describe the career goals you had when you were a child and how they have changed.

Information technology

The way information is stored and used in a computer or computer system

Database

Stored information

Network

A group of computers linked together

Related School Subjects
English
Math
Science
Technology

Related Abilities
Interpersonal
Language
Mathematical
Organizational
Scientific

Related Values
Good Salary
High Achievement
Independence
Leadership
Prestige
Variety
Work with Mind

The occupations in this cluster relate to computer jobs. Careers in the **information technology** field can be grouped into four areas. The areas are 1) network design and database administration, 2) technical writing and support, 3) interactive media, and 4) programming and software development.

The Information Technology Workplace

People who work in the Information Technology cluster may work in offices or in their own homes. Some workers might travel to different businesses. Most of the jobs in this area involve sitting at a computer for long periods of time. People who work in this cluster need to be aware of physical problems they could encounter. These problems include eyestrain, back and arm pain, and stiffness and soreness in the hands, wrists, and fingers.

Network Design and Database Administration

Businesses store a lot of information on computers. Stored information on a computer is called a **database.** In order for a business to best use, store, and share information, its computers need to connect and communicate with each other. A group of computers linked together is called a **network.** There are many occupations related to computer networks and databases.

Network Design and Database Administration Workers
Systems analysts help plan and develop these networks for businesses. They help businesses to share and store information. Because technology keeps changing, systems and network analysts need to be current with new products.

Telecommunication specialists work on connecting computers and related equipment. Computer scientists are inventors and use research in developing theory. They can work on creating computer hardware. They might also develop language used in programming. They can be involved in designing computer games.

Database administrators use software programs to save and organize data on computers. They also keep the information secure. Properly managing saved information is very important so that no records will be lost.

Technical Writing and Support

When you work with computers you see text on the screen. Technical writers and desktop publishers write and prepare what you see on the computer screen. As more people use computers, e-mail, and the Internet, more people need help solving computer-related problems.

Technical Writing and Support Workers

Technical writers write and edit text. Desktop publishers create graphics, place photographs, and separate colors on a page. They can also be called electronic publishers, layout artists, or image designers. Computer support specialists and help desk technicians handle calls from people who need help. Because many users are not computer experts, they need the help of these experts.

Technology Note

Desktop publishing is a way to create professional-looking documents. A desktop publishing system can print a variety of typefaces. It can incorporate graphics and illustrations. Many companies use desktop publishing to create newsletters and brochures. Knowing how to use desktop publishing software is an impressive skill for your résumé.

Interactive Media

Software
Program that tells a computer what to do

Interactive media occupations involve work on computers. Workers in this field help people and companies do business on the Internet. They might be Web page designers, Web editors, art directors, graphic designers, or media designers.

Interactive Media Workers

Web page designers put text, photos, videos, or sounds on the Internet. They create Web pages for individuals or businesses. Web editors make sure that the information on a Web page is correct. They also make sure that people who use the Web site get the information they need. They might make sure that Internet links take users where they need to go. Art directors, graphic designers, and media designers are in charge of the photos, illustrations, and art that go on a Web page. They choose the art that best helps a business get its message to users.

Programming and Software Development

To do work on a computer, you use **software,** or a program that tells the computer what to do. There are many jobs related to computer software. Computer software engineers design, build, test, and maintain computer software. They tell a computer how to perform a task.

Programming and Software Development Workers

Computer systems software engineers work for companies that design, build, and install complete computer systems. Programmers write, repair, update, and maintain programs or software packages. Programmers and software testers check their work to make sure programs work without any problems.

Information Technology Workers

People who work in the Information Technology cluster have scientific interests. They are able to think logically and make good decisions. They pay close attention to detail. They communicate well. They value high salary, mental challenge, and variety in their work.

Key to Education and Training Needed

1—Entry Level

2—On-the-Job Training

3—Apprenticeship

4—Technical/ Vocational Program

5—College

Sample Information Technology Occupations	
Computer Programmer	4 or 5
Computer Software Engineer	5
Computer Support Specialist	4
Computer Systems Analyst	4 or 5
Database Administrator	4 or 5
Desktop Publisher	3 or 4
Network Systems and Data Communications Analyst	4 or 5

(See the key on the left.)

Information Technology Outlook

Information Technology is a fast-growing career cluster. All occupations in this field are expected to continue growing. Jobs that will see the most growth by 2012 are systems analysts (57 percent), database administrators (44.2 percent), and software engineers (45.5 percent). Jobs for Web designers, desktop publishers, and computer support specialists are all expected to increase from 20 to 30 percent by 2012.

Most occupations in information technology require a high level of education. Pay depends on how much education a job requires. Here are average wages based on education for information technology jobs:

College Degree (4 years)	$52,600
Advanced Degree (more than 4 years)	$62,900

Lesson 8 Review Write your answers to these questions on a sheet of paper.

1. Explain what a systems analyst, a database administrator, and a technical writer do.

2. Why is information technology a fast-growing field? Give specific examples.

3. People in the Information Technology cluster may work in their own homes. Explain why you think this is an advantage or not.

This career cluster includes only a few workers in a small number of occupations. However, the work they do impacts almost everyone. Workers in the area write what you read in newspapers and books. They create what you see and hear in the movies, on television, or at a theater. The cluster includes four areas: 1) literary, 2) the arts, 3) music, and 4) entertainment.

Literary

Work in the literary field involves writing and communication. There are writers for newspapers, TV news, magazines, movies, radio, books, and the Internet. Another set of literary occupations is editors and copywriters. They review the writing for news, newspapers, magazines, and books.

The Literary Workplace

People with literary occupations may work in offices or newsrooms. They may also work from their own homes. Others may work at a variety of locations, interviewing people for stories. Meeting time deadlines is important in this line of work.

Literary Workers

Literary workers include news writers, authors, technical writers, script writers, editors, and copywriters, and translators. They write and edit a variety of material including news stories, books, and movie scripts. Translators help people who speak different languages to communicate.

Sample Literary Occupations	
Columnist	5
Copywriter	5
Film and Video Editor	5
Interpreter	5
Novelist	5
Reporter	5
Script Editor	5
Technical Writer	5
Translator	5

People with literary occupations must be able to express ideas clearly. They need to use correct grammar. They need to make sure they get the facts.

(See the key on page 107.)

Sample Arts Occupations

Occupation	
Camera Operator	3
Cartoonist	3
Commercial Designer	4
Floral Designer	2
Graphic Designer	4
Interior Designer	5
Painter (Artist)	3
Photographer	3 or 4

Sample Music Occupations

Occupation	
Composer	5
Dancer	3 or 4
Musician	3 or 4
Singer	3

(See the key below.)

Key to Education and Training Needed

1—Entry Level

2—On-the-Job Training

3—Apprenticeship

4—Technical/ Vocational Program

5—College

The Arts

This area involves visual art and design. Arts occupations include painters, sculptors, photographers, cartoonists, designers, and illustrators. There are also technical behind-the-scenes jobs in the art field such as camera operators, multi media artists, editors, and photographers.

The Arts Workplace

Artists may work in studios. They may also work for design firms. Many artists work out of their own homes or in a variety of locations.

Arts Workers

Workers in the art field need to understand color. They pay attention to detail, size, and proportion. They need good eye-hand coordination. They often need computer knowledge. They view themselves as creative.

Music

There are three groups of performers in the music field: 1) dancers and choreographers, 2) singers, and 3) musicians. Dancers and choreographers perform and create dances. Singers sing all types of music. Musicians play instruments. Composers write and arrange music for these three groups to perform.

The Music Workplace

Performers usually work in theaters, recording studios, or concert halls. They often travel throughout the country to perform. Composers may work almost anywhere. Many work in their own homes or in studios.

Music Workers

In the music field, preparation and practice are important. Singers and musicians need to know different forms and styles of music. They must be able to read and understand music. Dancers need to be strong and move gracefully.

Entertainment

The entertainment field includes announcers, performers, and directors. These people work in radio and TV, in the theater, and in movies.

The Entertainment Workplace

Entertainers can work almost anywhere. They work on TV and movie sets, in radio studios, and on stages. Many of them travel all over the world for their jobs.

Entertainment Workers

Radio and television workers include news announcers, sports announcers, talk show hosts, and disc jockeys. Announcers and disc jockeys must have nice-sounding voices. They need to pronounce words clearly. Sports announcers need a good knowledge of sports, their rules, and well-known athletes. Talk show hosts usually have a nice appearance and are good at making conversation with others.

Other performers include circus performers, comedians, and actors and actresses. Actors need to have good memories to learn their lines. They should be able to project their voices. Actors should appear comfortable in front of many people.

Directors put together the production of a show. They are managers who hire the cast, direct practices, and approve set designs, costumes, and music. Producers handle the business and financial decisions of a production. They are administrators who hire the director and rent the facilities where the show will occur.

Sample Entertainment Occupations	
Actor/Actress	3, 4, or 5
Announcer	3, 4, or 5
Radio/Movie/TV Producer	3, 4, or 5
Radio/TV Program Director	3, 4, or 5

(See the key on page 107.)

Arts, Audio-Video Technology, and Communications Workers

Most people working in this career cluster are interested in literary, musical, and artistic expression. They value creativity, imagination, and independent thought. Most jobs require a high level of education or training because there are many more people who want these jobs than there are opportunities. Job applicants must be very talented. Most people in this cluster are good communicators. They are friendly and enjoy being with others.

Arts, Audio-Video Technology, and Communications Outlook

There will be a very small amount of job growth in this cluster. It will be difficult to find a job in the entertainment field. There are very few popular singers or movie stars. The occupations that support these people are what make the entertainment industry large. These occupations include food service workers, event promoters, and security personnel. Jobs that will see the most growth in this cluster by 2012 include technical writers, translators, and film and video editors.

Only 1.6 percent of all employed workers in 2012 will have literary, arts, music, drama, or entertainment jobs. The average wages for occupations in this cluster depend on how much training and education a job requires.

On-the-Job Training	$25,100–$26,600
College Degree (4 years)	$36,500
Advanced Degree (more than 4 years)	$42,100

Lesson 9 Review Write your answers to these questions on a sheet of paper.

1. Give an example of a worker in each of these fields: literary, arts, music, and entertainment.

2. What are some behind-the-scenes jobs in the arts cluster?

3. The arts cluster employs a very small number of workers. Yet many people would like to work in these fields. Explain why.

This career cluster includes education, training, and library occupations. These occupations make up the largest group of professional workers—31 percent of all professional occupations.

The Workplace

Educators and librarians usually work in schools or colleges. They may work in public or private schools. Many preschool teachers work in places other than a school, such as child care centers, churches, or their own homes. Trainers may work in schools or businesses. They may travel to different places to do their jobs.

The Workers

Teachers help students to learn. They also need to make sure students follow the rules. Teachers work with every age group. Early childhood and preschool teachers work with young children. Elementary school teachers work with children between the ages of five and 11. Middle and high school teachers work with older students. Special education teachers, teacher assistants, physical education teachers, and coaches can work with any age group.

Besides teachers, there are many other occupations in the education and training fields. Some examples of these occupations are school counselors, principals, librarians, college professors, and corporate trainers. School counselors help students with their problems. They can help students adjust to school. Counselors help students choose classes. They help students plan for a future career. Principals oversee the work of teachers and school support staff. Librarians buy materials for and run the school library. College professors teach a variety of subjects at colleges and universities. Corporate trainers or training and development specialists work in business and industry. They provide programs for workers and managers to learn new information and skills.

Related School Subjects
Clerical Studies
English
Languages

Related Abilities
Clerical
Language
Leadership
Organizational
Persuasive
Social

Related Values
Creativity
Good Salary
High Achievement
Job Security
Leadership
Variety
Work with Mind
Work with People

Education and Training Occupations

Corporate Trainer	5
Elementary Teacher	5
Librarian	5
Postsecondary Teacher	5
Preschool Teacher	3 or 4
School Counselor	5
Secondary Teacher	5
Special Education Teacher	5
Teacher Assistant	3
Vocational Education Teacher	3 or 5

(See the key below.)

Key to Education and Training Needed

1—Entry Level

2—On-the-Job Training

3—Apprenticeship

4—Technical/ Vocational Program

5—College

In general, workers in this cluster have social interests. They are good at talking with and working with others. They value using their minds and working with people. They like to express their creativity. They enjoy variety in their work. Administrators and trainers are also good with people. Some might have business interests. Some teachers are well organized and serious. Others are friendly and outgoing.

Outlook

Education, training, and library occupations will see a large amount of growth by 2012. This field is one of the largest-growing career areas. By 2012, there will be a 38.1 percent increase in jobs for college or postsecondary teachers. Jobs as preschool and kindergarten teachers will increase by 33.6 percent. Child, family, and school social workers will see job growth of 23.2 percent.

By 2012, workers in the Education and Training cluster will make up 8.3 percent of all workers employed. Pay for jobs in this cluster can vary, depending on how much preparation a job requires. Here are the average wages for education and training jobs:

On-the-Job Training (Long-Term Preparation)	$19,000
College Degree, Teacher (4 years)	$42,600
Advanced Degree, Teacher (more than 4 years)	$57,000
Advanced Degree, Administrator (more than 4 years)	$71,500

Lesson 10 Review Write your answers to these questions on a sheet of paper.

1. What percent of all professional occupations is made up by the education and training occupations?

2. What are three different jobs included in the teaching profession?

3. Why do you think there are so many workers in education and training occupations?

Psychological

Having to do with the mind or brain

Psychologist

Someone who studies the mind and human behavior

Related School Subjects
English
Languages
Science
Social Science

Related Abilities
Interpersonal
Language
Leadership
Organizational
Persuasive
Scientific
Social

Related Values
Creativity
Good Salary
High Achievement
Independence
Job Security
Leadership
Prestige
Variety
Work with Mind
Work with People

The Human Services cluster covers four main service areas: 1) preschool and early childhood, 2) **psychological** and counseling, 3) community, and 4) personal care. Workers in each area need different levels of education and skills. The occupations in this cluster are located in almost every community.

Preschool Services

Child care work employs a large number of people, about 1.3 million workers. Child care providers and preschool teachers work with young children. They help the children to learn, play, and get along with others.

The Preschool Services Workplace

Child care workers may be employed by child care centers or nursery schools. Many people provide child care services out of their own homes.

Preschool Services Workers

Child care workers involve children in games, art, and storytelling. They help children to create relationships. They teach children about rules for playing with others. Preschool teachers need to know how to judge what things a child is good at and what things need more work. Then, they help that child learn new skills.

Psychological and Counseling Services

Psychological workers, called **psychologists,** study the mind and human behavior. Some study memory, learning, and mental health. Most psychologists work directly with people. Counselors help people in non-medical ways. They talk with people about personal, family, education, mental health, or career problems.

The Psychological and Counseling Services Workplace

Counselors and psychologists can work in hospitals, colleges, or schools. Many of these workers have private practices, or offices they own themselves.

Psychological and Counseling Services Workers

Psychologists help people with their emotional or mental problems. They work with people who are depressed or have other mental health issues. Some psychologists help people deal with things like divorce, family arguments, or the death of a loved one. Other psychologists work with children.

Counselors help people with their problems as well. They use different skills for different things people need help with. For example, substance abuse counselors help people who have problems with alcohol, drugs, gambling, and eating disorders. School counselors help young people deal with crises they may experience at school, at home, or with classmates.

Clergy
People who do religious work, such as priests, rabbis, ministers, nuns, or pastors

Community Services

The community services area includes religious occupations, social workers, and human services assistants. These workers provide help to people in different ways.

The Community Services Workplace

Clergy and religious workers usually work in churches, synagogues, mosques, temples, and other places of worship. They may also travel to visit community members. Social workers and human services assistants work in many different offices and settings. They might work in schools, medical centers, or places of business.

Community Services Workers

Clergy and religious workers might counsel people when they need religious or moral advice. They visit the sick. They help families deal with problems. They also perform funerals, weddings, and other religious ceremonies. Most clergy members do not work regular hours and many work longer than an average workday.

Social workers help people solve personal and family problems. Social and human service assistants usually help professionals such as psychologists, rehabilitation counselors, or social workers. They provide services or support for families. Some human service assistants provide emergency relief in disasters.

Personal Care Services

Personal care services occupations include personal and home care aides. These people work with elderly, disabled, or sick people. This area also includes hairdressers, hair stylists, and barbers.

The Personal Care Services Workplace

Personal and home care aides work in private homes, residential care centers, or nursing homes. Hair stylists work in salons. Many hair stylists own their own businesses.

Personal Care Services Workers

Personal care aides might help parents who need help caring for their children. They might also help people after they return home from the hospital. They work with the person to do everyday activities like feed and dress themselves. Home care aides may clean a person's house, do laundry, or plan meals. Hairdressers, hair stylists, and barbers shampoo, cut, color, and style hair. They provide a personal appearance or beauty service.

The number following the occupations below represents the minimum education and training needed for each occupation.

Key to Education and Training Needed	Sample Human Services Occupations	
1—Entry Level	Child Care Worker	**1 or 4**
	Clergy	**5**
2—On-the-Job Training	Clinical Psychologist	**5**
	Counseling Psychologist	**5**
3—Apprenticeship	Hairdresser, Hairstylist, and Cosmetologist	**3**
	Mental Health Counselor	**5**
4—Technical/ Vocational Program	Personal and Home Care Aide	**1**
	School Counselor	**5**
5—College	School Psychologist	**5**
	Social and Human Services Assistant	**2 or 4**
	Social Worker	**5**
	(See key on the left.)	

The main interest of human service workers is social. They need to be good communicators. In general, they are sensitive to people and their problems. Psychologists usually have scientific interests. Religious workers, counselors, and social workers are very good at teaching and leading others. Child care workers are energetic. They must be able to deal with children who misbehave.

Human Services Outlook

All occupations within the Human Services cluster are expected to increase by 2012. Jobs that will see the most growth include mental health and substance abuse social workers, mental health and rehabilitation counselors, social and human service assistants, personal aides, and home care aides. These occupations are expected to grow between 26.7 and 48.7 percent.

Human services workers will account for 3.3 percent of all employed workers by 2012. The average wages for occupations in this cluster varies. Here is a list of average wages based on training and education:

Entry Level	$16,300
On-the-Job Training/Apprenticeship	$17,800–$19,000
College Degree	$39,200–$44,100

Lesson 11 Review Write your answers to these questions on a sheet of paper.

1. Do you think child care jobs will increase or decrease in the next few years? Explain why.

2. What are two different jobs in the personal care services field?

3. Why do you think clergy and psychological workers are included in the same career cluster?

This cluster includes occupations in **hospitality** and **tourism.** Tourism is the largest industry in some states, cities, and regions. For example, Las Vegas, Nevada, is a well-known attraction for visitors. Other tourist locations include beaches and national parks, as well as historical and cultural places. This cluster also includes the cruise ship industry.

Hospitality

Taking care of guests or customers

Tourism

Business of providing services to visitors and travelers

The Workplace

People employed in hospitality and tourism can work in many different places. They may work in hotels, motels, at national parks, or on cruise ships. Others work at resorts, amusement parks, and restaurants. Some workers might drive buses or cabs. People who work for travel agencies usually work in an office.

The Workers

Tourism includes transportation workers such as bus and cab drivers. Travel agents are another transportation-related occupation in the tourism industry. Travel agents help people plan trips. Tourism workers have many interests.

Related School Subjects
Family/Consumer Science
Health
Math
Social Science

Related Abilities
Clerical
Interpersonal
Language
Manual
Organizational
Persuasive
Social

Related Values
Outdoor Work
Physical Activity
Risk
Variety
Work with Hands
Work with People

Sample Hospitality and Tourism Occupations

Chef	**3, 4, or 5**
Food Services Manager	**3, 4, or 5**
Hotel Desk Clerk	**2**
Lodging Manager	**3, 4, or 5**
Maid/Housekeeper	**1**
Meeting and Convention Planner	**5**
Recreation Worker	**3 or 5**
Reservation and Transportation Ticket Agent	**2**
Restaurant Host/Hostess	**1**
Short Order Cook	**1**
Travel Agent	**2**
Tour Guide	**2**
Waiter/Waitress	**1**

(See the key on page 117.)

Hospitality means giving good service to visitors. People want to be treated nicely when they check into a hotel, motel, or resort. Hotels and motel clerks, reservation agents, housekeepers, groundskeepers, and bellhops all try to make the guests comfortable.

Other hospitality occupations are tour guides, food service workers, chefs, and meeting planners. Tour guides show visitors around an area. Waiters, waitresses, and food service workers prepare and serve food at restaurants. Chefs supervise cooks and food service workers. They plan menus and cook meals. Meeting planners make arrangements for events to take place at a hotel or convention center.

Outlook

The hospitality and tourism industry is expected to grow. People want to take vacations and be entertained. Food preparation and serving occupations will see a 20 percent increase in jobs by 2012. There will be 21.3 percent more jobs for meeting and convention planners. Job growth for hotel and motel desk clerks is expected to be 23.9 percent. The employment of travel agents is expected to decrease. This is because more people use the Internet to make travel plans on their own.

Hospitality and tourism is a large industry. By 2012, workers in this industry will make up 11.4 percent of all employed workers. The amount of training and education a job requires determines the wages.

Entry Level	$15,500
On-the-Job Training/Apprenticeship	$20,500–$21,900
Technical/Vocational Program	$32,300
College Degree (2 years)	$32,300

Key to Education and Training Needed

1—Entry Level

2—On-the-Job Training

3—Apprenticeship

4—Technical/Vocational Program

5—College

Lesson 12 Review Write your answers to these questions on a sheet of paper.

1. Why do the hospitality and tourism fields differ from place to place?

2. Which jobs in tourism are growing? Which are not?

3. What are some positive features of working in the hospitality and tourism industries? What are some negative features?

Career Profile

Paralegal

Have you ever pictured yourself before a jury, arguing an important case? Perhaps you should become a lawyer. You might also consider other legal careers, such as a paralegal. Paralegal, or legal assistant, is a rapidly growing law career. A 28.7 percent growth in the paralegal field is expected between 2002 and 2012. Paralegals cannot argue cases before a jury. But they can do many varied tasks related to law.

Paralegals may conduct interviews with clients and witnesses. They may research cases for lawyers. They may attend hearings or trials with lawyers. Beginning paralegals may do many routine administrative tasks. Experienced paralegals do more difficult work such as drafting legal documents.

There are several different career paths for paralegals. Paralegals must pass the Certified Legal Assistant exam. Some paralegals get a four-year college degree. Then they get on-the-job training or take a 60-hour paralegal course. Others have a paralegal major or minor in college. Others get a two-year degree with a paralegal major. Paralegals are interested in business and law and have good writing and speaking skills.

This cluster covers occupations in the legal system as well as in law enforcement and **corrections.** It also includes emergency medical, fire, and security services.

The Legal System

The legal system deals with laws. Governments, courts, and elected officials are all part of the legal system.

The Legal System Workplace

Legal workers live within most communities. They work in courthouses, government buildings, and offices. Some legal workers own their own businesses.

Legal System Workers

Many different people are part of the legal system. Legal workers include judges, lawyers, and legal assistants. Judges oversee what goes on in court. They also make decisions about cases. Lawyers, also called attorneys, make arguments in court. They might work for the government or for the person they are defending. Law is a large field, so lawyers usually focus on one type of law such as family, business, or real estate. Legal assistants, or paralegals, research topics or prepare documents for lawyers or judges.

Legal workers have many interests. They usually like to be involved in business. Judges and lawyers have good language and persuasive skills. They like to be in leadership positions.

Law Enforcement

Law enforcement occupations include corrections officers, police officers, detectives, sheriffs and deputies, and dispatchers.

Corrections

Field that involves the treatment and rehabilitation of prisoners in jails

Related School Subjects
Clerical Studies
English
Science
Social Science

Related Abilities
Clerical
Interpersonal
Language
Leadership
Manual
Organizational
Persuasive
Scientific

Related Values
Creativity
Good Salary
High Achievement
Independence
Job Security
Leadership
Physical Activity
Prestige
Risk
Variety
Work with Mind
Work with People

The Law Enforcement Workplace

Corrections officers work in jails and prisons. Police officers, detectives, and sheriff's deputies might work on patrol in cars. They might also work in offices or police stations doing work related to solving cases. Dispatchers usually work at police stations.

Law Enforcement Workers

Corrections officers include jailers, guards, and wardens. They watch over the prisoners in a jail. They also help move prisoners throughout the jail or to other places. Wardens oversee everything that goes on at the jail. They make sure the jail operates safely.

Occupations related to corrections officers are probation and parole officers. These people work with people on probation or people who have been released from prison. Their job is to make sure these people follow the rules of their release from prison.

Police officers provide public safety. They do this by preventing crime. Police officers, sheriffs, and deputies enforce speed limits. They stop the destruction of property. They keep people from hurting others or themselves. Police officers might arrest criminals, resolve arguments, or help at traffic accidents. Detectives are police officers who investigate crimes. They try to figure out how and why a crime happened. They often try to find out who committed a crime.

Dispatchers use radios and other equipment to help police, firefighters, and emergency workers communicate with each other. Dispatchers answer 911 calls or other calls to the police or fire departments. They give the call information to police, fire, or emergency workers.

The United States government has its own law enforcement system. The Federal Bureau of Investigation (FBI) investigates all violations of federal laws. Other government agencies enforce different laws related to things such as money, taxes, the postal service, drugs, alcohol, and firearms. Other law enforcement occupations in the government include customs agents, federal marshals, immigration officers, and park rangers.

Law enforcement officers must be in good physical condition. They should be alert and be able to work well with others. They need to know how to investigate. They often have to make decisions quickly. They have social interests and enjoy working with people. They like to be in control of situations and are good problem solvers.

Emergency Services

Workers such as firefighters, emergency medical technicians (EMTs), and lifeguards deal with fire and medical emergencies. Security workers at airports or malls also handle emergencies. Emergency services workers often put themselves in personal danger on the job.

The Emergency Services Workplace

Firefighters and EMTs usually travel to the location where help is needed. They drive or ride in fire trucks and ambulances. Life guards and ski patrol workers usually work outdoors. Security guards can work almost anywhere, including airports, malls, and banks, and other businesses.

Emergency Services Workers

Firefighters and EMTs help people by putting out fires and providing medical care. They need to think and act quickly. They might not know what kind of emergency they are going to handle. Other protective workers like lifeguards and ski-patrol staff work to make sure people stay safe. They may need to rescue people who are hurt. Guards and security officers work to prevent fire, theft, vandalism, or other illegal activities. They protect airports, homes, businesses, and factories.

Emergency service workers need to have physical strength. They should be able to work as part of a team. These workers often deal with the public. They need to be able to communicate well.

Sample Law, Public Safety, and Security Occupations

Occupation	
Corrections Officer	2
Detective	3, 4, or 5
Dispatcher	2
Emergency Medical Technician (EMT)	3 or 4
Immigration and Customs Inspector	3 or 4
Lawyer	5
Legal Secretary	4
Paralegal	4
Police Officer	2
Security Guard	1

(See the key below.)

Key to Education and Training Needed

1—Entry Level

2—On-the-Job Training

3—Apprenticeship

4—Technical/ Vocational Program

5—College

Law, Public Safety, and Security Outlook

The job outlook until 2012 for this cluster is excellent. All occupations in this cluster are expected to see job growth. EMTs can expect to see 33.1 percent job growth. Jobs for security guards will increase by 31.9 percent. Police and sheriff patrol officer jobs will increase by 24.7 percent. Corrections officer occupations will grow 24.2 percent.

Law, public safety, and security workers will make up 4.3 percent of the workforce by 2012. There can be a big difference in wages for occupations in this cluster. Usually, pay depends on the amount of training and education a job requires.

Entry Level	$19,100
On-the-Job Training/Apprenticeship	$30,200
Technical/Vocational Program	$42,900
College Degree (4 years)	$38,000
Advanced Degree (more than 4 years)	$90,300

Lesson 13 Review Write your answers to these questions on a sheet of paper.

1. How do the jobs in the legal system and the law enforcement fields differ?

2. Name three jobs in the emergency services field.

3. Why do you think the job outlook for jobs in this cluster is excellent for the next few years?

4. What are some positive and negative features of jobs in the law enforcement field?

This career cluster includes occupations in the **finance** industry. The finance industry involves the management of money.

The Workplace

Finance workers do their jobs at various financial institutions such as banks, insurance companies, and investment companies. Banks are located in most cities. Insurance agents visit clients' homes or businesses. Financial companies are usually located in large cities around the country.

The Workers

There are four groups of workers in this career cluster: 1) administrative support workers, 2) salespeople, 3) financial analysts, and 4) administration and professional staff. Each group of workers has different skills and interests.

Administrative support workers are involved in office operations. They gather information, fill out forms, and record data. They answer customer questions. They enter data into computer systems, calculate numbers, and prepare reports. One example of an administrative support worker is a bank teller.

Salespeople sell products. They learn about the products and services their company sells. They help customers decide what to buy and how to pay for it. **Commodity** sales agents are a type of salespeople. They buy and sell products. Commodity sales agents might buy eggs from farmers. Then, they sell the eggs to stores to sell to customers. Insurance agents are also salespeople. They sell customers protection against car, home, or fire damage. They also sell medical insurance to handle health problems. Real estate agents are also salespeople. Real estate involves buying and selling homes, hotels, factories, and buildings.

Finance
Management of money

Commodity
Something that is bought or sold

Related School Subjects
Clerical Studies
English
Finance
Management
Math

Related Abilities
Clerical
Interpersonal
Language
Leadership
Mathematical
Organizational
Persuasive

Related Values
Good Salary
High Achievement
Job Security
Leadership
Prestige
Work with Hands
Work with Mind
Work with People

Financial analysts study trends related to money. They collect information by reading company reports, interviewing business executives, and studying related laws. Then they make decisions about how a company should use its money. They often give reports about investments to managers and decision-makers.

Administration and professional staff plan and manage banking, investments, and insurance. They are decision-makers and supervisors. They use information from financial analysts to make decisions about handling money. Financial managers fall into this group. These managers keep track of how much money a business has. They invest available money. They prepare required financial reports. Local bank branch managers are financial managers. Banks also offer services like investments and business, personal, and home loans. Bank managers oversee all of these services.

In addition to the four groups of workers you just read about, home builders and real estate developers are a part of the financial industry. Land developers buy land and plan for how it will be used. They plan to build shopping centers, houses, apartments, office buildings, or industrial parks.

Workers in the financial industry are excellent communicators. They are good at working with numbers. They also have good computer skills. People working in finance value making money. They enjoy being recognized for doing their jobs well. They have business and office operations interests.

Key to Education and Training Needed

1—Entry Level

2—On-the-Job Training

3—Apprenticeship

4—Technical/Vocational Program

5—College

Sample Finance Occupations	
Bill Collector	1
Brokerage Clerk	3 or 4
Credit Analyst	5
Finance Manager	5
Financial Analyst	5
Insurance Claim and Policy Processing Clerk	2
Insurance Sales Agent	3 or 5
Insurance Underwriter	5
Loan Officer	5
New Accounts Clerk	3
Purchasing Agent	3
Sales Agent: Securities and Commodities	5
Tax Preparer	2

(See the key on the left.)

Outlook

The finance industry is expected to grow by 12.3 percent from 2002 to 2012. There will be more jobs for accountants, tax preparers, and those in payroll services. The real estate area will add the most jobs. This is because the demand for housing will grow as the population grows.

By 2012, workers in finance occupations will make up 3.2 percent of all employed workers. Average wages for finance occupations vary. Here is a list of average pay, based on training and education:

On-the-Job Training (Moderate-Term Preparation)	$27,900
Technical/Vocational Program	$37,800
College Degree (4 years)	$50,300
Advanced Degree (more than 4 years)	$55,100

Lesson 14 Review Write your answers to these questions on a sheet of paper.

1. What are some places where finance workers do their jobs?

2. Why will the real estate field grow in the next few years?

3. Why must workers in the financial industry be excellent communicators?

Occupations in the Marketing, Sales, and Service cluster deal with how businesses get their products to customers in order to make money. Marketing is creating an awareness and desire for products and services. The sales field involves getting customers to buy products or services. Service is providing customers with answers to their questions about a product or service.

The Marketing, Sales, and Service Workplace

Sales and marketing workers can work almost anywhere. They may work in offices or they may travel to cities all over the country. Many sales workers also use the Internet or telephone to do business. Most salespeople prefer to have personal contact with buyers.

Marketing Workers

Marketing workers get customers to buy a product. They do this by advertising. Marketing occupations include marketing managers, promotions workers, and advertising representatives.

Marketing managers oversee the creation of good advertisements or promotions. They use information to plan the best way to sell a product to customers. These people need good judgment. They often have to make decisions or solve problems quickly.

Promotion workers plan and set up displays of products. They try to make the product look good to the customer. These workers usually have art or photography experience. They must be good at communicating a message. They are creative people.

Advertising representatives sell businesses time or space to advertise their products. They may work for radio or TV stations, newspapers, magazines, or other industries that get messages to the public.

Marketing workers usually have business interests. They value challenges. They enjoy solving problems creatively. People in marketing occupations should be good at working with others.

Related School Subjects
Art
Clerical Studies
English
Finance
Languages
Math
Management
Social Science

Related Abilities
Artistic
Clerical
Interpersonal
Language
Leadership
Mathematical
Organizational
Persuasive

Related Values
Creativity
Good Salary
High Achievement
Independence
Leadership
Variety
Work with Mind
Work with People

Sales Workers

Most of the workers in this cluster are sales workers. Other sales occupations include buyers, manufacturer's representatives, real estate agents, and customer service representatives.

Most sales workers are cashiers and retail salespeople. Cashiers and retail salespeople need good math skills. They should know how to use a computer and make change. They also need to be friendly when dealing with customers. Customers want salespeople to know about the product they are selling. Salespeople should be able to answer questions about the product.

Buyers or purchasing agents buy products directly from the manufacturers. They then resell the products to stores that will sell the products to customers. Buyers decide what products and services to sell in their stores. They need to predict what people will like and want to buy. Planning is an important skill for buyers. For example, swimsuits need to be in stores in early spring. The buyer needs to plan when to order them so the stores get them in time for the summer season.

Manufacturer's representatives can sell machinery and equipment. The manufacturer's representative tries to persuade the buyer that this is the best machinery available. If a business buys the machine, the manufacturer's representative may demonstrate how to use the machine and train workers to use it. These sales workers must be able to answer questions about the product. They may need to be able to read blueprints or engineering plans.

Gender and Careers

Some careers have traditionally been closed to women. For example, 50 years ago there were few female doctors and lawyers. The job of secretary, however, was almost exclusively filled by women. Today, both men and women work as secretaries, receptionists, and administrative assistants. Workers in all these jobs support managers. They schedule appointments and handle mail. They communicate with employees, customers, and clients. They often use photocopiers, word processors, and other office technology. All secretaries or administrative assistants must be organized and be excellent communicators.

Specialty sales occupations are also part of the sales cluster. Two examples of specialty sales are interior design and real estate. Interior designers plan how to decorate a room. They may work for large department stores or they may own their own businesses. Interior designers help a customer decide what to buy for a room. They decide where to place the furniture and what colors and patterns go together.

Real estate agents usually have their own businesses within a community. They find people who want to sell or rent their homes or business buildings. They also help buyers find homes to purchase. When a match is found between a buyer and seller, real estate agents help both sides decide on the final price of the property. Real estate agents can also help buyers with financing options for buying a house.

People in sales value mental challenges. They have business interests and they like to persuade and influence others. Salespeople usually are good communicators and enjoy being around people. They like competition and they value a good salary.

Service Workers

Customer service workers handle customer complaints. They might handle complaints such as billing errors or product repairs. They also deal with customers who are returning products and want their money back. They need to keep a written or computer record of the return. Customer service workers need excellent communication skills. They should be very good at working with people.

Key to Education and Training Needed	Sample Marketing, Sales, and Service Occupations	
	Advertising and Promotion Representative	3, 4, or 5
1—Entry Level	Buyer	3
	Cashier	1
2—On-the-Job Training	Customer Service Representative	2
	Interior Designer	5
3—Apprenticeship	Manufacturer's Representative	3
	Marketing Manager	3, 4, or 5
4—Technical/ Vocational Program	Real Estate Sales Agent	3
	Retail Salesperson	1
5—College	Sales Manager	3, 4, or 5
	Sales Worker Supervisor	3
	Wholesale Sales Representative	3

(See the key on the left.)

Marketing, Sales, and Service Outlook

Work in sales is expected to grow. Most new sales jobs will be for retail salespeople and cashiers. There will be more than one million new workers in these two occupations by 2012. Jobs for sales managers will increase by 30.5 percent. Occupations in advertising and marketing are expected to increase between 25 and 30 percent.

The Marketing, Sales, and Service cluster employs many people. Workers in this cluster will account for 12.6 percent of the workforce by 2012. Pay for sales occupations depends on the amount of training and education a job requires.

Entry Level	$15,400
On-the-Job Training (Moderate-Term Preparation)	$38,500
Technical/Vocational Program	$35,250
College Degree (4 years)	$58,200

Lesson 15 Review Write your answers to these questions on a sheet of paper.

1. If you were a creative person and wanted a job in the Marketing, Sales, and Service cluster, what job or jobs would you seek?

2. Name five specific kinds of sales workers.

3. What are some positive features of being a sales worker? What are some negative features?

Business generally refers to the making, buying, or selling of products and services to make money. The Business Management and Administration cluster includes management and administrative support occupations. Every company, business, organization, and school needs leadership. The occupations in this cluster relate to two kinds of leadership: administrative leadership and managerial leadership. Administrators make the plans and policies for a business. Managers put those plans and policies into action. For example, in a school the administrators decide what classes and programs to offer to students. They decide what school rules will be. The managers, such as principals and teachers, teach the students and make sure students follow the rules.

The Business Management and Administration Workplace

People with occupations in the Business Management and Administration cluster can work for very large companies or for small companies. They often work in office buildings. Many of these workers travel as part of their jobs.

Management Workers

Management workers include accountants, human resources workers, computer and information systems managers, budget analysts, operations research analysts, and administrative services managers.

Accountants keep track of money for a business. They prepare financial reports. They give the business team advice on taxes. They study how a business uses its money and find ways to help the business spend its money wisely.

Related School Subjects
Clerical Studies
English
Finance
Languages
Management
Math
Social Science
Technology

Related Abilities
Clerical
Interpersonal
Language
Leadership
Manual
Mathematical
Mechanical
Organizational
Persuasive
Scientific

Related Values
Creativity
Good Salary
High Achievement
Independence
Job Security
Leadership
Prestige
Variety
Work with Hands
Work with Mind
Work with People

Human resources workers help businesses find people to hire. Some human resources workers visit colleges to recruit new hires. Human resources workers also make sure that businesses follow proper legal procedures. They help employees with benefits like insurance and retirement funds. They also help workers resolve work-related problems. Human resources workers also handle training of new employees.

Another part of management is overseeing information and computer systems. People in these jobs study what people want and need computers to do. They meet with workers to decide how to design new computer programs or change old ones. They also provide help when computers do not work. Sometimes, they provide training. They also make recommendations when new equipment or software packages are needed.

Budget analysts are in charge of monitoring the spending of money. They want to help the business make money. They talk with supervisors and accountants. They give advice on how to solve money-related problems. They find good ways to deal with financial emergencies.

Operations research analysts are mathematicians. They study a business and test out their ideas by using mathematical models. For example, they might develop airline schedules to make the best use of fuel, pilots, airplanes, and time. Or, they might plan delivery schedules to make sure the right parts arrive at a manufacturing plant on time. These analysts try to find creative ways to solve problems a business might have.

Administrative services managers can be vice presidents or mid-level managers. These people make sure that business operations like payroll, planning and travel, mail, security, parking, and scheduling happen. In a large business, an administrative service manager may handle just one or two of the tasks listed. In smaller companies, one person may handle all of the tasks.

Sample Business Management and Administration Occupations

Accountant	5
Administration Services Manager	3, 4, or 5
Computer Systems Manager	5
Management Analyst	5
Office Manager	3
Operations Research Analyst	5
Personnel Recruiter	3, 4, or 5
Training and Development Specialist	5

(See the key on the left.)

Managers and administrators need leadership skills. They should be self-confident. They often need to work with a variety of people. They need to be able to communicate and to make quick decisions. Managers and administrators are good at gathering facts and making a plan. They have business interests.

Office and Administrative Support Workers

Office and administrative support workers provide support to business managers. Occupations in the support area include administrative assistants, receptionists, secretaries, office clerks, data entry workers, word processors, and customer service representatives.

Administrative assistants schedule, plan, and give important information to employees and the public. Receptionists answer phones. They connect customers to the right people in the company. Secretaries write reports, research and answer questions, take notes, and help managers with other tasks. Office clerks may run photocopiers and fax machines. They get mail ready to send. Data entry workers and word processors enter information into computers. Customer service representatives answer customer questions. They also handle customer complaints.

Administrative and office support workers need good listening skills. They also need to be good at spelling, punctuation, and grammar. They are expected to be excellent communicators and to be very organized. They have office operations interests.

These workers need to stay updated on the latest technology and computer programs needed to do their jobs. They should also be good at working under pressure when they need to meet deadlines.

Sample Office and Administrative Support Occupations

Administrative Assistant	4
Customer Service Representative	2
Human Resource Assistant	2
Medical Transcriptionist	4
Office Clerk	1
Receptionist	1
Secretary	4
Word Processor/Typist	2

(See the key on page 132.)

Business Management and Administration Outlook

Management jobs in companies and organizations will increase by about 195,000 by 2012. Occupations in the administrative support area, such as customer service representatives, are expected to see a lot of growth. Jobs as secretaries and data entry workers are expected to decrease. This is because most workers have their own computers and do typing tasks themselves.

The Business Management and Administration cluster is large. By 2012, workers in business occupations will make up 14.2 percent of all employed workers. Average wages for occupations in this cluster depends on the amount of training and education a job requires.

Entry Level	$17,500
On-the-Job Training	$25,900
Vocational Program/College (2 years)	$39,100
College Degree (4 years)	$49,200

Lesson 16 Review Write your answers to these questions on a sheet of paper.

1. Name three business management jobs included in the Business Management and Administration cluster. Name three administrative support occupations.

2. Administrative support occupations will decrease while customer service representative occupations will increase. How do you think these two facts are related?

3. The business management and administration cluster covers many different kinds of jobs. Which one appeals to you most? Explain why.

Governments may be small or large. There are federal, state, county, and city governments. They collect taxes, pass and enforce laws, and provide for the safety and protection of their citizens. Several government occupations are not found in other career clusters, such as tax collectors and military personnel. Other government jobs, however, are similar to jobs in other clusters. For example, governments operate hospitals, airports, schools, and parks. They also run tourism agencies, power plants, highways, courthouses, and research laboratories.

The Workplace

Government workers may work anywhere. Governments operate in every city or town across the country. Government employees might work at a county courthouse, a military base, or at a national park. The workplace is different according to the job.

The Workers

Governments employ people in all six interest areas: business, office operations, social, the arts, scientific, and crafts. Many government jobs are similar to jobs in the other industries and clusters you have learned about. There are some jobs, however, that are specific to government. These include occupations in the armed forces and occupations in public administration.

Armed Forces

The military provides a country's national security. The United States Military, or the Armed Forces, includes the Army, Navy, Air Force, and Marine Corps. Members of the Armed Forces are not considered to be part of the work force. In 2003 more than 2.5 million people served in the Armed Forces. More than 1.4 million people were on active duty. In addition, more than 1.1 million people serve in the Reserves and the Air and Army National Guard. Fifteen percent are officers who are the leaders, managers, and supervisors. Eighty-five percent are called enlisted personnel.

Enlisted personnel are involved in combat, transportation, construction, healthcare, and more. Also, 38,000 people served in the Coast Guard, which is now part of the U.S. Department of Homeland Security.

Government Agencies and Public Administration

Government agencies such as the Central Intelligence Agency (CIA), Federal Bureau of Investigation (FBI), Customs, the Drug Enforcement Agency (DEA), and the Internal Revenue Service (IRS) provide several different employment opportunities. Workers in these agencies include police officers, detectives, accountants, and tax clerks. The federal government also employs workers in countries all over the world. These workers help American citizens who visit those countries. They also help citizens from other countries visit the United States. They help businesspeople trade or do business with one another. Other government jobs provide services to the public. For example, government workers might arrange for the care of children, families, or the elderly who are having troubles.

Most administrators have business interests. They need to communicate and write well. They should be able to work with all kinds of people. Government administrators should pay attention to details and be organized. They need to be able to make good decisions.

Get Involved

What is more basic than having a comfortable home? That is the philosophy of Habitat for Humanity. This organization helps families build new homes. All the work is contributed by volunteers. Many teens contribute their services. In one community in Michigan, 60 percent of the volunteers are teens. Josh, one volunteer there, said, "I've worked with Habitat at least 50 hours this year. I've learned new things, and I really felt like I helped people." For safety reasons, there are rules about the jobs teens can do. They can use hand tools but not power tools. They cannot climb ladders. However, they can help clean sites, clean up after workers, paint, and landscape. Teen volunteers for Habitat enjoy the comforts of their own homes. They help others share this pleasure.

The number after each occupation shows how much education and training is needed for that occupation. See the key on the left.

<table>
<tr><td colspan="2">Sample Government and Public Administration Occupations</td></tr>
<tr><td>Animal Caretaker</td><td>1</td></tr>
<tr><td>Building Inspector</td><td>3 or 4</td></tr>
<tr><td>Computer Programmer</td><td>4 or 5</td></tr>
<tr><td>FBI Agent</td><td>5</td></tr>
<tr><td>Firefighter</td><td>2</td></tr>
<tr><td>Government Administrator</td><td>5</td></tr>
<tr><td>Mail Carrier</td><td>1</td></tr>
<tr><td>Military Officer</td><td>5</td></tr>
<tr><td>Police Chief</td><td>3, 4, or 5</td></tr>
<tr><td>Police Officer</td><td>2</td></tr>
<tr><td>Post Office Clerk</td><td>2</td></tr>
<tr><td>Public Relations Specialist</td><td>5</td></tr>
<tr><td>School Administrator</td><td>5</td></tr>
<tr><td>Surveyor</td><td>4</td></tr>
<tr><td>Translator</td><td>5</td></tr>
</table>

Key to Education and Training Needed

1—Entry Level

2—On-the-Job Training

3—Apprenticeship

4—Technical/ Vocational Program

5—College

Outlook

Government workers can work in any cluster. The outlook for new jobs depends on the cluster. Occupations in the postal service are expected to decrease slightly by 2012. Postal service occupations are found only in government. Most other government-related occupations are expected to grow.

The wages for most occupations in this cluster are the same as for those in other industries. The average wage for government supervisors and managers is $64,100 in 2003. Wages for government administrators can vary widely. For example, a small-town city council member may earn little or no pay. The president of the United States earns $400,000 per year. For people serving in the armed forces, starting pay in 2003 ranged from $12,780 to $26,208. Military personnel also receive free housing, food, healthcare, and clothing.

Lesson 17 Review Write your answers to these questions on a sheet of paper.

1. What are two government occupations not found in other career clusters?

2. Name two cities where you might find a larger than average number of government workers.

3. What are some positive features of working for a government?

What Career Is Right for You?

Each career cluster has a wide variety of occupations. As you learn about each cluster, you can decide whether the careers interest you. You may change the opinions you have had about a particular career. For example, you may find that the tourism industry offers more potential than you thought. You might find there are fewer administrative assistant jobs available than you realized. Think about your responses to the careers and career clusters described in the chapter. Then answer the questions on page 139. Put the answers in your portfolio.

You can learn about a career by going to work with an experienced worker.

1. What is one career cluster in which you have had work or volunteer experience? Describe the experience. Describe its positive and negative features. Explain whether you would consider the cluster for a future career.

2. What is one career cluster in which someone you know is employed? Describe the person's job.

3. Learning more about a career can change a person's opinions about it. Choose one career cluster that you might reconsider after having learned more about it. Explain why your opinion has changed.

4. Which career cluster appeals to you most? Name two or three jobs in the cluster that especially interest you. Describe the features, such as good pay, prestige, or outlook, that are attractive.

5. Choose one of the jobs you named in question 4. Summarize what you have learned about the job's tasks, pay, workplace, and outlook. You can find additional information about jobs by using the CDMCareerZone Web site or the *Occupational Outlook Handbook.*

Vocabulary Review

Choose the word or phrase from the Word Bank that best completes each sentence. Write the answer on your paper.

> **Word Bank**
>
> career ladder
> commodity
> corrections
> engineering
> finance
> hospitality
> information technology
> industry
> manufacturing
> offshore outsourcing
> tourism

1. The science of planning and building machines, tools, and transportation systems is _____.

2. Giving jobs to workers in countries outside the United States is _____.

3. The management of money is _____.

4. The _____ field deals with the way information is stored and used in computers.

5. A large-scale business or service area that provides a product or service is a(n) _____.

6. The business of providing services to visitors and travelers is _____.

7. Taking care of guests or customers is _____.

8. You can move up a _____ by getting more training and education.

9. Turning material into products people use every day is _____.

10. Something that is bought or sold is a(n) _____.

11. The field that involves the treatment and rehabilitation of prisoners in jails is _____.

Concept Review

Choose the word or phrase that best completes each sentence. Write the letter of the answer on your paper.

12. On average, the highest yearly pay is earned by people with _____.

    A long-term on-the-job training

    B an Associate's degree

    C a postsecondary vocational award

    D a Bachelor's degree

13. _____ workers enjoy working with their hands.

A Sales   **C** Manufacturing

B Tourism   **D** Finance

14. An occupation in the education and training field is _____.

A school counselor   **C** technical writer

B customer service representative   **D** loan officer

15. A field in which workers get customers to buy a product is _____.

A extraction   **C** marketing

B logistics   **D** public administration

16. An industry that distributes materials and products is _____.

A mining   **C** information technology

B transportation   **D** hospitality

17. One job that is specific to government is _____.

A truck driver   **C** hotel clerk

B engineer   **D** military officer

Critical Thinking

Write the answer to each question on your paper.

18. Why is it a good idea to know which career areas will grow and be in demand in the future?

19. Do you need to decide on a particular career before planning further education? Or can you just decide on a career cluster? Explain.

20. Which career cluster interests you more after reading about it? Explain why you are interested in that cluster.

Test-Taking Tip

When studying for a chapter test, review the topics in the chapter. Then make up a practice test for yourself.

5

Your Preferred Careers

Do you ever wish you could look into the future? It would be great to see yourself in your chosen career in five or 10 years. Of course, no one can see the future. But you can prepare for it. You must actively make choices and take steps. These choices and actions will lead you to where you want to be five or 10 years down the road. This chapter will help you make specific career and education choices that will lead you to a bright future. It provides a plan to help you talk with your parents or guardians about your future.

Goals for Learning

◆ To make a career plan

◆ To explore the education and training needed for a chosen career

You have learned about many different occupations. Now, you can decide what occupations interest you. You can begin to explore these occupations. You can learn more details about the jobs you want. As you explore, you are gathering information. This information will help you make decisions about your future. You are starting a career plan.

What Are the Steps of a Career Plan?

The first step in a career plan is choosing the careers you are interested in. The second step is identifying what you need to learn in school. It is important to take classes that will prepare you for the occupation you want.

Taking science classes is one way to prepare for a career in math, science, or technology.

The third step is to see what abilities you need for the career you want. You may need to work on some abilities to get better at them. The fourth step is thinking about what work-related values you can fulfill in the career you choose. The fifth step is researching the job outlook for a career. See what occupations will have new job openings. Find out what certain jobs pay. The sixth step is deciding what your plans will be after you finish high school. The final step is sharing your plan with parents or guardians. You need to think about how you are going to reach your career goals. Reaching a career goal will cost money. How will you pay for training or a college education? You need a plan that shows your parents or guardians that you have given some thought to your future.

Before you start your career plan, let's first review what you have discovered so far. In Chapter 1, you learned what work is. You learned how work affects your life. Think about how the job you want will impact your life. It may seem too early to decide the exact job you want. However, it is never too early to begin thinking about and planning for your future career.

In Chapter 2, you practiced self-assessment. You stated what school subjects you like. You named the skills you are learning in each subject. You identified your work-related abilities. You also explored the values that are most important to you. You examined your interests. Finally, you thought about how much time and energy you want to invest in more education and training.

In Chapter 3, you learned the five decision-making steps.

1. Set Goals

2. Make Priorities

3. Explore the Options

4. Assess the Risks

5. Make a Plan

You learned about the major industries in the United States in Chapter 4. You learned details about many occupations by reading about career clusters. Now, you will make a specific career plan based upon everything you have learned.

Career Plan

Preferred Careers

First you need to choose the careers that interest you. Select two occupations. Be specific. For example, you may know you like science, but what scientific occupation do you want to prepare for? Do you want to be a biologist, a pharmacist, or an engineer? Maybe you are interested in business and the tourism industry. Do you want to be a travel agent, a hotel manager, or a chef? Identify two occupations you want to look at more closely.

School Subjects

Use the resources such as the CDMCareerZone Web site or the *Occupational Outlook Handbook* (OOH) to find out what school subjects you need to take for the careers you chose. Have you completed the classes required for each of your chosen careers? Do you still need to take certain courses?

Abilities

Recall the abilities you wrote down on your Self-Assessment Profile in Chapter 2. Remember that an ability is something a person does well. Think about some skills you have developed that are related to your abilities. Recall that a skill is a competency that comes from training or practice. For example, a skill related to artistic ability would be the good use of colors in a painting. How do your skills relate to your two chosen careers? What skills must you develop in order to be prepared for these careers?

Values

Remember that work-related values are things people want to get from performing a job. Fulfilling certain work values can bring you job satisfaction. What values could you fulfill in both of your chosen careers? Think of work-related values for each career. If similar values appear in both careers, this means they are strong beliefs of yours. If different values appear in the two careers, this means you may have several strong values. Try to prioritize your values. Decide which ones are most important.

Employment Outlook and Wages

For each of your chosen careers, you should examine two pieces of information. First, will jobs be available in this field when you are ready to begin work? Second, how much money will you be paid for doing the work? You can find this information on CDMCareerZone, in the OOH, or in other materials available at libraries or in your school's career center.

Career Profile

Television News Producer

On a television news program, the anchor gets most of the attention. But have you ever thought about the people behind the scenes? Many reporters, camera operators, videotape editors, and producers combine their talents to create television news.

Many people in television news start their careers as news producers or production assistants. The job of a producer varies according to the size of the station. At a small station, a producer keeps a close eye on news from wire services, newspapers, and cable news networks. Then he or she might schedule the stories that will air. He or she might write the stories to be read by the news anchor. A producer or production assistant might edit video clips to show during the program. A producer must communicate with reporters, camera operators, and anchors. He or she has responsibility for coordinating the news program.

A degree in broadcast journalism is the best background for the job of news producer. Many television stations offer unpaid internships for college journalism students. These help students learn about television news.

Plans After High School

What are your plans after you finish high school? Do you want to find a job right away? Do you see the military as an opportunity? Would you move to a different location to receive training for a specific job? Do you want to travel or stay at home? Think about the two careers you chose. How would deciding on one or the other change your plans after high school?

Postsecondary Education

Employers today expect job applicants to have better job skills than they once did. To learn these skills, more and more students are going on to **postsecondary** education. Postsecondary means after high school. Postsecondary education can include technical school or college. How do you decide which school to attend? You need to do some research. You have identified two occupations that interest you. Now you need to identify the schools and institutions that offer the program or programs you want to study. You can find this information in your school's guidance office or career center. Most schools have catalogs or videos about postsecondary schools. Your local library also is a good resource for information. You can search for schools using catalogs or the Internet.

As you find schools that offer a program that interests you, you will see that schools are different. Tuition, fees, and room and board charges vary. Some schools have more modern equipment than others. Other schools have more instructors and course offerings. Some schools are very proud of their graduates and will tell you the names of employers who hire their graduates.

Writing Practice

Spend a few minutes thinking about yourself in a specific career. Use your imagination to picture yourself and your workplace. Picture the people you are with and what you are saying, doing, or thinking. Now write a journal entry about your thoughts. Describe them in as much detail as possible.

A positive attitude is one of the best educational tools there is. All students have classes in which they perform better. For example, perhaps math comes easily to you while writing is more difficult. A positive attitude about writing will give you confidence in your abilities. It will give you the extra energy you need as you work on writing better.

Conclusion

Your career plan includes the main points to talk about with others. Your plan should help you get the information you will need to make one or more of these decisions:

- Choose one career over another career
- Select to go to work or school or
- Choose one postsecondary school over another

Lesson 1 Review Write your answers to these questions on a sheet of paper.

1. Why is it important to share your plans for the future with your parents or guardians?

2. Why is it wise to consider two different careers when making plans for the future?

3. Suppose the two careers that interest you have very different values. What does this tell you?

What are you going to do after high school? You need to decide how much education and training you will complete. Your parents or guardians can help you make this decision. Do you know what you want to do after high school? Now is the time to decide. The decisions you make now about your future can affect the rest of your life.

Why Is It Important to Finish High School?

About one-half of students who do not finish high school will not find work. Those who do find work usually do not have year-round, full-time jobs. Of the students who graduate from high school, about two-thirds will continue their training and education. On average, they will earn more money than those who do not continue their education.

High-school graduates are more likely to get jobs and be paid more than students who do not graduate.

Deciding to get more education is an **investment.** An investment is time, effort, or money you spend to get something in the future. Making an investment can mean taking a risk. Read the example below.

It is a hot summer day. You decide to buy some lemonade. You pay cash for the lemonade and then drink it. You pay for and receive the benefits of your purchase at the same time. You are very certain of the benefits of your purchase. You will get to enjoy a cool, refreshing drink. There is little risk involved in your decision.

Now let's look at the decision you will be making. Should you get more education after high school? It might not be easy to answer that question. It is a much bigger decision than buying lemonade. You might not see the benefits of more education right away. The benefits come later. For example, people with more education make more money on average throughout their lifetimes. By deciding to continue your education, you make an investment in your future.

There are four questions you should consider when deciding whether to continue your education: 1) Do you have basic math, reading, and writing skills? 2) Do you have work experience? 3) How will you develop job skills? and 4) How many years of education do you want to complete?

Gender and Careers

For many years, some women had to choose between having children and having a career. If a woman was able to take a maternity leave, it was most likely unpaid. In addition, she lost seniority at work. Now, many companies have become more generous with parental leaves. Federal law now says that new parents must receive up to 12 weeks unpaid leave upon the birth or adoption of a child. This applies to both men and women. Unfortunately, many workers cannot afford several weeks of unpaid leave. More and more companies are granting paid parental leaves to both mothers and fathers. For example, one company gives up to 12 weeks paid parental leave to the primary caregiver in a family. It gives the other caregiver one week paid leave. In 2003, 12 percent of American companies offered paid parental leave.

Do You Have Basic Math, Reading, and Writing Skills?

Employers want to hire people who have basic math, reading, and writing skills. They want workers who can think, solve problems, and communicate well. Employers are very good at identifying those who have poor basic skills in reading, writing, and mathematics. Having poor basic skills can keep you from being hired. People who have strong basic skills often earn higher salaries. Students who take math, science, reading, and writing courses will have more career choices. The career plan you will complete at the end of this chapter will help you identify your strengths. It can also show you the areas in which you need to improve your skills. You may need to take more classes to get the skills an occupation requires.

The Economy

When you set career goals, retirement is probably the last thing on your mind. The end of your career seems a long way off. But retirement is a reality that even the youngest workers must consider. When you work, the federal government withholds part of your paycheck for Social Security. Every American worker contributes to Social Security throughout his or her working life. When workers retire, they receive money back each month. However, Social Security payments alone do not provide a comfortable retirement. Also, a huge number of American workers will retire in the next 20 years. Some people doubt that all Americans will receive the Social Security funds they have counted on. Financial experts advise workers to create their own retirement accounts. Many companies have retirement plans in which workers invest a percentage of their salary. When they retire, workers receive benefits from the plan. Another option is an Individual Retirement Account, or IRA. People can contribute a certain amount of money to the account each year. An IRA offers tax advantages and a good way to invest money for retirement.

Do You Have Work Experience?

Do you have a job now? Working while you are still in school has several benefits. You can learn more skills. You may have more chances to learn about different careers. Working part time can help you build skills and behaviors that employers value. On the job, you learn to show respect to others. You also can show a willingness to learn new things. Employers also value people who can communicate well. They want to hire people who can follow directions and be on time. Working while in school also gives you a chance to learn about a specific industry. You can learn the skills needed for an occupation. You can practice these skills while working. You can see what other skills you need to learn.

There are even more benefits to working while in school. Teens who work while in high school continue to work as adults. They are less likely to be unemployed. If they become unemployed, they are able to find work more quickly than those with no high school work experience. Young adults who worked 20 hours a week in high school have higher yearly pay after they graduate. They earn 25 to 30 percent more than young adults who did not work in high school.

Get Involved

Have you ever considered teaching preschoolers? Three-, four-, and five-year-olds often love the attention of young people. Head Start is an organization that provides education for preschoolers from low-income families. It helps prepare children so that they do their best when they enter school. Head Start was started by the federal government in 1965. It has helped more than 15.3 million children. There are many volunteer opportunities with community Head Start organizations. High school and college students participate by helping provide educational play for the preschoolers. They also help get buildings ready for Head Start classes. Volunteering for Head Start gives students an opportunity to practice teaching while helping people.

How Will You Develop Job Skills?

If you do not work while in high school, you need other ways to develop job skills. One way you can do this is by continuing your education after high school. This will help you to be ready to enter an occupation. Graduates of educational programs are better trained to immediately enter jobs than non-graduates. Most college graduates have more employment opportunities than those who do not graduate. You need to think about the occupations you want to pursue. Then decide how you will study and prepare for those occupations.

How Many Years of Education Do You Want to Complete?

If you decide to get more education after high school, how much should you get? Students who graduate from two-year degree programs earn 25 to 30 percent more each year than high school graduates. Students with four-year degrees make 75 percent more money each year than high school graduates. You can see that investing in more education can result in increased pay.

How Can You Pay for a Postsecondary Education?

Training and education beyond high school is a big investment. For many people, it is the biggest investment they make. You have seen the many benefits of continuing your education. But how will you pay for it? Postsecondary education is expensive. However, **financial aid** can help with the cost. Financial aid is money available to students to help pay for postsecondary education. It includes scholarships, grants, loans, and work-study programs. It is important to get information about school costs and financial aid. Share this information with your parents or guardians. This will help them plan financially for your education. If you are well-informed about costs and financial aid, you can make good decisions. The career plan you will complete on pages 156–157 will help you do this.

Lesson 2 Review Write your answers to these questions on a sheet of paper.

1. Explain why deciding to finish high school is important.

2. Why does the decision to get more education after high school involve risk?

3. Why do you think young adults who worked part-time in high school have more success in later jobs than those who did not?

Technology Note

You can find out a lot about colleges and other postsecondary schools on the Internet. Almost all colleges and schools have Web sites. They offer all kinds of information about courses of study, students, and teachers. Many also have e-mail addresses. You can e-mail people at the school and ask questions you have about the school.

Your Career/Education Plan

Complete each part of this career plan. Write your responses on a separate sheet of paper. Include this activity in your career portfolio.

Part A: Preferred Careers

After you identify two careers you want to explore further, write a brief description of what you would do in each. Also indicate whether each career is available in your community or within driving distance from your home. To do this, use resources such as the CDMCareerZone Web site mentioned in Chapter 3 or the list of careers included in the career clusters in Chapter 4.

Part B: School Subjects

Write down the school subjects required for each career. Have you studied the school subjects required for each of your chosen careers? Do you still need to take certain courses? Write down any courses you still need to take to prepare for each career.

Part C: Abilities

What abilities do you have? How do your skills relate to your two chosen careers? What skills must you develop in order to be prepared for your desired careers?

Part D: Values

What values can you fulfill in each of your chosen careers?

Part E: Employment Outlook and Wages

Will jobs be available in this field when you are ready to begin work? How much money will you be paid for doing the work?

Part F: Plans After High School

What are your plans after finishing high school? (Other than going to college or other postsecondary school.)

Part G: Postsecondary Education

What schools offer the programs you are interested in? How are these schools similar? How are they different?

It is important to share and explain your career plan with a parent or guardian.

Chapter 5 REVIEW

Word Bank
financial aid
investment
postsecondary

Vocabulary Review

Choose the word or phrase from the Word Bank that best completes each sentence. Write the answer on your paper.

1. The time, effort, or money spent to get something in the future is a(n) _____.

2. Money available to students to help pay college costs is _____.

3. The time after high school is described as _____.

Concept Review

Choose the word or phrase that best completes each sentence. Write the letter of the answer on your paper.

4. Two-year college degree graduates earn about _____ more than high school graduates.

   A 10 percent

   B 30 percent

   C 50 percent

   D 5 percent

5. The best advice for a classmate considering a part-time job is that _____.

   A it is a bad idea because it is too time-consuming

   B it is a poor choice because it will not pay well

   C it is a good way to develop valuable skills

   D it is necessary in order to be employed later

6. An important piece of information to examine when choosing a career is _____.

   A how many jobs are available right now

   B whether more men or women work in it

   C its history

   D how much it pays

7. Choosing postsecondary education _____.

   A is something everyone should do

   B is not necessary for most careers

   C always pays off

   D is an investment that involves risk

Critical Thinking

Write the answer to each question on your paper.

8. Why do you think a willingness to learn new things is a behavior that employers value?

9. A friend does not take math courses because she says math is not necessary in her chosen career. Explain why this is a good decision or not.

10. A friend says he is not going to college because he cannot afford it. What would you tell the friend?

6 Opportunities in Your Community

Going to college is a unique learning experience. Students learn subjects such as math and English that will help them in their careers. They also learn about other people and about themselves. They learn more about living in a community and their own responsibilities as citizens. What are some opportunities in postsecondary schools and your community after high school? In this chapter, you will find out.

Goals for Learning

◆ To recognize career opportunities in one's community

◆ To understand how networking can help in finding a job

◆ To learn how to select a postsecondary school or college

◆ To realize the importance of getting along with others

◆ To learn conflict-resolution skills

Core services

The 11 industries a community needs in order to function

Your community can be an important resource as you plan your career. By learning about the economy in your community, you can find opportunities to learn about occupations. Think about the occupation you want to explore. Do you know anyone in your community who has that occupation? You may be able to talk to that person to get more information. What companies or businesses related to that occupation are in your community?

What Industries Does a Community Need?

A community needs industries in 11 of the 16 career clusters (covered in Chapter 4) to function. These 11 industries are referred to as **core services.** Read the 11 core services listed here. Sample careers in each area are provided.

Natural Resources

People need electric power in their homes. Farms and businesses also need power. Electric lines bring power where it is needed in a community. Cities and towns also need to treat drinking water and wastewater. Most communities employ power line, telephone, and cable repairers. Water treatment plant operators are also employed in most communities.

Architecture and Construction

Some areas have a lot of new construction. Other areas have none. Even if there is no new construction in your area, many workers provide the maintenance and repair necessary in every community. Workers who fix and maintain homes and buildings include roofers, electricians, carpenters, plumbers, and heating and air-conditioning mechanics. Roads also need to be repaired. Road-paving and surfacing operators do this job.

Education and Training Services

Schools are located in all communities or regions. Some communities have many schools. Smaller towns may have only one or two schools. Teachers and administrators work in schools.

Finance

Banks are needed in each community so people can manage their money. Most people must also pay taxes. Bank managers, tellers, accountants, and tax preparers are needed in each community.

Government and Public Administration

Government provides the structure for a community to exist. It keeps the community organized. Administrators, tax collectors, and highway maintenance workers are some examples of government workers.

Health Science

People need medical care close to where they live. Health science occupations include doctors, therapists, and nurses. These people provide necessary medical care at clinics, hospitals, or private offices.

Hospitality and Tourism

Many communities have hotels or motels and restaurants to serve visitors. Motel desk clerks, housekeepers, cooks, and food servers are employed in most communities. Some communities also have tourist information centers.

Human Services

Usually a community has one or more churches or places of worship. Communities also have barbershops and beauty salons. Other services provided in the Human Services cluster include funeral services, child care, and mental health care. Occupations related to human services include clergy members, hairdressers, barbers, and funeral directors. Child-care providers, social workers, and counselors also work in the community.

Law, Public Safety, and Security

Police, fire, and emergency medical services need to be near where people live. Law enforcement officers are in every community.

Marketing, Sales, and Service

Most communities have grocery and retail stores. Store managers and salespeople work in these stores. Some cities or towns might have small stores that are owned by someone who lives in the community.

Transportation, Distribution, and Logistics

People need to be able to get the things they need to their homes or businesses. People also need to be able to travel within their community. Some communities have airports, bus and train stations, and taxis. Occupations that help connect and serve communities include truck drivers, bus drivers, service station attendants, and mechanics.

Look at the map of Millberg on page 165. Use the key to locate industries in each of the 11 core services. Do you know the location of these services and industries in your community?

Millberg

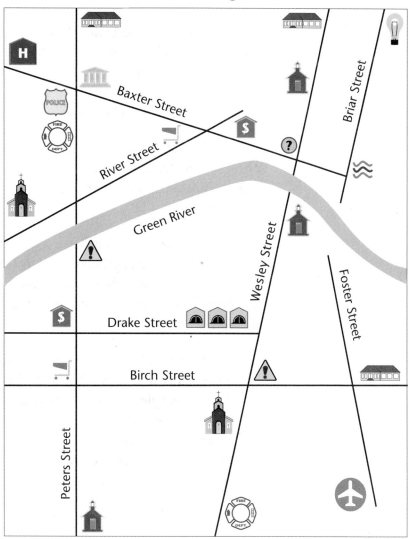

KEY

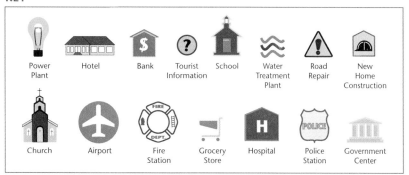

Knowing the industries in your community also tells you what type of work and careers are available locally. The yellow pages of the telephone directory can be very helpful in finding addresses and telephone numbers. You can also find out where industries are located by searching for them on the Internet. Another way you can find information is by asking police officers or mail carriers. They are familiar with the community and can help you locate businesses, schools, and other places.

Lesson 1 Review Write your answers to these questions on a sheet of paper.

1. What are core services?

2. What are some examples of human services found in every community?

3. Name two specific companies or organizations in your community that provide core services.

The Economy

The industries in your community can be an important resource as you seek an occupation. The stronger your community's economy, the better resource it is. What makes a community's economy strong? Money comes into a community when people there sell products or services to others. The following industries bring a lot of money into a community: farming, mining, forestry, fishing, manufacturing, tourism, and government. Many communities encourage new businesses such as banks that serve a large area. Amusement parks or large shopping centers would also bring in money. They would attract people from other cities and states. On the other hand, when people must go outside the community for services, money leaves the community. So if a community had no hospital or medical services, the community would lose money. Building a hospital in the community would improve its economy.

Networking

The exchange of information or services among individuals, groups, or institutions

Internship

Doing work for an employer for a specified period of time to learn about an industry or occupation

You have now learned about the core workers in your community. These people can be a great resource as you plan your career. They can answer your questions about certain occupations. Meeting and talking with a person about his or her job experience can give you information you cannot get by doing research or reading a book.

What Is Networking?

Most people know very little about how to get a job. It can take months. A job search is more than filling out applications, mailing out résumés, and having interviews. One of the best ways to get a job is **networking.** Networking is talking to people you know to learn about possible job opportunities. Networking is the most productive of all ways to do a job search. Personal contact with someone you know can give you valuable information about a company. You can find out who to talk with at the company. You can also find out whether the company is hiring. Personal contacts can be parents, guardians, relatives, neighbors, friends, part-time employers, classmates, or church members. Building relationships with these people can help you find a job.

What Is an Internship?

Networking can help you find a job. It might also help you get an **internship.** An internship involves working for an employer for a specified period of time to learn about a certain industry or occupation. An internship provides an opportunity to develop specific job skills. Some internships pay a wage. Others do not. You can often complete an internship while you are still in school. Some schools offer credit for an internship.

Have you ever gone to work with your parent or guardian for a day? If so, you probably got to see what he or she does on the job. An internship is different. It is more detailed than observing what a person does on the job. An internship gives you an opportunity to do a job. It is like a job tryout. In an internship, you might complete special projects. You might perform a variety of tasks from different jobs. Or, you might focus on a single occupation. For example, suppose your career goal was to be an accountant. You could get an internship doing accounting work. You would be supervised by an accountant. An internship offers a chance to learn about an occupation by experiencing it.

How Can I Begin Networking?

In Chapter 4 you identified the names, addresses, and telephone numbers of contact people in your community. Now is the time to use this information.

1. Identify a company or organization that employs people in a career that you would like to enter. Write down the address and phone number.

2. Identify a person within the company or organization in a career area of your choice. Write or call this person and ask for an **informational interview.** An informational interview is an opportunity to talk to someone at a business to gather information.

3. If there is nobody in your region in the career area you want to explore, try to identify someone in a related career. Suppose you want to be an engineer. You might interview a science teacher in physics or chemistry at your school. He or she would have knowledge related to engineering.

You can call someone you know in a business or company to set up an informational interview.

Here are some things to keep in mind as you interview someone about his or her work.

- Communicate clearly to the contact person that this is not a job interview.
- Set a time limit for the interview. Thirty minutes is a reasonable amount of time. Ask the person to answer some questions to help you in your decision making about the career area.
- Prepare for the interview. The more you know about the career you are discussing and your abilities, the better the interview will go.
- Keep a record of your interview dates. In your initial contact, mention that you are a student and give the name of your school. Tell the interviewee who suggested that you contact him or her. State that you have researched the career.
- Conclude by thanking the person for the interview. Ask for a business card or get the person's correct title and address to send a thank-you note.

It is best to write down your questions before the interview. Having questions ahead of time may make you more relaxed. You will know what to ask. Many people enjoy talking about themselves, so the interview may be easier than you think. Remember that first impressions are powerful. Be sure to dress appropriately, be on time, and be polite. Practice asking and answering questions before an interview. You can find sample interview questions in the Portfolio Activity on pages 182–183 in this chapter.

Lesson 2 Review Write your answers to these questions on a sheet of paper.

1. Why is networking one of the best ways to get a job?

2. Suppose you had an internship at an advertising agency. Describe some ways you would probably spend your time.

3. Suppose you are interviewing someone about his or her job. Why should you inform the person that you do not expect this to be a job interview?

Get Involved

The United Way is a non-profit organization that exists in many communities. Here's how it works: individuals and companies contribute money to the United Way fund. The United Way distributes the money to many local organizations that help people. These organizations range from the Red Cross to local food banks. There are many volunteer opportunities for young people at local United Way organizations. For example, the Lubbock, Texas, United Way sponsors a program for young people. The students are in charge of distributing several thousand dollars. These high school students quickly learn about the many organizations that need money and volunteers. They also develop valuable management skills.

Knowing what you want to do after high school is a big challenge. Many high school students think they need to decide what they want to do for the rest of their lives. This is not true! In fact, most adults make six or seven job changes in their working lives. The world of work is continually changing. It doesn't make sense to decide now what job you will do for the rest of your life. However, you can identify what direction you want your career to take immediately following high school.

How Do I Choose My Career Direction?

To make this decision, you can use the information you learned about yourself in Chapter 2. For example, based upon your abilities, interests, and values, you can decide whether to pursue work immediately after high school graduation. Maybe you would prefer to enroll in postsecondary training. You might decide that you want to attend college. Once you are clear about your plans after high school, the next step is deciding where you want to work or study.

What Should I Consider When Choosing a School?

Deciding which school to attend is a hard decision. How can you sort through the options available to you? If you are planning to attend a college or university, then there are several things for you to consider. Think about the following questions:
- Is it important for you to stay close to home?
- What amount of tuition can you and your family afford?
- Does a school have the areas of study you are considering?
- Would you feel more comfortable in a large, medium, or small school?

As you think about these questions, keep in mind your past and current experiences. Your experiences can guide you in making plans about your future. To begin narrowing down school options, consider your current situation. For example, ask yourself how you feel in your current school. Do you like the size of your school? What are some of the things you wish were different about your school? What are some of the things that you really like about your school? You may attend a small high school and you feel comfortable there. A large state university might be a shock to you. Or, you might feel limited by your small school and wish you had more opportunities. In that case, you might consider a larger college.

Consider the same sort of questions about the community in which you live. What do you like about it? What do you wish was different? Think about your values. How might they influence your decisions? For example, suppose you value being close to family. How would you feel about going to a school several states away? Perhaps you value living in a city. It is important for you to consider these things as you make your plans. Using your values in this way will help you to make a good decision.

Your thoughts about these questions can help you plan for your future. If you are planning on attending college, then you need to decide what kind of college is right for you. Perhaps you know that a smaller college is right for you. Then you can cross large state universities off your list. If a college does not offer the courses you are interested in, you can stop researching that school.

Writing Practice

To better understand your attitudes about your current school, keep a journal. Write every day or so about what you like and what you wish were different. After a few weeks, reread your journal. What does it tell you about the sort of school you might prefer after high school? Use your journal entries to help you decide.

If you still cannot decide, ask others for help. Discuss your thoughts about school options with school counselors, parents, or guardians. Share your thoughts and ask for their input. Even if they haven't attended college, they can help. They may be able to help you with your career plans.

How Can I Learn More About Schools?

You may find it helpful to visit several schools that vary in size and location. This strategy helps you to compare what you like about different schools. It also helps you to see if your ideas about what kind of a school you'd like are correct. As you gather information, keep in mind that schools have Web sites. Use the Internet to get information about schools you might be interested in. A school's Web site can give you information about programs or majors, application materials, application deadlines, and financial aid. You can also learn about activities and services available to students. For example, many schools have clubs, sports teams, and support services such as career counseling, tutoring, and academic advising.

Once you have gathered information about schools that interest you, identify specific schools to visit. Discuss your thoughts about the sort of school you might prefer with your parents or guardians. Try to identify at least three schools to visit. Talk with your school counselor about your choices.

Technology Note

You can use e-mail to communicate with college administrators. Many admissions offices provide names and e-mail addresses of people who can answer your questions. Take advantage of this quick and easy way to get information.

What Should I Ask When I Visit a School?

When you have identified schools to visit, contact each school's admissions office. To help with your visit, admission offices offer tours and information sessions. Here are some questions to ask admissions office representatives:

- What is your student-to-faculty ratio (the number of students for each professor)?
- What assistance is provided to students who need help deciding what to study?
- What assistance is provided to graduating students who are looking for jobs?
- How many of your students get jobs after graduation?
- What is your school most known for?
- What percent of your students receive financial aid?
- What is the average financial aid package?
- What clubs, sports teams, and other activities are available?
- How many students apply and are accepted each year?
- How many of your classes are taught by graduate students?

Try to meet with a faculty member from the program(s) of study you are considering. Here are some questions you might ask:

- What are the special strengths of your program or major?
- What priority do faculty members place on teaching?
- Do students have the chance to meet with their advisors on a regular basis?

Think about other questions you might have about the faculty or the program. Try to get a good sense of how much support faculty members will offer you in your area of interest. Pay attention to how enthusiastic faculty members are about their work. When teachers enjoy what they do, they are more likely to provide a positive learning experience.

What Should I Do After Visiting Schools?

Keep a record of your thoughts and impressions of every school you visit. Pay attention to whether the people you met with were friendly, knowledgeable, and helpful to you during your visit. After you have completed your visits, discuss your experiences with your school counselor and your parents or guardians. How did your experiences compare with the preferences you identified before visiting? Review your thoughts about each school. What did you like and dislike? In what ways did each school meet or not meet your expectations? Based upon what you know now, what are your thoughts about the school you would prefer? Is your preferred school a realistic option? To which schools should you apply?

Take time to research and visit schools you think you would like to attend. The more information you have, the better decision you will make. If you base your decision upon your experiences, you will be happier with your choice.

Lesson 3 Review Write your answers to these questions on a sheet of paper.

1. What are three options people may choose after high school?

2. When choosing a college, you should consider what you like and dislike about your current school. Why is this useful?

3. What are two steps to take when you research a college?

On the Job

Are you overwhelmed by all of the paperwork involved in choosing a college or other school? You may be juggling college and test applications, financial aid applications, and other resources. Keeping organized is a valuable skill in any occupation. It can help you now as well. Spend time each day organizing paperwork into files. Keep material on your computer organized as well.

Do you prefer to work with people? If you do, you probably enjoy talking with others. Or, would you rather work with things? Perhaps you are more comfortable working with machines and computers. You may have to answer questions like these when you are looking for a job. No matter what job you choose, you will have some contact with people. Learning how to work well with others is an important skill for all jobs. Many people think it is the most important skill for a successful career.

What Are Some Challenges of Living and Working with Others?

You might think that learning to live and work with others is simple. Many times, this is true. It is easy to interact with people you know or people who are similar to you. However, in your community and at your job, you will meet many different people. Some may have different backgrounds from yours. They may have different religions or cultural traditions, and may speak different languages.

Communication Connection

How do people in your community tend to behave toward one another? Do strangers speak to one another? Do you and your neighbors know one another? How might communications with others differ in cities, suburbs, and rural areas? How might they differ in another country?

You might find it challenging to interact with people who are different from you. Perhaps this is because you don't know about their culture. For example, in some cultures it is important to make eye contact with the person you are talking to. Eye contact lets that person know you are interested in what they are saying. It also makes them feel you are being truthful. Making eye contact is considered a basic communication rule. In another culture, however, it may be considered rude for a person to make eye contact, especially with an older person.

You also need to know how to talk to different people. For instance, you probably would not talk the same way to your school principal as you talk to your best friend. You change the way you communicate depending on who you are talking to. Likewise, it is important to develop communication skills for different living and work situations. Living and working with others can be pretty complicated.

How Can I Show Respect to Others?

Attitude

How someone thinks, feels, and acts

One thing you want to do in all of your interactions with others is show respect. When you show respect to others, you treat people like you would want to be treated. To show respect to others you need to listen to what they say. You can also learn about people who are different from you. The more you know about them, the more respect you will have for them. All of these things help build good communication.

When talking with someone, carefully listen to what the person is saying. For example, you might start thinking about your response while someone is still talking. This distracts you from really listening. The next time someone talks to you, practice listening to what he or she is saying. Focus only on understanding what he or she says. When he or she is finished talking, you will have time to form your response. You may even respond by summarizing what the other person said. This will confirm that you heard the person correctly. It will also communicate to the other person that you did really listen!

Everyone deserves respect. If you believe that everyone is worthy of respect, you make it a habit to treat them well. With this **attitude,** you show that you believe everyone matters. Helping people feel that they matter is a powerful communication tool. You can help people feel that they matter by taking time to learn about them. Learn what other people like and what their values are. You might be scared by what you do not know. But that doesn't mean you should avoid interacting with others who are different from you. There is little chance for good communication when there is no communication at all. Spend time learning about cultures and traditions that are different from your own. You will find that people who seem different might actually have a lot in common with you. You might also discover that it is fun learning about different cultures and traditions. Imagine how dull the world would be if everyone was exactly alike.

How Can My Attitude Affect My Job?

You have seen that showing respect toward those with whom you live and work is important. Other ways to live and work well with others include being honest, trustworthy, reliable, and having a positive attitude. Often employers state that these key traits are the main reasons why they hire someone. Likewise, employers may fire people who do not have these traits.

How Can My Friends Affect My Behavior?

In order to demonstrate positive behaviors, spend time with people who do the same. Your friends can affect your behavior. For example, you might say that you would never damage someone else's property. However, if you were in a group of friends who decided to paint graffiti, you might join them. Being part of the group makes it easier to do so. You may even feel pressure to go along with everyone else. Your friends can have a similar influence on you when it comes to using drugs and alcohol.

Career Profile

Chef

Have you ever helped prepare a big dinner for a dozen friends and family members? Then you have an idea of the excitement and challenges of being a chef. A chef spends his or her day testing recipes and planning menus. He or she is in charge of buying fresh meats and vegetables. Some chefs prepare most food themselves. Others manage a large team of workers.

Being a chef is a physically demanding job. Most chefs work nights and weekends, and their families must adjust to their unusual work schedule. Chefs work in a wide variety of places. These include formal restaurants, cafés, hotels, resorts, hospitals, corporations, and schools. Some chefs train at independent cooking schools. Others graduate from two-year or four-year college programs in hospitality or culinary arts.

When your friends show negative behaviors or have a negative view toward life, you may begin to think more negatively. People who have a negative attitude are usually not as valued by their friends, teachers, and employers. Think about how you feel after you have interacted with someone who is very negative. How is that different from how you feel after you interact with someone who is very positive? Attitudes and behaviors can catch on. Try to demonstrate positive behaviors and attitudes rather than negative ones.

How Can I Resolve Conflict?

Even when you choose positive-thinking friends, conflicts can arise. Relationships are complicated. It can be easy to have your feelings hurt. It can be just as easy to hurt someone else's feelings. However, you can learn to handle conflict situations effectively. Conflict will occur in school and it will occur when you are at work. It is just part of life. The key to handling these situations is in what you do when a negative interaction happens.

The first response you might have to conflict is anger. This is normal. But acting on that anger may make the problem worse. When someone makes you angry, try to stay calm. Take a deep breath or count silently to 10. This will give you time to collect your thoughts before reacting. Let the other person know how you feel, but do not attack the other person. If you hurt another person's feelings, apologize. When people try to communicate well and show respect, the result is almost always positive.

How Should I Interact with Authority Figures?

So far, you have learned how to have good relationships with your friends. You must also communicate well with parents, teachers, and work supervisors. These people have roles of **authority** in your life. Knowing how to communicate effectively with people in authority is important. Some people find it is hard to accept advice and directions from others. They might react with anger when they are "told what to do." People in authority roles have the power to make decisions regarding rules and behavior. In fact, it is their job to do so.

Express your opinion respectfully if you disagree with someone in authority.

You are expected to work and live by the rules. If you are not clear about a rule or decision, speak up. Respectfully ask the person in authority to explain why an action was taken. If you think a rule or decision is unfair, explain why you think so in a respectful way. As you have learned, it is important to respect everyone. It is possible to disagree with people and also show them respect.

Living and working with others is not always easy. You need to respect other people. Listen to them when they talk to you. If you have a disagreement with someone, stay calm. Let that person know how you feel, and do so respectfully. You will find it is easier to live and work with others if you treat them well.

Lesson 4 Review Write your answers to these questions on a sheet of paper.

1. Why is learning to work well with others an important job skill?

2. What are some ways to show respect when you are talking with someone?

3. Suppose a person in authority takes an action with which you disagree. Describe the best way to communicate with the person.

4. Think of a time when you had a disagreement with an authority figure in your life. Did you act respectfully? If not, how might you have responded differently to show your respect?

Gender and Careers

American women did not have equal rights in education for many years. Harvard, the first college in America, was founded in 1636. It admitted only men. Many people felt that women should focus on taking care of children and the home. In fact, many felt that women were unfit for both physical and mental exercise. But in 1833, Oberlin Collegiate Institute opened. It was the first college for both men and women in the United States. In 1837, Mary Lyon founded Mount Holyoke Female Seminary. This was one of the first colleges for women in the United States. Many women who graduated from Mount Holyoke became teachers. In 1910, only 2.7 percent of American women had completed four or more years of college. By 2000, this number had risen to 25.6 percent. In comparison, in 2000, 27.8 percent of men had completed four years of college.

Conducting an Informational Interview

Identify a company or organization that employs people in a career that you would like to enter. Now, identify a person within the company or organization in a career area of your choice. Contact this person and ask for an interview. If there is nobody in your region in the career area you want to explore, try to identify someone in a related career. For example, if you want to be a music director, you might interview a band or choir teacher at your school.

Introduce yourself to the person you are interviewing with a firm handshake.

Ask the following questions during the interview. Write down the interviewee's answers. Include this information in your Career Portfolio.

1. How did you get into this occupation?
2. What attracted you to this career/organization?
3. What is the way people usually begin in this career area?
4. What does the company expect you to do in your job?
5. What are your company's products, services offered, customers, and competitors?

6. What are the essential abilities and skills you need to do your job?

7. What is the preparation and training required for your position?

8. What personal satisfactions do you get from doing your job?

9. What is it like to work at this company? Do you need to work with many different people? Is there good morale in your company?

10. What personal traits are helpful to succeed in your position?

11. What creates dissatisfaction in this type of work?

12. Can you tell me about working conditions that I should be aware of? For example, what is the dress code? Does the job require extra work after hours?

13. What is the beginning wage? Do you get yearly raises?

14. Who makes the decisions and how are they made in this company/organization?

15. What is a typical day like working here?

16. Are there any opportunities to work part-time or during the summer?

17. Is this company/organization going to grow? Or, will this company get smaller in the future?

18. Do you have any advice for me?

19. Could I contact you again if I have other questions?

20. Could you suggest someone else I might talk with? Could I use your name as the person who suggested I contact him or her?

Conclude by thanking the person for the interview. Ask if he or she has a business card or at least be sure to get his or her correct title and address to send a thank-you note.

Chapter 6 REVIEW

Vocabulary Review

Choose the word or phrase from the Word Bank that best completes each sentence. Write the answer on your paper.

1. Working for an employer for a specified period of time to learn about an occupation is a(n) _____.

2. How someone thinks, feels, and acts is that person's _____.

3. The 11 industries a community needs in order to function are known as _____.

4. The exchange of information or services among individuals, groups, or institutions is _____.

5. The power to enforce rules is _____.

6. An opportunity to talk with someone at a business to get information is a(n) _____.

Concept Review

Choose the word or phrase that best completes each sentence or answers each question. Write the letter of the answer on your paper.

7. Which of the following is NOT a core service?

   A transportation   **C** arts

   B natural resources   **D** sales

8. The most productive way to do a job search is _____.

   A filling out applications **C** mailing out résumés

   B scheduling interviews   **D** networking

9. Many people think the most important skill for a successful career is _____.

   A word processing   **C** public speaking

   B working well
   with others   **D** computer programming

10. To find out more information about a college, you could _____.

    A visit the campus   **C** ask a student at the college

    B check the college Web site   **D** do all of these

11. One thing people should do in all interactions with others is _____.

    A make eye contact   **C** accept advice

    B ignore conflicts   **D** show respect

Critical Thinking

Write the answer to each question on your paper.

12. A friend refuses to use networking to get a job. She wants to get hired based on her merits and not on whom she knows. Do you agree or disagree with her? Explain your thoughts.

13. Why is it important for a job seeker to know about his or her community's core services?

14. Describe some ways to be a good listener.

15. Deciding on a single career course in high school does not make sense in today's world. Explain why.

Test-Taking Tip

Do not wait until the night before a test to study. Plan your study time so that you can get a good night's sleep before a test.

7

Job Training Readiness Skills

Paperwork is a part of every job search. Whether it is filling out a job application, preparing a résumé, or taking a skills test, you will need to write. Good writing will go a long way toward helping you get the job you want. Making the best impression during the hiring process requires plenty of research and preparation. While your self-assessment has been helping you think about careers you might pursue, it has also been helping you organize the information you will want to include on an application and in your résumé. You want to use this information to get an employer's attention. In this chapter, you will learn more about the hiring process and steps you need to take to apply for and get a job.

Goals for Learning

◆ To understand the hiring process

◆ To prepare a personal goal statement

◆ To learn how to write an effective résumé

◆ To obtain references

Résumé

A summary of knowledge, abilities, and experience that shows how a person is qualified for a particular occupation

Recruitment

Getting a number of applications from which to choose new employees

Screening

Going through a number of applications to pick out the most suitable people for a job opening

Selection

Choosing a person for a job opening

In your everyday life, you may hear about or see advertisements for jobs that you would like to get. You might see a job advertised while you are at school or work. Or you might hear or see a job advertisement when you are spending time with your friends. You probably know that in order to get a job, you need to send a **résumé** to the employer who is advertising the job. But what happens after employers receive your résumé? How do they go about selecting the person they think is the best qualified for the job? After you send your résumé, you may be nervous. You might feel as if you are in the dark as you wait to hear from the employer. However, once you know a little more about the hiring process, you can relax and continue your job search with confidence.

What Is the Hiring Process?

Not all employers have the same process for hiring people. As a result, you may have different experiences with different employers. Generally, the size of the company is a factor. Larger companies usually have a human resources department. Workers in this department are involved in the different stages of the hiring process. In smaller companies, department managers may be responsible for taking care of the entire hiring process for their departments. As a result, even within the same company, employees may be hired in different ways. In spite of these differences, there are steps in the hiring process that most employers follow. **Recruitment, screening,** and **selection** are the three basic steps in the hiring process.

Recruitment

The hiring process starts when the manager of a department needs to fill a job opening. In large companies, department managers send written requests to the human resources department. These requests state the requirements for the job and how soon a new employee is needed. The human resources department checks to see if there are any applications on file that fit the job. If there aren't any or if there aren't enough, the human resources department advertises the job opening.

Some companies list all new job openings on a bulletin board or on a Web page that contains company career opportunities. This practice helps to build employee morale by offering career advancement within the company. Letting people know about the job opening so they can apply for it is called recruitment.

Advertising in the newspaper is a common method used by employers to recruit applicants. This is an excellent way for employers to advertise because they can get the information about their job openings to a lot of people at a relatively low cost. However, you should be aware of a few things when looking for job openings in the newspaper.

First, the need for employers to reach as many people as possible may be a sign that they are having trouble keeping employees. This doesn't mean you should not respond to newspaper advertisements, but you should be aware of problems the company may be having. For example, you should be prepared to ask questions about workplace conditions, wages, and other factors that could affect your decision to accept the job.

Second, because job openings advertised in the newspaper are seen by more job seekers, the competition is much greater. The number of people applying for a job may be very high. An employer may decide to look at only the first 100 applications they receive. So you need to respond immediately to newspaper advertisements. If you don't, your résumé may not even be seen.

Finally, newspaper advertisements represent only a small percentage of available jobs. Some authorities suggest only about 20 percent of available job openings are found in help-wanted advertisements. Many employers use other ways to recruit applicants. Here are some other places where you may see or hear about job openings.

- Job fairs
- Youth centers
- Employment offices
- Business windows
- Radio
- Television
- The Internet
- People you know who are working

Finding job openings in the newspaper may be easy. There may be a lot of jobs listed. However, you should not focus your efforts on newspaper advertisements alone. Remember that networking, discussed in Chapter 6, is the most effective way to find a job.

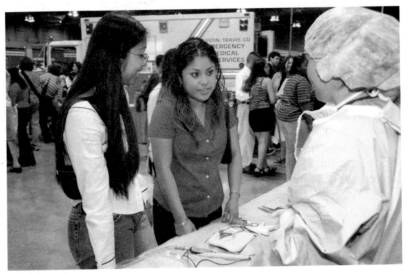

You can find out about job openings at job fairs.

No matter where you see or hear about a job advertisement, you must make sure you read it carefully. Look for clues that tell you what an employer really wants. An employer might expect applicants to have knowledge of a specific computer language, good communication skills, or a willingness to work flexible hours.

Screening

The next step in the hiring process is screening. When employers begin looking at the applications and résumés they have received, they are screening for a qualified applicant. The more résumés an employer receives, the longer time screening takes. To save time, employers may spend less than a minute reviewing each résumé. Employers expect résumés to be organized. They should have correct spelling, punctuation, and grammar. Employers quickly reject résumés that are sloppy and disorganized.

Suppose you have a great job interview. You feel confident about getting the job. But the company hires someone else. Remember that hiring decisions depend on many factors. For example, the other applicant may have had more experience than you. Stay positive. You know you have good interviewing skills. Next time you may be more fortunate.

Employers also want to be able to tell quickly which applicants have the basic qualifications for the job. If your résumé highlights important information, you are more likely to be considered for the job. Employers receive so many applications for each job that they often don't have the time to respond to every applicant. Many employers respond only to those applicants who have been selected for an interview.

Selection

After employers narrow down the number of résumés, they begin looking more closely at the job applicants. They compare the qualifications of applicants. They contact applicants' employers to verify work history. Then, they choose the applicants they would like to interview. In the interview, employers can collect more information about an applicant. Then, they make their final selection for who will fill the job. Usually, the manager or person who will be supervising the new employee will be involved in the interview. That person will either do the interview alone or will be a member of the team that is doing the interview.

What Will Employers Ask During an Interview?

Employers usually ask questions to verify that the applicants have the knowledge, skills, and other requirements that are needed for the job. To get that kind of information, employers may ask applicants what they would do in certain situations. Besides knowledge and skills, employers will also try to find out which applicant has the qualities they are looking for. Here are some qualities that employers would expect job applicants to have.
- Dependability
- Leadership
- Creativity
- Positive attitude
- Willingness to learn new skills
- Passion for doing excellent work
- Ability to work with others

What Else Do Employers Expect from Applicants?

Employers will also expect applicants to be familiar with the job requirements. If you hear about the job from a friend, for example, it is important for you to find out specifics about the requirements you need to have. Some employers may even expect applicants to have some knowledge of the company. This means taking the time to do some "homework" that will show your interest in working there. You can learn what a typical work day is like at the company by talking to people who work there. You can also read brochures that the company uses to recruit applicants. The interview is the last opportunity you have to let the employer know that you are the best person for the job.

What Happens After the Interview?

After your interview is finished, you may be told how many other people are being interviewed for the position. You will also learn how long you will have to wait for the final decision. If the number of applicants is small and you did well in your interview, you may receive a call on the same day. Usually, the manager or supervisor of the department with the job opening decides who to hire. That person will call you if he or she wants to offer you the job.

If you don't get the job, the hiring manager may call you to tell you so. Or, the employer may send you a letter saying so. If your interview went well, you might not know why you did not get the job. Sometimes, the hiring manager may tell you the reasons they hired someone else. However, employers usually are not specific in their letters about the reason why applicants did not get the job. They may briefly state that they had many well-qualified people apply for the job.

Sometimes, you will not get offered a job, even if you are qualified. You may never know why you didn't get called for an interview or why your interview was not successful. Many factors in the hiring process are beyond your control. These factors include the reason why an employer advertised a specific job opening, the amount of time an employer has to screen applicants, and the interviewer's personal opinions about qualities necessary for the job. You may not be aware of any of these things when you apply for the job.

It can be discouraging when you don't get a job you thought was perfect for you. However, it is important for you to continue your job search. A well-planned job search will help you find suitable job openings in your career area.

Lesson 1 Review Write your answers to these questions on a sheet of paper.

1. How does the hiring process of larger companies differ from that of smaller companies?

2. What are two reasons that newspaper ads may not be the best way to find a job?

3. What are some reasons that you may not get a job for which you are qualified?

The Economy

City or suburbs? Not only individuals, but companies too, must make this decision. In the early 1900s, most large companies were located in big cities. In the 1950s and 1960s, many people moved out of cities into nearby suburbs. Soon more and more people had to commute into cities to work. Many companies moved to the suburbs too. This made them attractive to employees. Workers could live near their work. They could save time and money on commuting.

Today some companies that had moved to the suburbs are moving back to cities. They find that many creative people like living in cities more than in suburbs. For example, one company moved into a poor area of Baltimore. Many of the company's employees wanted to be near the city's cultural attractions. The company also hired some people from nearby neighborhoods. These workers appreciated the steady jobs with good wages. The company participated in community projects such as tutoring. Soon the neighborhood improved, and the company's profits increased. Moving to the city was a plus for everyone.

Personal goal statement

A description of a career goal along with the knowledge, abilities, skills, and personal values that are related to the goal

When you are going on a road trip, you need a road map. A road map guides you on your trip. It shows you how far away your destination is. It also shows the various routes you can take to get there. A map even shows places where you can stop along the way.

What Is a Personal Goal Statement?

A **personal goal statement** is similar to a road map. It helps you to reach the goal you have in mind. The goal may be to change a specific behavior, increase your grade point average, get a specific job, or gain admission to college. A personal goal statement also contains information that makes it easy for you to identify the various things you may need to learn or do in order to achieve the goals you have in mind.

Personal goal statements are useful in many parts of your life. In this lesson you will learn how to prepare a personal goal statement that will help you reach your career goal. A clear and focused personal goal statement is the first step for a successful job search.

A personal goal statement can be a guide, much like a road map.

So far, you have done self-assessment and career research activities. These activities helped you to identify the careers you would like to pursue. In selecting those careers, you collected some important information. You identified your favorite school subjects, your abilities, and your personal values. You also learned about the occupations and jobs that are available in the career that interests you. With the information about yourself and the careers you chose, you are ready to prepare your personal goal statement.

What Is Included in a Personal Goal Statement?

Your personal goal statement will include the following sections:
- Your name and present situation
- A description of your career goal or the job you would like to have
- The knowledge, abilities, skills, and personal values required for the career goal or job
- The knowledge, skills, abilities, and personal values you have
- The requirements you still need to get to achieve the career goal or get the job
- In-between or short-term goals to be achieved in order to reach your career goal

Name and Present Situation

In this section you may use your educational level, employment position, or volunteer experience to indicate your present situation. For example, you may describe your situation as middle school student, cashier at a store, high school student, or volunteer community organizer.

Writing Practice

Where you want to live is an important lifestyle decision. It affects your career goals. Write a comparison and contrast of city, suburban, and country living. Discuss the positive and negative features of each kind of living as you see them.

Description of Your Career Goal or Job

This section contains the description of the goal you are focusing on. It may be to get a part-time job or to gain admission to a college. You may also write the description for a career goal that is further into the future, after you have finished college.

When you write the description of your goal, you want to make sure that the description of your goal is as complete as possible. There are two ways to make sure that this happens. First, try to be as specific as you can be about your goal. For example, if your goal is to become a nurse, in what area of nursing do you want to work? Do you want to be a nurse who takes care of babies, the elderly, or patients who just had an operation? Or, if you want to work as a salesperson, would you prefer to work in a sports, electronic, or general department store? When you make the description of your goal specific, it helps you to see more clearly the knowledge, abilities, and skills you already have. It also helps you identify the knowledge, skills, and abilities you need to reach your goal.

Lifestyle is the second point to consider when you want to make sure that the description of your goal is as complete as possible. Your lifestyle is the kind of life you live as a result of the personal values you have. Often, the jobs people have and the lifestyle they live are closely related. Here are some lifestyle questions to consider:

- How important to you is helping to make things better for others?
- How important to you is spending time with your family?
- Does involvement in a lot of different activities make your life more satisfying?
- Do you prefer to live in the city, suburbs, or a rural area?
- How important to you are financial success and fame?

When the description of your goal includes lifestyle information, you get a better chance to see how all the requirements of your goal may fit together in the best way for you.

Requirements for Your Career Goal or Job

You use this section to record the requirements needed for the job or career goal you described earlier. The requirements include the knowledge, abilities, skills, and lifestyle that are necessary for the career or job you identify as your goal. You may organize these requirements in your own way under various headings such as Knowledge, Abilities/Skills, and Lifestyle/Personal Values. The more you know about what your goal requires, the more confident you will be later when you are checking off the requirements you already have and getting an idea of how much learning you have ahead of you.

Your Personal Resources

Your **personal resources** are all the skills, abilities, knowledge, personal qualities, and values that you have learned and developed over the years. You already have much of the information for this section from the self-assessment activities you did in Chapter 2 of this textbook. Review the information you collected about your interests, abilities, school subjects, volunteer and work experience, and personal values. Add more information if you can.

Skills Needed

Compare the requirements of your career goal and your personal resources. What skills or experience do you still need to get? For example, suppose your career goal requires you to have computer skills. You don't have the skills required. You will need to get computer skills.

Steps to Reach Your Career Goal or Job

This section is useful for making a note of the in-between goal or goals that you need to fulfill before you achieve your main career goal. For example, to get the computer skills you need for a job you might take a computer class or read a book. Or, if you want a job at a department store, you might first need to get retail experience at a fast food or convenience store. Getting a job at a fast food or convenience store becomes an in-between goal.

If you have a long-term plan to get the job you want, that is excellent. However, it is okay if you have only an idea of the career you would like to pursue. You may have chosen a career in the social service area but you are not sure if you want to become a social worker, a counselor, or a psychologist. Your personal goal at this point may be to get a job in which you can learn about the social service field after you graduate from high school. You can write an effective personal goal statement for that goal.

As you get ready to prepare your personal goal statement, remember that your idea of where you want to end up in life may change. As circumstances change in your life, they may influence your personal goal. For example, you may plan on becoming a professional sports player. Later, you may realize that you would rather be a high school coach. Or you may plan on becoming an English teacher. Later, you discover that you would rather use your creativity to be a writer. You may even change careers completely. It is not unusual for someone to change careers several times. It is important to remember that your personal goal statement is an indication of where you want to be in the future. You can change it as your goals change. You can add to and reshape your personal goal statement as you move toward your goal in life.

Look at the example of a personal goal statement on page 199. It shows how you can arrange information in each section.

Personal Goal Statement

Name and Present Situation

- Miko Tanaguchi
- Student
- Employed as a cashier at local convenience store

Description of Career Goal or Job

A part-time sales position in the clothing section of a department store within walking distance of my home or on bus route

Requirements for Career Goal or Job

Knowledge:
- High school
- Clothing/fashion
- Dealing with cash, credit cards, and personal checks

Abilities/Skills:
- Dealing with the public
- Good spoken and written communication
- Measuring clothing for alteration

Lifestyle/Personal Values:
- Shift work
- Weekend work
- Well-groomed

Personal Resources

Knowledge:
- High school senior
- Top of my class in English language arts
- Cash registers, computer programming, Excel

Abilities/Skills:
- Experience dealing with the public
- Good written and spoken communication skills

Lifestyle/Personal Values:
- Like variety in activities
- Like talking to people
- Like looking well-dressed
- Honest
- No car but can get a ride sometimes

Skills Needed

Abilities/Skills:
- Measuring clothes for alteration
- Credit cards and personal checks transactions

Steps to Reach Career Goal or Job

Not applicable

Lesson 2 Review Write your answers to these questions on a sheet of paper.

1. What is a personal goal statement?

2. Explain why your personal goal statement might include an in-between goal.

3. How does this statement relate to lifestyle and personal values?

> I want a part-time position in a community center in which I can lead exercise programs. I prefer working with the elderly.

Action verb

A word that shows action

Writing a résumé is an important part of preparing to search for a job. Your résumé represents the skills, accomplishments, and qualifications that you want employers to know about you. The purpose of your résumé is to convince employers that you are the person they should hire. If your résumé gets you an interview, it means you were successful in preparing an effective résumé. You presented yourself as qualified for the job that you are seeking. In this lesson, you will learn how to prepare an effective résumé.

How Do I Start to Prepare a Résumé?

To prepare a good résumé, you need to do some planning. In Lesson 2, you wrote your personal goal statement. This included a description of the occupation or job you would like to have. You also identified the qualifications that the occupation or job requires. You will need to use this information as you write your résumé.

You will also need to gather information about your past employment, related experiences, awards, and accomplishments. You can mention these things in your résumé. Keep a record of places you have worked and the job titles you had. Note the exact dates you worked at each job. Keeping careful records will help you make sure that there are no mistakes in your résumé.

You may have made a list of your skills. Now you need to identify examples of places where you've used your skills. Stating the skills you used during employment is very effective on a résumé. Employers are interested in the skills you have used while on the job. What you say is important, but how you say it is just as important. In stating your skills, use language that highlights them. One way to do so is to use **action verbs.** Look at the list of common action verbs on page 201. Keep the list nearby as you write your résumé.

What Are the Different Types of Résumés?

There are many ways to present your qualifications in a résumé. However, most résumés can be grouped into three types: chronological, functional, and combination.

Chronological résumé

A résumé that focuses on the history of an applicant's education and work experience

Functional résumé

A résumé that focuses on the job tasks or skills that the applicant can perform

The **chronological résumé** focuses on education and work or volunteer history. Your education and work or volunteer history are given in chronological order with the most recent dates listed first. Your education or work history can come first depending on which one relates better to the requirements of the job you are applying for. A sample chronological résumé is shown on page 206.

The **functional résumé** focuses on skills you acquired from various experiences. Instead of focusing on individual work experiences, you put the emphasis on particular skills in such areas as dealing with the public, supervision, communication, and leadership. A sample functional résumé is shown on page 207.

The combination résumé shows specific work experiences as well as areas of skills. It combines the format of a chronological and a functional résumé.

Each of these three résumés contains basically the same information. However, the information is organized or arranged differently. You want to arrange the information to get the attention of employers. The chronological résumé is the type of résumé that most employers are familiar with, so this lesson will focus on the chronological résumé.

Common Action Verbs

Achieved	Encouraged	Invented
Applied	Enlarged	Investigated
Arranged	Equipped	Maintained
Awarded	Established	Recorded
Built	Estimated	Researched
Coached	Examined	Reviewed
Compared	Excelled	Revised
Composed	Expanded	Scheduled
Controlled	Formed	Secured
Convinced	Grouped	Selected
Created	Guided	Sold
Designed	Handled	Solved
Developed	Improved	Succeeded
Directed	Increased	Supported
Distributed	Installed	Taught
Earned	Introduced	Translated

What Information Is Included in a Résumé?

Career Tip

Keep your résumé short. One page is long enough for a first-time job seeker. An employer may be screening dozens of résumés. He or she does not have time to read several pages on each applicant.

A résumé should contain the following information:

- Personal information
- Career objective
- Education
- Work history
- Related information

Personal Information

This section tells employers who you are and how they can contact you. Personal information appears first in your résumé. It is the section of the résumé that includes your name, address, telephone number, and your e-mail address if you have one. It is important to respond promptly to messages from someone who is considering hiring you. Therefore, you must be sure that you can get your messages from the telephone number and the e-mail address you put on your résumé.

Although the purpose of your résumé is to introduce yourself and your qualifications as clearly as possible to employers, it is not necessary to put certain information on your résumé. For example, information about your age, height, weight, gender, race, religion, and any disabilities is not necessary.

Career Objective

This section briefly states your career goal. You can use information from the personal goal statement you wrote in Lesson 2 for this section. The purpose of your career objective is to let employers know quickly the type of job you want and the qualifications you have. Employers usually read the objective first. If it catches the employer's attention, he or she is very likely to read the rest of your résumé.

It is important to write your career objective according to the job you are applying for. However, the objective is not the place to be too specific. If you are too specific about the duties you wish to perform, and such a job does not exist in the company, you may not be considered for other jobs that you might be suitable for.

In most cases, you will be sending your résumé to an employer in response to a specific job opening. In those cases, your career objective must show the employer that you have the required qualifications for that specific job. Here is an example of a career objective for a specific job and one for a more general approach.

Specific:

Seeking a position in a high school teaching grades 11 and 12 math and computer science with responsibility for coordinating the computer lab.

General:

Seeking a position teaching English in a high school that can benefit from my experience in student leadership programs and community literacy.

Education

This section lists the education you are completing or have completed. In this section, you put the names of the schools you attended with the city and state where they are located. You also include what years you attended each school. If you are completing high school, list your expected graduation date. You do not need to include any other schools. If you have attended more than one high school, include all of them and the years you attended each one. Your major subject areas or courses that are relevant to the job are also important to include here. Other information related to your education includes honors and awards received for your performance in particular courses.

It is important to take the time to think of things related to your education that could make you stand out as the best person for the job. Suppose you had a part-time job during the year or semester. You worked to gain experience in you career field. While working, you maintained a GPA of 3.5. This information would be an excellent selling point to employers. It shows that you have the ability to balance work and study. It also shows you are committed to the career you want to pursue.

Work History/Experience

This section lists the jobs or work experience you have. If you have no work experience but a lot of volunteer experience that is relevant to the job you are applying for, include it here. The idea is to show that you have the skills that the job requires. The information in this section will be arranged with the latest dates first, just as you did with the information in the education section. List the names of the places you worked, including the city and state. Under each place of employment, include the position(s) or title(s) you held and awards and other accomplishments earned from your work.

Related Information

This section may include extracurricular activities, special skills, and awards outside of school and work. They should be relevant to the job. Mention accomplishments that reflect your energy, interests, successes, and other strong qualities you have. Some examples include involvement in 4-H organizations, obtaining cardiopulmonary resuscitation (CPR) certification, teaching a computer course to other teenagers or adults. Depending on the type of activities you list, this section of your résumé may have a heading such as Extracurricular Activities, Other Experiences, or Volunteer Experiences.

You can include job-related volunteer experience on your résumé.

Remember, you want to make your résumé stand out from others. When you have completed a draft of your résumé, here are some questions you should ask:

- Could someone reading my résumé easily understand what my skills are?
- Does my résumé specify what I can do to help the employer?
- Have I included only those items that are directly related to the specific job opening?
- Is the content of my résumé organized and attractive?
- Does my résumé give someone a desire to learn more about me?

Finally, you will write, rewrite, and edit until your résumé is perfect. It is a good idea to have someone else read your résumé. You may also want someone to read aloud your résumé so you can hear what it says. Keep your résumé up-to-date. As you grow by learning more skills and achieving more accomplishments, your résumé should grow with you. Its development should match a similar development in the personal goal statement you wrote in Lesson 2.

Career Profile

Personnel Specialist

Did you ever wonder who reads your résumé when you send it to a company? Or who interviews you for a job opening? If you apply to a fairly large company, chances are the person is a personnel specialist. Personnel specialists work in the human resources department of a company.

Some personnel specialists help hire new employees. They communicate with all the departments of their company to find out about job openings. Then they are responsible for advertising the job openings. Next they receive and review résumés. They may interview applicants or schedule interviews with department managers. Finally, they make job offers and help new employees learn the company ropes.

Other personnel specialists work with employee benefits. They inform company employees about their insurance and retirement programs. Still others work to train both new and veteran employees.

If you are organized and enjoy meeting people, you might enjoy working in human resources. Depending on the position, human resources work requires a high school diploma or a two-year, four-year, or even a graduate degree.

Sample Chronological Résumé

Leslie M. Student

1234 High School Street

Philadelphia, PA 19019

888-555-1234

Personal Information

CAREER OBJECTIVE

Career Objective

Seeking a position teaching English in a high school that can benefit from my experience with student leadership programs and community literacy.

EDUCATION

Education

July 2004	Earned Pennsylvania teaching certificate
June 2004	Graduated from Bingham Teachers' College in Philadelphia, PA, with majors in English Literature and United States History
June 1999	Graduated from Western High School in Johnstown, PA

EXPERIENCE

Work History

| 2003–2004 | Volunteered as literacy tutor to non-reading adults in Philadelphia, PA |
| 2000–2003 | Worked summers at Western Community College in Johnstown, PA, as program coordinator of youth leadership development |

EXTRACURRICULAR ACTIVITIES

Related Information

2003–2004	President, Society for Educators-in-Training
May 2001	Elected Education Department Representative to student government association
April 2000	Winner of Joe Ford Scholarship for Student Educators

Sample Functional Résumé

Diego Employee

98765 Working Avenue

San Diego, CA 92101

888-555-9876

`Personal Information`

CAREER OBJECTIVE

`Career Objective`

Seeking a position as a hotel desk clerk.

SUMMARY OF QUALIFICATIONS

- 10 years experience in the hotel industry as a housekeeper and desk clerk
- Excellent communication skills
- Enjoy talking with and helping people
- Hard working, reliable, and organized

RELEVANT SKILLS AND EXPERIENCE

`Related Information`

Customer Service
- Treated customers with respect
- Greeted customers with a smile
- Answered customer questions in a friendly way

Supervision
- Prepared work schedules for 12 employees
- Trained new clerks
- Trained new housekeepers

Administrative
- Answered telephones at front desk
- Organized time cards and payroll for 12 employees
- Handled credit card, check, and cash payments from customers

EMPLOYMENT HISTORY

`Work History`

2000–present	Front Desk Clerk	Hotel La Bienvenida	San Diego, CA
1996–2000	Assistant Clerk	Comfort Hotel	Coronado, CA
1995–1996	Housekeeper	Comfort Hotel	Coronado, CA

EDUCATION

`Education`

Hospitality and Tourism classes, 1996   Coronado Community College

What Is a Cover Letter?

When you send your résumé to an employer, you should also send a **cover letter** with it. A cover letter introduces you to the employer. It should be written specifically for the job opening you are applying for. Its main purpose is to tell the employer briefly and clearly why you are qualified for the job. Here are some general guidelines for writing a good cover letter.

- Address the letter to the appropriate person. If you don't know that person's name, call the company and ask. If you are responding to an advertisement, address the cover letter to the person listed in it.
- State the job you are applying for.
- Say why you are interested in the position.
- Highlight your qualifications that are relevant to the job.
- Say that you will call to arrange an interview.

You may be able to submit your résumé and cover letter electronically. If you will be faxing your résumé and cover letter, make sure the copies are clear. Use a plain font and do not use extra formatting. If you are sending your résumé and cover letter by e-mail, you can send attachments. Some companies may also have a form for your résumé that you fill out online. Make sure you follow the instructions for such forms.

Gender and Careers

Child care has helped women become more active in the work force. Up until the 1960s, many women with children stayed at home. In the 1960s and 1970s, more mothers wanted or needed to work outside their homes. But who would care for their children? At first, many women had to depend on family, friends, and hired babysitters for child care. Soon, private child care centers began opening. They were bright and cheerful but often expensive. Women often spent much of their salaries on child care. They asked their companies to provide child care. Today, many large companies have on-site child care. Parents can bring their young children to their workplaces. Their children are nearby all day. Mothers and fathers can often spend lunchtime or playtime with their children during the day. The companies pay part of the child care expenses. Of course, not all companies can provide this service. Still, parents have more options than they had in the past.

Sample Cover Letter

July 28, 2004

Ms. Pat Brown
Brighton School District
456 Lee Road
Philadelphia, PA 19019

Dear Ms. Brown:

I am writing in response to your teacher recruitment brochure given out at Bingham Teachers' College. I am very interested in a position as an English teacher at a high school in your school district.

As my résumé shows, I am a certified English and History teacher. I am prepared to teach both English and History courses. I understand that your district is trying to promote community literacy. My experience as a literacy tutor could make me a valuable addition to your school district. Also, my involvement in student leadership development can help to combine students' activities and community literacy efforts.

I would appreciate it if you considered my application. You may reach me at 888-555-1234 to schedule an interview. I look forward to meeting with you.

Sincerely yours,

Leslie M. Student

Leslie M. Student

Lesson 3 Review Write your answers to these questions on a sheet of paper.

1. What is the main purpose of a résumé?

2. Why might a person choose to write a functional résumé instead of a chronological résumé?

3. Why is it important to send a cover letter with a résumé?

Technology Note

You are probably an expert at using e-mail. But are you familiar with faxing? Using a fax machine is a good way to send important letters and documents. By dialing a telephone number, you can send pages that are received almost immediately. Many companies encourage job applicants to send résumés by fax. Find out if this is an option when you apply for a job. Sending a résumé by fax gets your application process off to a quick start.

Reference

Someone who can share your skills, personal qualities, and job qualifications with an employer

You want your résumé to give employers a good impression of yourself. When employers are considering hiring you, they want to make sure that the information in your résumé is correct. To get that information, they talk to people who know something about you. It is your responsibility to provide the names of those people to the employer. These people are your **references.**

Why Do You Need References?

It is important to have references who can speak positively about who you are and what you can do. Some employers may ask for a list of references with the application. These employers check your references before the interview. Other employers may ask for your references at the interview. The important thing is not to wait until the last moment to find people who will be good references for you.

Who Can Be References?

Your references can be former employers, teachers, coaches, sponsors of clubs that you are involved with, and other adults who know you well. Your employer is an ideal person to ask to be a reference. If you've been a good worker and are leaving your job on good terms, your employer is in the best position to speak about your job skills. However, certain laws permit previous employers to discuss only job-related issues with other employers who are asking about an applicant. Therefore, you will need to make sure you include other references who can speak on your behalf about other matters besides work-related things.

Teachers and guidance counselors can also be good references. Those who know you are dependable, cooperative, and hard working would be happy to help you. They can tell employers about your personal qualities. Coaches, sponsors of community clubs, and other adults who know you well could also give employers the information they are looking for about your personal qualities.

It is not a good idea to include relatives as references. It is very unlikely that employers would call them to find out if you are suitable for a job. Employers expect relatives to say only positive things about you because they are related to you.

How Can You Get Good References?

When you have selected three or four people to give references on your behalf, the next step is to get permission from them to give their names to employers. Most people will agree to be a reference for you. However, you need a good reference. If a reference will not speak positively about you, it will not do you any good. You don't want a negative reference to keep you from getting a job.

Therefore, it is important to ask the people you have selected if they think they know you and your work well enough to give you a good reference. If you are honest, most people will be honest with you in return. If they say they are unable to give you a positive reference, thank them for their honesty and move onto the next person on your list. You can be sure that those who say "yes" will be good references. They can be even better references if you let them know what type of job you are applying for. They will have a better idea of how to present your abilities and qualities to fit the job opening.

When you have three or four people who have agreed to give you references, prepare a reference list. Type your list or prepare it on a computer. At the top of the sheet of paper, include your name and address and then the heading "References." List each person's name, title or occupation, the company where he or she works, address, daytime phone number, and e-mail address. If the advertisement for a job does not ask for a list of references with the application, it is still a good idea to have a copy with you at the interview.

Lesson 4 Review Write your answers to these questions on
a sheet of paper.

1. Why is it a good idea to have a list of references before you
apply for a job?

2. In general, who are some people who might make good
references? Who are some people who would not make
good references?

Get Involved

Have you ever wanted to become a teacher? Or do you
simply want to help others? Tutoring is a great way to get
involved in your community. Many organizations such as
Boys and Girls Clubs and Big Brothers/Big Sisters sponsor tutoring
programs. Tutors may be matched with one or two young people
who need help in reading or math. A tutor may lead a group of
small children in educational games. Tutors may read to children or
help them with computer skills. In fact, tutors do many of the same
jobs a teacher does each day. Tutoring teaches valuable skills and
helps others. It can become a valuable addition to your résumé.

Personal Goal Statement

In Lesson 2 you learned the importance of a personal goal statement. You saw an example of a statement. Read through the main parts of a personal goal statement below. Then, answer the questions on page 215 on a sheet of paper. Add the activity to your career portfolio.

Name and Present Situation
• include your name
• include whether you are a student
• include the job or jobs you currently have

Description of Your Career Goal or Job
• describe your career goal
• describe the job you want to get

Requirements for Your Career Goal or Job
• include what knowledge is required
• include what abilities and skills are required
• include the lifestyle and personal values required

Personal Resources
• include what knowledge you have
• include what abilities and skills you have
• include your lifestyle and personal values

Skills Needed
• include abilities and skills you need to get

Steps to Reach Your Career Goal or Job
• if there are in-between goals you need to reach before you reach your main career goal, include them here

1. Write your name and present job. Also write whether you are a student.

2. Describe your career goal or job.

3. What knowledge does your career goal or job require?

4. What abilities and skills does your career goal or job require?

5. What knowledge do you have now that relates to your career goal or job?

6. What abilities and skills do you have now that relate to your career goal or job?

7. How does your lifestyle relate to your career goal? What personal values do you have that can help you reach your career goal?

8. What knowledge do you need to gain to reach your career goal?

9. What abilities and skills do you need to gain to reach your career goal?

10. If you need to reach in-between or short-term goals before you reach your career goal, what steps do you need to take?

<table>
<tr><td>

action verb

chronological
  résumé

cover letter

functional résumé

personal goal
  statement

personal resources

recruitment

reference

résumé

screening

selection

</td></tr>
</table>

Vocabulary Review

Choose the word or phrase from the Word Bank that best completes each sentence. Write the answer on your paper.

1. A person who can share your personal qualities and job qualifications with an employer is a(n) _____.

2. Going through a number of applications to pick out the most suitable people for a job opening is called _____.

3. A description of a career goal along with information related to the goal is called a(n) _____.

4. A résumé that focuses on job tasks or skills of an applicant is a(n) _____.

5. The knowledge, skills, abilities, and personal values a person can use to be successful are known as _____.

6. A summary of knowledge, abilities, and experience that shows how a person is qualified for a particular occupation is a(n) _____.

7. Getting a number of applications from which to choose new employees is known as _____.

8. A one-page letter sent with a résumé is a(n) _____.

9. A résumé that focuses on an applicant's education and work experience is a(n) _____.

10. Choosing a person for a job opening is called _____.

11. A word that shows action is a(n) _____.

Concept Review

Choose the word or phrase that best completes each sentence or answers each question. Write the letter of the answer on your paper.

12. Which is an important lifestyle question to consider in making a personal goal statement?

   A What career cluster do you like most?

   B What job do you want to get?

   C Do you want to live in a city, a suburb, or the country?

   D What is your in-between career goal?

13. Which information is not needed on a résumé?
    - **A** career goal
    - **B** high school attended
    - **C** last job
    - **D** gender

14. An example of a good reference is _____.
    - **A** your grandfather
    - **B** your basketball coach
    - **C** your best friend since first grade
    - **D** your cousin

15. About how many of the available job openings are found in newspaper help-wanted ads?
    - **A** 5 percent
    - **B** 20 percent
    - **C** 60 percent
    - **D** 90 percent

16. The first step in the hiring process is _____.
    - **A** a job interview
    - **B** selection
    - **C** recruitment
    - **D** screening

Critical Thinking

Write the answer to each of the following questions.

17. Do you need to know your specific career goal before looking for your first job? Explain why or why not.

18. Why is it important to create a strong résumé?

19. A friend has an excellent job interview with a company. When the company does not hire her, she is upset. What might you say to help her feel better?

20. A friend is applying for jobs. He says he does not need to ask people to be his references yet. He will wait until he is called for an interview. Explain why you think this is a good plan or not.

Test-Taking Tip

Look over a test before you begin answering questions. See how many sections there are. Read the directions for each section.

Communication Skills

When you speak with a possible employer, you want to give a specific message about yourself. You'll have a short amount of time to communicate your qualifications and the reasons you're right for the job. Simple, right? Not really. Like any other skill area, good communication requires practice and preparation. In this chapter, you will learn some techniques and tips for getting a strong, positive message across to an employer. A good interview could make the difference between being one more applicant in a crowd to being the stand-out applicant the interviewer remembers—and hires.

Goals for Learning

◆ To understand the purpose of an interview

◆ To prepare for an interview

◆ To learn the importance of self-advocacy

Communication Connection

You may not think of hand shaking as a kind of communication. However, it is a form of body language that may have a big impact in a job interview. Always be ready to shake hands with your interviewer. Practice a handshake that is not weak but also not too hearty. With your handshake, offer a smile and a polite greeting.

Many people feel nervous or afraid before an interview. They imagine being put on the "hot seat" and being asked all sorts of questions that they will not be able to answer. Some people describe this as the "sweaty palms" experience. The good news is that you can be prepared for these situations. You might still be nervous, but you can avoid being surprised by the questions that come up. By preparing effectively for an interview, you will be able to handle any situation that arises.

How Can You Prepare For an Interview?

By doing the activities in the previous chapters of this book, you have already done much of the work that you need to do to prepare for an interview. Being effective in an interview is based on knowing yourself and having a clear sense about why you are a "good fit" for the position for which you are applying.

The interview is where you get to share important information about yourself and your goals. The information you share focuses on the skills, interests, experience, and values that connect you to the job. If you are interviewing for a job in carpentry, for example, you need to share the skills you have that relate to the work a carpenter does. Specifically, you need to tell the interviewer the things you have done in the past that demonstrate that you could do the job successfully.

What Is the Interviewer Looking For?

The interviewer is looking for someone who can do a specific job. The interviewer has identified the skills and experiences necessary for doing the job well. The interviewer also has an idea of the type of person needed in a particular work situation. When you have done a good job preparing for an interview, you have taken the time to do self-assessment (Chapter 2) and to research career options (Chapters 3 and 4). You have also learned how to connect information about yourself with appropriate careers. By doing these activities, you have become the expert about why you are an excellent fit for the job for which you are interviewing.

Then, all you need to do is to communicate to the interviewer what you know about yourself. Your job is to convince the interviewer that you are the best person for the job.

Many people are scared or nervous about interviews because they do not know the questions that will be asked ahead of time. This may be true. Even though you do not know the exact questions, keep in mind that most interviewers want to know the same things:

1. Can you do the job?
2. Will you do the job?
3. Will you fit into the job situation?

Almost all interview questions will relate to one of these three questions. While the words may be different, the information is the same.

Can You Do the Job?

This question asks you to identify the skills you have that connect with the job. To answer this question, think about how you can communicate your skills in terms of accomplishments. For example, consider the difference between a baseball player saying "I can catch, hit, and throw the ball" and "My batting average is .303 and I did not make any fielding errors last season." The first example simply communicates that the baseball player has the relevant skills.

Career Profile

Retail Merchandise Buyer

There are many job opportunities in retail sales. Sales clerks and sales managers work for small shops, large discount stores, and department stores. They sell everything from gift items to clothing to furniture. One interesting retail job opportunity is that of a buyer.

A buyer is responsible for purchasing goods from a wholesaler to sell in a retail store. First a buyer must be in touch with his or her customers. He or she must understand the prices, quality, and styles of goods that customers want. The buyer must also communicate with the store or shop management. The buyer needs to know the store's selling philosophy. Finally, a buyer must work with wholesale salespeople. These are the people from whom he or she buys goods.

A buyer may travel to large markets several times a year. For example, a clothing buyer for a department store may go to New York City twice a year for big fashion shows. A furniture buyer may go to home fashion shows several times a year.

Many retail buyers start their careers as sales assistants. This helps them understand customers and merchandise. A two-year or four-year college degree is needed for many retail buying positions.

The second example communicates the player's skills in terms of accomplishments. The first statement communicated only that the player had the skills. The question remains as to how well the player can catch, throw, and hit. The second statement communicated not only that the player has the skills but also a high skill level. Thus, the second statement would be a better way to convince the interviewer that the player can do the job well. In a similar way, you should try to communicate your skills by describing accomplishments that involve using relevant job skills.

How Can You Communicate Your Job Skills?

At first, communicating your skills in terms of accomplishments may seem like a difficult task. A good way to begin is by making a list of the skills required to do the job in which you are interested. For example, a secretary must be able to follow directions, have computer skills, communicate effectively, and be organized. A bank teller must be good with details, have basic math skills, be able to work with a computer, and be reliable. Choose two jobs that you are currently interested in. For each job, make a list of the relevant skills.

How Are Skills and Experiences Related?

After you have made a list of relevant skills you can list your experiences related to those skills. List the times you have demonstrated the skills. (You may find it helpful to review the information in Chapter 2, Lessons 1 and 2.) Describe these times in terms of accomplishments. Use action verbs to begin the descriptions. For example, "managed," "organized," "coached," "planned, " and "filed." You can also work with a parent, teacher, or counselor to find ways to describe your skills in terms of what you have accomplished. Once you have done this, you can begin to practice how you will answer the question, "Can you do the job?" Your answers should be clear and to the point. You can practice stating these answers in a small group in class, with your counselor, with your parents or guardians, or with your teacher. Focus on the most important skills for the job in which you are interested.

Will You Do the Job?

To answer this question, focus on your interests. You must be able to communicate what it is about the job that you find interesting. This question gives you the chance to let the interviewer know you are excited about the job. (Referring back to the work you did in Chapter 2, Lessons 3 and 4 may be helpful.)

Identify the interests that connect most closely to those required for the job for which you are interviewing. Once you have connected your interests to those required for the job, begin transferring these connections into statements. For example, "I enjoy helping others and have done this in my role as a tutor to other students." You can practice your statements by rehearsing them with an interview partner. Your partner's task is to ask the question, "What about this job interests you?" Your task is to provide the answer in clear, direct statements.

Will You Fit into the Job Situation?

This is a very important question. You will have the chance to discuss your personal qualities, such as honesty and reliability that make you a good worker. Many people advance in their jobs because they are a good fit for their job situation.

Other people lose their jobs because they cannot fit in. Many times, this happens because people do not have positive attitudes and good social skills. For example, they are not reliable, they do not work hard, or they have trouble getting along with their coworkers.

Employers want to hire people who can work well as part of a team.

How Can You Connect Your Values with a Job?

Fitting in also includes being clear about your values and how your values connect with the job. (Remember, you learned about values in Chapter 2, Lesson 4.) It is important to note that although interviewers will very likely ask you direct questions about your skills, experiences, and interests, they might not ask you a direct question as to whether you will fit in. The interviewer will try to get clues by observing what you communicate through your body language and how you speak.

How Can You Show Interest in a Job?

Body language that demonstrates that you are interested in the job includes making good eye contact, maintaining good posture, having a firm handshake, dressing appropriately, and demonstrating that you have done some research about the employer and the job. Speaking with an appropriate level of enthusiasm is also important. If you speak too quietly, then you will communicate a lack of interest and energy. If you speak too loudly you will communicate insensitivity to others. Keep in mind that what you say and how you say it are equally important in the interview process.

Having a positive attitude is also important. Would you rather spend time with people who demonstrate positive behaviors and attitudes or negative ones? Most of us enjoy being around positive and optimistic people. Demonstrate in your interview that you are the sort of person with whom your prospective employer would want to spend time. Be positive, optimistic, and complimentary.

What Qualities Do Employers Want?

Although the answer to whether you will fit into any specific job situation requires you to know something about the particular job you are interviewing for, there are some factors that it is safe to assume are common across all job situations. For example, all employers want their employees to be honest, hard working, and reliable. Employers want people who will contribute to the work environment by displaying positive attitudes toward their jobs, their coworkers, and their supervisors.

How Can You Communicate These Qualities?

It is important for you to communicate that you have these qualities. You can do this by stating that you have them. You can also provide examples of times in your life when you have demonstrated them. For example, suppose you were involved in a group project at school. You could explain how you encouraged the group to take a positive approach to problem solving. Or, suppose you rarely miss a day of school and are always on time. This shows that you are dedicated and prompt. Sharing these qualities is important to demonstrate that you are a positive person and someone who works hard to fit in.

You can practice your responses to the question of how well you will fit in by making a list of all the qualities and values that you possess. Try to identify instances or experiences in which you demonstrated these qualities and values. Now turn those instances into statements. Practice stating the examples in ways that give the interviewer evidence that you will fit in. Practice your statements with peers, parents or guardians, your counselor, or your teacher.

Remember, even though you may be nervous about an interview, you know what the basic questions will be. The interviewer wants to know if you are the "right" person for the job. Your role in the interview is to convince the interviewer that you are the right person. You must connect your skills and experience to the job for which you are being interviewed. By preparing effectively for the interview, you will be ready to provide the answers. You can draw from your past and present experiences to convince the interviewer that you have the skills, interests, values, and experience necessary to perform the job well.

Lesson 1 Review Write your answers to these questions on a sheet of paper

1. What are the main things an interviewer wants to know when he or she interviews someone?

2. What is the best way to prepare to communicate your skills in an interview?

3. Besides skills and knowledge, what are the main things a person needs to fit into a job situation?

You have learned that you know much of what happens in an interview ahead of time. You have been preparing for interviews by completing many of the activities in this book. The interview is the time when you pull it all together and show that you are a good fit for a job. As you focus on the interview, remember that most interview questions will relate to the three basic questions discussed in the previous lesson. Here are some typical interview questions and suggestions for answering them.

1. **What experiences have you had that relate to this position?** This question requires you to discuss your relevant skills in terms of your accomplishments.

2. **What interests you about this job (or college or other postsecondary institution)?** This question requires you to discuss your relevant interests and activities and show how you have put your interests into action.

3. **What are your long-term goals?** This question requires you to discuss how your interests, skills, motivation, and values connect with goals that are a good fit for the job.

4. **In what kind of work environment are you most comfortable?** This question requires you to discuss how you fit in. This is the time to mention your positive qualities such as being reliable, hard working, and able to communicate well with others.

5. **What are your strengths?** This question gives you the chance to discuss your relevant skills in terms of your accomplishments.

Writing Practice

An interviewer might ask you, "How would your friends describe you?" Write an answer to this question. Give examples to support the descriptions.

6. **What are your weaknesses?** Be careful! An interview is not the time to discuss your shortcomings but rather to highlight your current skills. You can also mention the skills you would still like to learn and develop. This question provides you with the chance to discuss your interest in developing more skills related to the job.

7. **Describe a time when you have demonstrated the skills required for this job.** Show how you can connect your skills with the job.

8. **How would your friends describe you?** To answer this question, focus on the positive things your friends would say about you. For example, "My friends would describe me as honest, reliable, loyal, and hard working. They might also say that I try to see the positive in all situations."

9. **What do you think you could contribute to this organization?** This question provides the chance to talk about your skills, interests, and personal qualities that connect with the job. Remember you want to be a positive contributor to the environment and this is the time to let the interviewer know this.

10. **What two or three accomplishments have given you the greatest satisfaction in your life?** For this question, focus on the accomplishments that contain skills that connect with the job.

11. **What is most important to you in a job?** This question provides the opportunity to bring together your answers to all three questions in Lesson 1. Talk about how it is important for you to use your skills that connect with the job. Tell how the job you are interviewing for connects to your interests. Stress how it is important for you to be able to contribute positively to your work environment.

12. Describe a time when you failed to achieve a goal you had established for yourself. Focus on a time when you achieved some of what you hoped to achieve but maybe not everything. Tell also what you learned from the experience. For example, "As a newspaper delivery person, I set the goal of having 100 percent of my customers satisfied with my work. I came very close to achieving this goal. But, a couple of customers became upset when I was not able to deliver the paper at the usual time. As a result, I decided to contact my customers personally when I knew that the paper would be late. All of my customers appreciated this approach. Several customers even noted that they had never had such good service."

13. Why should I hire you? Once again, this is a question that provides the chance to share your answers to all three questions in Lesson 1.

14. What was your most rewarding experience in high school? To answer this question, try to identify a time when you were able to demonstrate positive personal qualities and use skills that are relevant to the job. For example, if the ability to set and achieve goals is important for the job, then the following example would be appropriate: "I tried out for the tennis team in 10th grade and barely made the varsity team. I decided that I would have the goal of being one of the top three players by my senior year. I worked hard. By the time I was a senior I was ranked number two on the team."

15. How do you feel about moving to take this job? The answer to this question is one that you need to be clear about. If moving is important for this particular job and you don't want to move, then the job may not be a good one for you. If you wouldn't mind moving, then say so.

16. Describe a time when you were faced with a major problem and tell me how you handled it. Identify a major "problem" as a major "challenge" that you experienced. Successfully learning a new skill or dealing effectively with a challenging task in school sports or in the community are good possibilities for an answer.

17. **How do you work under pressure?** To answer this question, you should note that you handle pressure effectively. Say that you stay focused on the job, work well with others, and keep a positive attitude.

18. **What would you contribute to our work environment?** For questions like this, it is helpful to develop a one- or two-sentence summary about your relevant accomplishments and your personal qualities. Once you develop this summary, write it down. Then practice saying it out loud.

19. **What do you know about our organization?** This is the time for you to share what you have learned about this particular organization. Note that "nothing" is never a good answer. You need to prepare for the interview by taking the time to learn something about the organization. Check it out on the Internet and talk to people who may know something about it. Do your homework and be ready to say something positive and specific about the organization.

20. **Do you think your grades are a good indication of how you would perform on the job? Why or why not?** If your grades are good, then it makes sense that they provide a good indication of your abilities. If your grades are not so good, then you may want to focus on areas in which you have been more successful. Some very good workers are better performers on the job than they are in the classroom. It is okay to say this if that is the case for you.

21. **How would you describe yourself?** This is another opportunity to use your summary statement of your accomplishments and positive personal qualities.

Technology Note

Computers have not only changed life for workers in offices. They have changed the way almost every business operates. Retail businesses rely on scanners for customer payment and inventory. Airlines use computers to book flights, check in passengers— and fly the planes! Factories use lathes and other machines that are computer controlled. Find out about the newest technology used in your career area of interest. This knowledge could pay off in interviews.

22. **Do you have plans for continuing your education?** Your plans should indicate your interest in continuing to learn and develop new skills.

23. **What do you see yourself doing five years from now?** It may be important to have a five-year plan related to the job. You might note that in five years you will have learned more about the industry in which the job is located, developed more advanced skills related to the job, and gotten additional education related to the job. For example, if the job is in the food service industry, you might note that you hope to have the chance to take on more responsibility. You want to learn more about the food service industry. You might also note that you hope that the organization will think of you as one of its best employees.

24. **Do you have any questions for me?** "No" is not a good answer to this question. It suggests that you are not interested in the job. There are some questions you can prepare ahead of the interview. For example, you can ask the interviewer to describe the ideal candidate for this job. You can ask the interviewer to share his or her opinion about what the biggest challenges are in this job. You can ask what the opportunities are for advancement. With each of these questions, the interviewer's response will give you important information. Note how you welcome the sort of challenges the interviewer identifies. If the interviewer said something earlier in the interview that you think would be helpful to learn more about, this is the time to ask. By responding with a few questions regarding the job, you will communicate that you are interested in the job and motivated to do the work.

Doing well in an interview requires preparation, homework, and practice. Find an interview partner and practice asking and responding to each of these questions. If you do this, you will notice that the more you practice, the easier interviewing gets. If you find that you cannot give a good answer to any of these questions, ask your teacher, parent, guardian, or counselor for help.

What Are Some Interview Dos and Don'ts?

Once you have prepared for an interview, there are some basic things you should keep in mind before the interview.

It is important to dress properly for an interview.

DO

- Dress properly for the interview. Wear clean, neatly ironed, and professional-looking clothing.
- Arrive on time for your interview. To be sure that you will arrive on time, know where the interview will take place. If it is somewhere that you are not familiar with, go to the location the day before the interview. Be sure you know how to get there and how much time it will take. If there is likely to be heavy traffic, plan for extra time.
- Make sure that you are well groomed for the interview. Make sure you hair is neat. Make sure you are clean and presentable. Keep in mind that an interview is not a time to splash on perfume or cologne.
- Be polite. The interview begins the moment you make contact with anyone who works for the organization. On interview day, it begins the moment you walk in the door. Treat everyone with respect.
- Act as if you want the job. Be sure to say so toward the end of the interview. Remind the interviewer why you are a good fit for the position before you leave.
- Ask the interviewer when you can expect to hear about the job. Find out what the time line is for the employer to make a decision.

DON'T

- Chew gum during an interview.
- Tell jokes or use inappropriate humor.
- Talk negatively about others or about previous employers.
- Use slang or improper language during an interview.
- Leave the interview without expressing your interest in the job.

What Should You Do After an Interview?

You have now learned what to do before and during an interview. The interview does not end, however, when you leave. You should write a thank-you note to the interviewer within 24 hours of the interview. Thank the interviewer for his or her time. Express your interest in the position. Restate how your skills and abilities qualify you for the position. If you thought of additional qualifications you have for the job, you can mention them in the note. The note should be brief and sincere.

What If You Do Not Get a Job Offer?

No matter how prepared you are for an interview, it is a fact of life that sometimes you will not get a job offer or be accepted into a school. This can be a difficult experience. When this occurs, there are several things that you can do. Review your interview experience. How well did you do? What could you do better in the next interview? The goal is to keep getting better at interviewing. Another thing you can do is call, write, or e-mail the interviewer. Express your thanks for having had the chance to interview. Also share your disappointment that it did not work out this time.

You can also ask what the interviewer thinks you could do to improve your chances in the future. Asking for feedback gives you the opportunity to find out what things you can do to get better. Thank the interviewer for his or her time. If an interview doesn't turn out how you expected, don't be discouraged. The more interviews you have, the better you will become at interviewing. Remember, everyone has had this experience. If you keep working at it, you will be successful!

Lesson 2 Review Write your answers to these questions on a sheet of paper.

1. In what ways is an interview a positive opportunity for the person being interviewed?

2. Why is it important to research an organization where you are interviewing?

3. An interviewer might ask a question such as, "What are your weaknesses?" Write an answer to this question.

The Economy

When the nation's economy is strong, many good jobs are available for people. Likewise, when the economy is poor, many people are unemployed. A time in American history when many people were unemployed was the Great Depression.

In 1929, the country had many economic problems. The stock market crashed. In other words, the value of most stocks fell or disappeared. Because people soon had little money to spend, businesses began to fail. Soon millions of Americans were unemployed.

Franklin Roosevelt became president in 1933. He started many programs to employ people. For example, he started the Works Progress Administration. This program employed people to build roads, bridges, and post offices. Roosevelt gave people confidence in the government and in the economy.

Roosevelt also signed the Social Security Act. Under this plan, money from each American's earnings was put into a special fund. When people retired, they received benefits. Although the Social Security program has some problems today, it has given key benefits to Americans for many years.

The Great Depression lasted for about 10 years. However, the government learned how to avoid similar problems in the future. Today there are many programs in place to prevent similar economic difficulties.

Self-advocacy

Supporting, defending, or speaking up for yourself

You have learned that in interviews, you must explain the reasons you are the right person for a job. The interview is not the time to be shy. You should say positive things about yourself. This is not always easy. You might not feel it is polite to speak very positively about yourself. You might feel like you are bragging. But, in an interview, it is important to speak up for yourself. This skill is called **self-advocacy.** You may not have heard the term "self-advocacy" before. Advocacy means "to defend or support a person or a cause." In self-advocacy, the person you are supporting or defending is you!

Why Are Self-Advocacy Skills Important?

Using self-advocacy skills is very important in an interview. During an interview you are required to "speak up for yourself." Self-advocacy skills are also important for other parts of the job search process. When you write your résumé, you put your strengths into words on paper. When you write a cover letter for an application, you include a summary of your strengths and accomplishments. When you engage in networking, you must use self-advocacy skills effectively. Being able to state your skills, interests, experience, and values is an important self-advocacy skill. Supporting yourself in this way can be useful throughout the job search process. Self-advocacy can help achieve your goals in work and in life.

When you use self-advocacy skills, you communicate clearly and effectively who you are and what you can do. Remember that stating your accomplishments is important. Your accomplishments are proof that you have the skills a job requires. It is one thing to *say* that you have a skill. It is even better to *show* that you have the skill. You can practice your self-advocacy skills as you prepare for interviews. The more you practice standing up for yourself, the better you will be able to show that you can get the job done.

When Will You Need to Use Self-Advocacy Skills?

You can use self-advocacy skills in situations other than job interviews. There will be other times in your life when you will need to support or defend yourself. Once you have a job, you will need to let your employer know you are doing a good job. You need to communicate the important contributions you are making. You can do this in the same way you communicate your qualifications and accomplishments during your job search. Find opportunities to let your employer know how you are contributing. Times when you can do this include your regular performance reviews, update meetings, written reports, or informal conversations with your supervisor.

How Can You Communicate Your Accomplishments?

Sometimes, you will communicate your accomplishments in terms of what you personally have been able to achieve. For example, in a performance review your supervisor may ask you to explain the work you have been doing. You might say, "In the past three months, I have helped increase sales at our store by 25 percent. I have done this by changing the displays in the store and creating new signs in the store window." Other times, you might communicate your accomplishments in terms of what your work group or team has accomplished. This is especially important if you are a supervisor or manager. For example, you might say something like, "In the past three months, we have increased sales at our store by 25 percent. We did this by meeting together to identify ways that we could better market our products. We changed the displays in the store and created new signs for the store window to attract new customers. It has really been a team effort."

Gender and Careers

Before the 1970s, many more men than women had full-time careers. Women had traditionally put caring for children and homes above a business or other career. Of course, this situation has changed. Women work in many careers that used to be mainly pursued by men. All aspects of employment have changed as a result. Even job interviews are different today. In the past, an employer might ask a woman if she planned to get married. An interviewer might ask a woman if she planned to have children soon. Employers sometimes thought that a woman would only work until she had children. Today, questions like these cannot be asked in a job interview. If an interviewer does ask a question like this, politely refuse to answer.

Think about a time you have been in a class, on a team, or involved in some other group activity. Your teacher or coach may want to know whether you have completed your homework or practiced on your own. The only way someone would know this is if you told them. If your teacher asked who had completed the required assignment, you would want to be sure that he or she knew you had done so. You would also want your coach to know if you had been doing extra practice. Letting a teacher or coach know you have been working hard creates a positive impression of the kind of person you are. If you do not complete your homework on a regular basis, what kind of impression do you think this creates? Your teacher probably won't have a very good impression of you. You want to be sure that you are doing the things that will help you to be viewed positively by others. More importantly, you need to let them know what you are doing.

How Can You Let Employers Know You Are a Good Worker?

It is important as a worker that you learn to communicate to your employer that you work hard and do your best to contribute. You can communicate this by volunteering for additional assignments, completing your assignments on time, and doing a good job on them. You can also try to provide answers to problems that occur, and maintain a positive attitude. These behaviors are ways that you let your employer know that you are a good worker. They are self-advocacy skills. The best time to start practicing them is right now. To start, think about ways in which others may view you. Do you think they see you as the sort of person who works hard and tries her or his best? Do they view you as a person who is reliable and positive? If the answer to these questions is "yes," keep up the excellent work! If the answer to these questions is "maybe" or "no," you may need to change some of your behaviors.

How Can You Change Your Behaviors?

Some ways in which you might change your behaviors and begin practicing self-advocacy skills include:

- Get your assignments done on time. Do them well.
- Volunteer to help when there is the chance to do so.
- Ask your teachers, coaches, and advisors if there are ways you can help them.
- Do more than what is expected. Do extra work on some assignments. Put in extra practice time. Then, let your teacher or coach know that you are working hard to do your best.
- Ask your teachers, coaches, advisors, parents, or guardians for feedback about how you can do better.
- Be reliable, on time, and positive.
- Try to provide solutions to problems when they occur.
- Express your thanks to others when they help you.

By practicing these behaviors, you can help others to see you positively. You are advocating for a very important person—you!

Lesson 3 Review Write your answers to these questions on a sheet of paper.

1. What is self-advocacy?

2. Why is self-advocacy important in a job interview?

3. Explain how you can practice self-advocacy skills in a job.

4. Describe two ways that you can start practicing self-advocacy skills right now.

Get Involved

Volunteers can work with a huge number of organizations that help people. Perhaps you have had the chance to help people with a variety of needs. But have you ever thought about forming your own organization to help others? Each year, individuals see a need and start a group to fill it. For example, one young boy discovered that people were cold and homeless in his city. He took coats to these people that very day. Then he formed a group to keep helping these people. High school students have started groups that befriend the elderly. They have collected food and clothing for victims of hurricanes and tornadoes. Look around you. Discover how you can help those in need. This will show the kind of spirit that most employers are looking for.

Interview Preparation

You have read about effective interview techniques. You have read some common interview questions. Answering these questions can help you prepare for an interview. Imagine you have been called for an interview for a job. On your own paper, write down the name of the job. Then answer the questions below as you would answer them in a job interview. Add this activity to your career portfolio.

1. What experiences have you had that relate to this position?

2. What interests you about this job?

3. What are your long-term goals?

4. In what kind of work environment are you most comfortable?

5. What are your strengths?

6. What are your weaknesses?

7. How would you describe yourself?

8. What do you think you could contribute to this organization?

9. What two accomplishments have given you the greatest satisfaction in life?

10. What is most important to you in a job?

11. Why should I hire you?

12. What was your most rewarding experience in high school?

13. Describe a time you were faced with a major problem. How did you handle it?

14. What would you contribute to our work environment?

15. Do you think your grades are a good way to see how you would perform in this job? Why or why not?

You can practice answering common interview questions with a friend or classmate to prepare for job interviews.

Chapter 8 R E V I E W

Vocabulary Review

Write the answer to this question on your paper.

1. What is self-advocacy?

Concept Review

Choose the word or phrase that best completes each sentence or answers each question. Write the letter of the answer on your paper.

2. Which question would most likely be asked in a job interview?

    A "How did you enjoy grade school?"

    B "Are you a good basketball player?"

    C "What is your favorite color?"

    D "What are your long-term goals?"

3. Which would be the most effective action verb to describe someone's accomplishments?

    A was   **C** invented

    B tried   **D** did

4. Which long-range goal would a successful job applicant most likely mention in an interview?

    A to make a lot of money

    B to become a sales manager

    C to have four children

    D to be able to retire young

5. Which is the best preparation for a job interview for an accounting firm?

    A reading a math book

    B buying a new outfit

    C practicing interviewing with a friend

    D researching the company president

Critical Thinking

Write the answer to each question on your paper.

6. Explain how an interview might be a positive experience even if you do not get the job.

7. Suppose you walk into a workplace for a job interview and are treated rudely by the receptionist. Explain how you would react and why.

8. Suppose you feel you have not had a chance to shine on a school athletic team. How might you use self-advocacy to change this situation?

9. Suppose you are a quiet, shy person. For this reason, you feel that an interview does not show your best traits. What might you do to improve this situation the next time you have an interview?

10. What are three questions you could ask an interviewer who asks, "What would you like to know about our organization?"

Test-Taking Tip
Before you take a test, skim through the whole test to find out what is expected of you.

Life Outside of Work

You already know that people have to work in order to make a living. You may even have heard the saying that all work and no play makes a person dull. Failing to balance work and free time doesn't just make a person dull. It can lead to stress and other negative factors. It can damage a person's health and relationships. It is important to develop interests outside of work and make choices that will enhance your health and well-being. Striking the right balance will help you work smarter and feel better in every area of your life.

Goals for Learning

◆ To understand the importance of developing interests and hobbies outside of work

◆ To learn time-management skills

◆ To realize the impact of life choices on personal health and well-being

◆ To recognize the effects of ethical decisions

Hobby

An activity done for enjoyment

Stress

A state of physical or emotional pressure

Obligation

Something that is required or must be done

Just as it is not too early to plan for your career, it is not too early to think about how you can develop your **hobbies** and interests. A hobby is an activity you do for enjoyment. Your job might help you fulfill some of your values. Hobbies and interests can also help you fulfill your values. You might think that hobbies and interests are not related to work at all. It may seem that an activity you do for fun is completely the opposite of an activity you do for pay. Some people might even have hobbies that give them a break from the **stress** of their jobs. Although that may be true in some cases, hobbies and interests have other connections with work. In this lesson you will learn about those connections. You will also discover some of the reasons people have hobbies and interests. Then, you will learn how you can find new hobbies to try.

How Is Work an Obligation?

You have learned that work is a specific activity that people do to earn a living. People work in order to provide for themselves and others. They work for wages. They need to be paid in order to fulfill their needs or to support a family. Work is an **obligation.** An obligation is something you have to do. If you want to earn a living, you must work. Another part of work is providing goods or services to others. For many people, providing for others is satisfying and enjoyable.

If you are in school, you are doing work when you study and complete assignments. Of course, you do not get paid for doing this kind of work. However, you get an education that prepares you for work later in life. Schoolwork is also an obligation. If you want to get an education, you must do schoolwork. Besides the work you do for school classes, you might also do other learning activities. If you want to be a musician, you might take music lessons. Practicing your musical instrument would be an obligation. You must practice if you want to develop the required level of knowledge and skill you need.

What Are Hobbies?

Hobbies are activities that people choose to do. They are not obligations. For example, you may decide to learn how to ski because you enjoy the activity. Hobbies also give you the chance to learn new skills. Because hobbies are fun, they can help you reduce stress in your life. Notice how you feel after participating in a hobby. You will probably feel more relaxed, happier, and calmer. The free time that you have when you are not performing work is called **leisure time.** The activities people do in their free time can range from playing sports to researching an interesting subject at the library. The list below includes some of the many different activities that people consider their hobbies.

Bicycling	Fishing	Photography
Boating	Gardening	Playing a musical instrument
Collecting coins	Going to sporting events	
Dancing		Rock climbing
Developing Web sites	Hiking	Reading
	Listening to music	Volunteering
Dining at restaurants	Painting	Writing poetry

How Are Hobbies and Interests Related?

You have learned that interests are things that people want to learn more about. For example, you might be interested in learning about rare coins. However, you do not collect coins. You just want to read about and learn more about them. In this case, your interest is rare coins. Your hobby is reading or learning about the coins. For the rest of this lesson, the word *hobbies* will be used to include interests as well.

Why Do People Pursue Hobbies?

People have different reasons for pursuing and developing their hobbies. Some people might really enjoy the things they do at work. So they transfer those skills to activities during their leisure time. Other people develop hobbies to do something different from their jobs. For example, suppose a person has a competitive job that has a lot of interaction with other people. He or she may turn to practicing yoga or sketching landscapes as a hobby. On the other hand, a person in a solitary, routine job may feel the need to participate in a competitive team sport as a hobby.

Think about your hobbies. What reasons do you have for doing these activities? If you said the reason for doing at least one of your hobbies is to keep physically fit, you are like a lot of other people. Next to keeping fit, relieving stress is another reason people develop hobbies. Almost everyone experiences stress at some time. Stress is physical or emotional pressure. It is built up tension that comes from trying to balance the demands of school, work, family, and friends. You most likely have experienced stress at some point. You might have felt stress when studying for final exams. Another time you may have experienced stress is when waiting to hear whether you made the team for a sport. Learning and getting used to the tasks that you have to perform in a new job might be stressful. When you are feeling stress, you may have headaches, back pain, and sore muscles. You might also have trouble sleeping. One way to relieve this stress is to do something you enjoy like jogging or reading.

Hobbies can help you develop new skills.

Career Tip

You might think your hobbies are not related to the career you pursue. But keep in mind that most activities contribute to your personal growth in some way. You can demonstrate that your hobbies and interests enhance your value to an employer. Be prepared to share your experiences.

Many people relieve stress by doing physical activity. For example, a hard-played game of basketball can be useful for releasing pent-up emotions. On the other hand, playing a competitive game might create more tension rather than relieve it. If this happens to you, you might consider other activities. Some of these non-competitive activities might be aerobics or weight lifting. Becoming aware of the activities that relieve or contribute to tension in your life will help you choose your hobbies.

Another reason people develop hobbies is to meet new people. For many people, belonging to a group is very important. You can meet new people by joining various clubs and organizations. Some of these clubs are devoted to arts and crafts, drama, and reading. Other clubs involve indoor and outdoor sports. There are also groups that do work for a cause, like taking care of the environment. By joining a club, you can spend time with friends doing something you enjoy. You also have the opportunity to make new friends. If you are shy and have a hard time meeting new people, pursuing a hobby that involves other people is a good way to make friends.

What Are Some Other Reasons to Develop Hobbies?

You have just read about three important reasons for having hobbies: keeping fit, relieving stress, and being socially involved with other people. These are not the only reasons you may have for your hobbies, however. Another reason might be to develop your skills in sports or a musical instrument. Hobbies can also provide you the opportunity to be recognized or rewarded for an ability you have.

Writing Practice

Take some time to write your hobbies on a sheet of paper so you can be sure that you have thought of all of them. Then write the reasons you do these activities. Check with your peers to see what their reasons are.

What are some of your hobbies? What needs do they fulfill? Let's look at an example of a hobby that might fulfill all the needs you have learned about. Basketball is a leisure activity that can have many purposes. Playing basketball can help you stay fit. It can also help you relieve stress. Basketball is a team sport, so it provides the chance to meet new people. Playing basketball will also help you develop skills like coordination, strategy, and working with others. Many sports besides basketball can fulfill these needs.

Some people prefer hobbies that are not physical activities. Playing a board game like chess, for example, will not help you stay in shape. However, it may be a way for you to relieve stress because it provides a break from your everyday life. You might also get better at thinking, planning, and making strategies as you play.

No matter what hobbies you pursue, think about how they meet your needs. People choose different leisure activities because they have different needs. You might find that physical activity is a good way for you to relieve stress. Or, you might find that reading is a better way to do so. Thinking about your needs will help you choose hobbies. To help you think about the needs your hobbies fulfill, look at this chart of hobbies and the needs they might fulfill.

Need Fulfilled	Hobby		
	⚽ Team Sports	🎲 Board Games	📕 Reading or Other Quiet Activities
Stay in Shape	✔		
Relieve Stress	✔	✔	✔
Meet New People	✔	✔	
Improve Skills	✔	✔	✔
Get Recognition for Ability	✔	✔	

How Can You Decide What New Hobbies to Pursue?

If the hobbies you have now are not helping you to fulfill your needs, you can find and develop new hobbies. This is a good time for you to explore leisure activities. You may have tried a hobby earlier in your life and didn't like it. Now, you might find it interesting. You might be physically stronger now or have greater coordination and concentration. These changes might make it easier for you to take part in physical activities. This is the time to develop interests and learn skills from leisure activities. These skills can help you throughout your life.

To start finding new hobbies, look at the classes you are taking in school. The activities you enjoy in your schoolwork can lead you to develop a hobby that uses those same activities. Here are some examples of activities from various school subjects.

Subject	Activities or Interests
Art	drawing, painting, sculpture, graphic design, photography
Science and Technology	electronics, computer programming, astronomy
Music and Theater	dance, drama, singing, instruments
English	fiction writing, poetry, public speaking
Family/Consumer Science	cooking, sewing, managing a budget
Shop	automotive, metal work, wood work
Physical Education	sports, exercise

Hobbies that you really love sometimes can guide you to a career that you will enjoy. Consider your hobbies and skills. What careers use the specific tasks or skills your hobby uses? You may be able to turn what you do in your free time into a career.

Another way you can find new hobbies is by looking at the clubs and teams that your school has. Many of these clubs or teams expand on class activities. Here are some examples: computer club, poetry club, and business club. Other clubs may not be based directly on classroom activities. Groups might meet to discuss ways to protect the environment or to do community service projects. Another way to find hobbies to try is by going to local community agencies such as the YMCA/YWCA or a community center. These places might offer activities like indoor and outdoor sports, and leadership, environmental, arts, gardening, and computer clubs.

What Are the Connections Between Hobbies and Work?

Hobbies can also help you develop skills you can use in your career. One of the greatest benefits of a hobby is when it turns into a career. For example, you might begin to learn playing the piano for fun. You take lessons and practice regularly. Perhaps you become good enough to be a piano teacher. Similarly, you might start playing basketball after school with your friends. Then you try out for and make the school team. You might go on to play at college or as a professional. Or, you might become a basketball coach.

Your hobby may not turn out to be exactly what you do for work later in life, however. Just because you like an activity as a hobby does not mean that you will want to do it as a career. Even if you become very good at your hobby, some jobs are very difficult to get. For example, very few people end up being professional basketball players. You might enjoy basketball and also have strong business skills. You might enjoy working in a management position for a basketball team. Perhaps you have artistic ability. Then, you might become an illustrator for a sports magazine. For most careers, you use skills from more than one hobby. For example, an illustrator for a sports magazine combines the hobbies of sports and art.

Pursuing your hobbies and developing new ones can help you learn new skills and meet new people. You can also stay physically fit and find good ways to relieve stress. Taking part in leisure activities that you enjoy can also help develop skills you can use in your career.

Lesson 1 Review Write your answers to these questions on a sheet of paper.

1. How are hobbies and interests different from work?

2. What are some reasons for pursuing hobbies?

3. How can hobbies be directly related to your career? How are they indirectly related?

Career Profile

Personal Trainer

Some career paths combine hobbies and health with earning a paycheck. Professional trainers often begin with a personal interest in health and wellness. They develop this personal interest through education and practice. Personal trainers work in a variety of settings: health clubs, medical and chiropractic practices, rehabilitation centers and hospitals, and community centers. They might also work for a sports team or club. They work with a wide range of clients. But the goal is always similar: to help a client get stronger and healthier. Personal trainers provide information about safe exercise programs, develop training plans, monitor progress, and provide feedback to people.

Personal trainers generally have to be certified. They need to demonstrate an understanding of how exercise and diet affects the body. Trainers who work with athletes, people with diabetes, or individuals learning to use an artificial limb also spend time learning about the special needs of their clients. In addition, personal trainers have to pay close attention to their own health and fitness. Helping people achieve their health goals can be rewarding and meaningful work for a person with a passion for personal wellness.

Think Positive

Searching for a job can be frustrating and exhausting. During this stressful time, it is very important to eat right, exercise regularly, and get plenty of sleep. These steps will help you keep stress under control.

This lesson is about managing your time. **Time management** is how you use your time to complete your activities and achieve your goals. It involves deciding what activities you want to participate in and how much time you want to give to each of them. Time management also involves discovering what activities are taking up more time than you want them to. You can call these activities "time wasters."

This lesson will help you understand time management and practice time management skills. It will guide you through a survey of how you spend your time. Then you will make some decisions about the time you spend on those activities. The decisions can help you subtract time from some activities, add time to others, or even get rid of "time wasters." These time management skills will be useful throughout your life. It is important to start developing them now.

How Do You Spend Your Time?

It is important to have a clear idea of how you spend your time. What activities are you involved in? How much time do you spend on them? One way to answer these questions is to do a personal time survey. Make a list of the activities you participate in each day. Use the chart on page 253 for activity suggestions. Then determine how much time you spend on each activity. Finally, total the hours to find out how much time you spend doing the activities.

You should do your personal time survey for at least a week. There are 168 hours in a week. (24 hours $\times$ 7 days = 168 hours) Estimate the amount of time you spend on each activity each day. Then multiply that time by seven to get the total for a week. You will need to multiply your time spent in school by five instead of seven. You are in school only five days each week. Make sure that your total hours do not add up to more than 168.

Here is an example of a completed personal time survey.

Activity	Hours Per Day		Hours Per Week
1. Number of hours for sleep	8	× 7 =	56
2. Number of hours for meals	$1\frac{1}{2}$	× 7 =	$10\frac{1}{2}$
3. Number of hours for homework	$1\frac{1}{2}$	× 7 =	$10\frac{1}{2}$
4. Number of hours for chores, errands, etc.	$\frac{1}{2}$	× 7 =	$3\frac{1}{2}$
5. Number of hours for scheduled activities (clubs, church, family events, etc.)	1	× 7 =	7
6. Number of hours for sports	1	× 7 =	7
7. Number of hours traveling to and from activities	1	× 7 =	7
8. Number of hours spent with friends	$\frac{1}{2}$	× 7 =	$3\frac{1}{2}$
9. Number of hours on the phone	$\frac{1}{2}$	× 7 =	$3\frac{1}{2}$
10. Number of hours watching TV	$1\frac{1}{2}$	× 7 =	$10\frac{1}{2}$
11. Number of hours on the computer	$\frac{1}{2}$	× 7 =	$3\frac{1}{2}$
12. Number of hours at school	$6\frac{1}{2}$	× 5 =	$32\frac{1}{2}$
Total	24		155

Notice that the total of 155 hours is less than 168. This is because the number of hours in school is counted for only five days. Now that you have completed your personal time survey, look at the total for each item and compare them. Make a note of anything you find interesting or had not realized about the way you spend your time. Are you spending too much time preparing for school? Not enough time sleeping? How much time is spent on the phone compared to socializing in person? Answering these questions is part of balancing your time between work and leisure.

How Can You Use Your Time Survey Results?

Career Tip

Remember that networking is a very effective way to find a job. Developing interests that bring you into contact with a variety of people is a great way to develop a relationship that will lead to a good job.

Your personal time survey has given you a better picture of how you spend your time. Now you can think about how you might want to change the amount of time you spend on your activities. Are you spending too much time on one activity or too little on another? Are there any time wasters? As you subtract or add time to the activities, just remember to keep the total for the week at or less than 168 hours.

Once you have made changes to your personal time survey, you can make a schedule. A schedule will help you remember the things you have to do and how much time you want to spend doing them. A good way to start is to make a simple "To Do" list. Include activities you have to do for the week, when they need to be done, and the amount of time they will take. The activities should be things you have committed yourself to doing, such as homework, practice for a sports team, and family functions. This schedule will ensure that you have time to complete your most important activities.

If you have a lot of activities to fit into your week, you may need to create a more detailed schedule. Making time for all of your activities and obligations can be a lot to handle. You need a well-organized plan to manage your time. This kind of plan involves making a schedule for the week. For each day, write the activities that you must do. These would be the same activities you wrote in your "To Do" list. Also include the activities you would like to do.

A proverb says, "The journey of a thousand miles begins with one step." Thinking about your career and all the coming changes may feel overwhelming. Instead of focusing on this enormous task, think about the small steps. This will help you see your progress day by day. Instead of being overwhelmed, you will be encouraged and challenged with each new step.

Making a schedule can help you manage your time effectively.

You will need to take some time to set up your time-management schedule. It may take effort and persistence to make it work. If the first attempt with your time-management plan does not work, go over the plan again and make changes as necessary. For example, make sure that you are setting aside enough time to complete the activities you have on your plan. You should also make sure that you are not spending more time on activities than you have planned. You may have set aside one hour for leisure reading, for example. When the hour is up, you may need to stop reading and move on to the next activity.

Learning how to make and use a time-management plan will help you complete work. It will also help you use your leisure time wisely. If you follow your plan, you may have more time to include other valuable activities you would like to do.

Here are some hints to help you make your time-management plan work well.

- Put aside some time to prepare your schedule, preferably on a weekend.
- Schedule the most important activities first. Important activities might include homework, family functions, and research projects for school.
- Allow time to get from one activity to the next one. For example, if your last class of the day finishes at 3:00 P.M., don't schedule the next event for 3:00 P.M.
- Allow some non-scheduled time. If you fall behind in your schedule, this time will allow you to catch up. If you stay on schedule, this non-scheduled time can be free time to fill however you like.
- Consider the times of the day when you work best. Some people work best right after school. Others work best early in the morning.

Recognize the difference between activities that require the best of your mental and physical abilities and those that don't. You need to place these activities at suitable times in your schedule. Some household chores such as vacuuming the carpet or washing the car demand little of your ability or skill. Other chores can be tiring, leaving you with little energy to focus on other activities. Do not participate in activities that are not on your schedule. For example, if watching TV is not on your schedule for a particular day, don't give in to the temptation.

You can get an idea of how to arrange your time by studying the sample schedule on page 257.

🕐 Time Schedule

SATURDAY

9:00–9:30 A.M.	Breakfast
10:00–12:00 P.M.	Work on science project
12:00–1:00 P.M.	Lunch
1:30–3:30 P.M.	Work on friend's car
4:00–6:00 P.M.	Soccer practice
6:30–7:30 P.M.	Dinner
7:30–8:00 P.M.	Household chores
8:00–9:30 P.M.	Socialize with friends

SUNDAY

9:00–9:30 A.M.	Breakfast
10:00–11:00 A.M.	Finalize science project with classmate
11:30–1:30 P.M.	Family function and lunch
2:00–4:00 P.M.	Soccer game
4:30–5:30 P.M.	Mow lawn
6:00–8:00 P.M.	Go to see a movie with friends
8:30–9:30 P.M.	Prepare schedule for week

Lesson 2 Review Write your answers to these questions on a sheet of paper.

1. What are some benefits of good time management?

2. How is a "To Do" list different from a schedule? How are they related?

3. Why is it important to leave non-scheduled time in your schedule?

Diet

The food that you regularly eat and drink

Nutrient

A substance in food that your body needs to work properly

Part of having a successful career is living a healthy lifestyle. Your career choices can be limited by not making healthy choices. Many employers require their workers to be in good physical shape. Employers also want employees who make good decisions about drugs and alcohol. Being unhealthy can affect your job performance. The information presented in this lesson focuses on making healthy choices.

Nutrition and Fitness

Food is fuel for your body. Food provides the energy your body needs to work properly. Deciding what food to eat is important. Good food choices help you stay healthy. Poor food choices can lead to poor health. Eating too much or not enough food also can cause problems.

Why Is Diet Important to Your Health?

Your **diet** is the food that you eat and drink. Your diet affects the way you look, feel, and perform. A healthy diet helps you look your best. It makes your hair shine and helps keep your skin clear. It gives you energy to do things you need or want to do. Eating healthy also contributes to your emotional health. It gives you energy to think clearly and to deal with stress.

Scientists have discovered that food contains about 50 substances that your body needs to work and grow properly. These substances are called **nutrients.** Foods vary in the nutrients they provide. For example, green beans have more nutrients than sugar. A healthy diet includes foods that are good sources of nutrients. If your diet does not include enough nutrients, you might experience headaches, stomachaches, tiredness, or depression. A lack of nutrients can lead to health problems.

To make sure you eat foods with the right amount of nutrients, you can plan your diet. The U.S. government publishes guidelines for a healthy diet. You can use these and other resources to make sure you are eating healthy.

Physical fitness
The body's ability to meet the demands of everyday living
Symptom
A physical sign or indication that you have an illness

Along with having a healthy diet, it is important to get physical exercise. Exercise keeps your body fit. **Physical fitness** is your body's ability to meet the demands of daily living. That means having enough energy to do all the things you want to do. Physical fitness is a key part of your overall good health. It affects your emotional, social, and physical well-being. Exercising regularly to be physically fit is another way you can take care of yourself.

To exercise means to move the larger muscles of your body, such as those in your arms and legs. Regular exercise can help build a strong heart and lungs. It helps build strong, firm muscles. It improves your body's ability to move in ways you want it to move, such as by twisting and turning. Exercise gives you more energy so you can do more without becoming tired. Active people sleep better, feel better, and are less depressed than people who are not active.

Exercise can reduce the chance for illness. For example, regular exercise reduces the risk of heart disease. Regular exercise can also shorten the time it takes to get well if you become sick. Not getting enough exercise can cause serious health problems. According to a government report, the lack of physical activity contributes to 400,000 preventable deaths (17% of total deaths) a year in the United States. You can keep yourself healthy by doing 30 to 60 minutes of physical activity a day.

Recognizing and Preventing Illness

Our bodies need food, plenty of fluids, exercise, and rest to stay healthy. However, there are times when the body does not work properly and an illness occurs. Being able to recognize the signs, or **symptoms,** of an illness will help you know when and how to get treatment.

What Diseases Are Considered Common?

Diabetes

A disease in which the body is not able to use sugar from food

The most common disease in the United States is the cold. A cold usually lasts from several days to more than a week. Symptoms include sneezing, cough, stuffy or runny nose, fever, headache, and sore throat. These symptoms differ throughout the time that you have the cold. They may also differ from person to person and from cold to cold. The flu, or influenza, has some of the same symptoms as a cold. Flu symptoms are usually more severe. Symptoms include fever, headache, sore throat, and coughing. Aching muscles, chills, nausea, vomiting, and diarrhea are some other flu symptoms. These symptoms also differ throughout the illness and from person to person.

In addition to the cold and flu, other common diseases include heart disease, cancer, and **diabetes.** Heart disease is the leading cause of death in the United States. You can protect yourself from heart disease, high blood pressure, high cholesterol, heart attack, and stroke by eating a healthy diet and getting enough exercise. Cancer is the second leading cause of death in the United States. Cancer is an abnormal and harmful growth of cells in the body. There are more than 100 types of cancer. Cancer symptoms can vary. Often, people will feel pain or discomfort in the area where the cancer is growing. Sometimes, a person will not feel well but not have specific symptoms. Unusual weight loss and poor appetite may occur as a result of cancer. The most important factor for cancer survival is finding the cancer early. Here are some warning signs of cancer.

Change in bowel or bladder habits

A sore that will not heal

Unusual bleeding or discharge

Thickening or lump in the breast or elsewhere

Indigestion or difficulty swallowing

Obvious change in wart or mole

Nagging cough or hoarseness

Another common disease is diabetes. Diabetes is a disease in which the body cannot use sugar and other food for energy. Type I and Type II are the two most common types of diabetes. Type I diabetes usually starts during childhood. Symptoms include frequent urination, extreme thirst and hunger, rapid weight loss, and tiredness. About 5 to 10 percent of people with diabetes have Type I diabetes.

Type II diabetes is the most common form of diabetes. It usually occurs in adults over age 40. Type II diabetes is milder than Type I. People who are inactive or overweight are at risk for getting Type II diabetes. Type II diabetes can often be controlled and prevented through weight loss and exercise. Symptoms include blurry vision, slow-healing sores, tiredness, and tingling in the hands or feet. Type II diabetes accounts for 90 to 95 percent of people with diabetes.

What Are STDs?

Sexually transmitted diseases, or STDs, are spread through sexual activity. In the United States, one in four people under age 21 has an STD. More than 20 diseases are transmitted sexually. Some of the most common and serious STDs are AIDS, gonorrhea, chlamydia, syphilis, and genital herpes. Except for genital herpes and AIDS, most sexually transmitted diseases can be cured when they are treated early. For diseases without cures, medical treatment can make people more comfortable. There are no vaccines to prevent sexually transmitted diseases. The best way to protect yourself from STDs is to refrain from sexual activity.

Technology Note

Keeping track of nutrition and exercise has never been as easy as it is today. Inexpensive electronic logs can help you keep track of eating patterns and daily activity. You can also go online to find "personal health assistants" and many other resources about developing healthy habits. Take advantage of these resources to help you make healthy choices.

How Can You Prevent the Spread of Illness?

Drug

Any substance, other than food, that changes the way your mind and body work

People cannot prevent all illnesses from happening to them. However, many diseases can be prevented. Diseases such as the cold and flu are spread from person to person. Germs that cause disease are passed from person to person. Other diseases are caused by a person's behaviors. For example, consider a person who eats many fatty foods, avoids exercise, and smokes cigarettes. The person's behaviors may cause high blood pressure or trigger a heart attack. Another way disease is spread is through the environment. For example, small children who eat chips of lead-based paint can get lead poisoning. Nonsmokers who breathe other people's cigarette smoke may get lung diseases, including cancer. Here are some things you can do to prevent illnesses from spreading.

- Avoid physical contact with a sick person
- Cover your mouth when coughing
- Wash your hands often
- Avoid second-hand smoke
- Protect yourself from STDs

Mood-Modifying Substances

Another part of having a healthy lifestyle is avoiding harmful **drugs.** Drugs like tobacco and alcohol have damaging physical and mental effects.

The Economy

Being overweight or obese can impair both physical and financial health. A study by the Medical Expenditure Panel Survey estimated that individuals, insurance companies, and government programs spent more than $51 billion in 1998 for illnesses directly related to being overweight and obese. The amount does not seem to be declining. As a result, health insurance costs have increased. People have to spend more of their own money for health care.

Other research has shown a direct impact on productivity in the workplace as well. Obese people have a significantly greater likelihood of developing illnesses. This means they are also much more likely to miss time at work. Between higher medical costs and reduced productivity, the overall cost of obesity has created both a healthcare crisis in this country as well as an economic dilemma.

How Does Tobacco Affect People?

Every time a person smokes, he or she breathes in about 2,000 harmful chemicals. One of the most damaging chemicals is **nicotine.** Nicotine is **addictive,** or habit forming. Nicotine is found in cigarettes, cigars, pipe tobacco, and chewing tobacco. It speeds up the heart rate and increases blood pressure. Long-term tobacco use can lead to a heart attack, stroke, or cancer. In fact, smoking is responsible for 87 percent of lung cancer deaths. Smoking can also cause other breathing diseases. Cigarette smoke also can harm nonsmokers. Studies prove that healthy nonsmokers can get breathing diseases and cancers by inhaling smoke from burning cigarettes. Because of the harm second-hand smoke causes, laws forbid smoking in many public places. In addition, many workplaces are smoke free.

How Does Alcohol Affect the Body?

People can become physically and psychologically addicted to the alcohol found in wine, beer, and hard liquor. People drink alcohol to feel more self-confident, to relax, or to escape uncomfortable emotions. In realty, alcohol doesn't help and instead often hinders people. Alcohol has a damaging effect on every major system in the body. Alcohol is not digested but absorbed directly from the stomach into the bloodstream and carried throughout the body. When people drink alcohol, their judgment, vision, reaction time, and muscle control are affected. The amount of alcohol in their blood begins to rise. Short-term effects of alcohol include slurred speech, dizziness, flushed skin, stumbling, and dulled senses and memory. Physical and mental dependence on alcohol or lack of control over drinking is called **alcoholism.** Alcoholism is classified as a disease.

Communication Connection

Many people who use drugs and alcohol believe these substances will help them feel relaxed around others. In reality, people who use drugs often say and do things they regret later. Instead of using substances to relieve your anxiety, try a more healthy way to deal with stress. For example, you can practice interviewing with a friend. Try to make it a fun activity. This will help you get used to asking and answering questions in a friendly setting. You can prepare for job interviews without any negative side effects.

What Other Affects Can Alcohol Use Have?

Alcohol use can also affect driving ability. About half of all teenagers who are involved in traffic accidents have been drinking alcohol. The penalties for drunken driving vary from state to state. Some penalties include spending the night in jail or having your driver's license suspended. Even if you do not drink alcohol, drunken driving can affect you. Some people accept rides from others who have been drinking alcohol. Turning down such an offer ensures your safety and protects you from injuries that could affect you for a lifetime.

What Are Some Other Harmful Drugs?

Besides tobacco and alcohol, other drugs can have harmful effects on a person's mind and body. These drugs include marijuana, inhalants, steroids, heroin, pain-killers, and hallucinogens. Many of these drugs are addictive. Marijuana affects each person differently. Long-term use of marijuana damages the brain, kidneys, liver, lungs, and reproductive organs. Inhalants are chemicals that people purposely breathe in. They include gasoline fumes, paint thinner, lighter fluid, glue, hair spray, and nail polish remover. Inhalants can harm the mind and body by slowing down the brain and nervous system. Steroids are often used illegally to boost muscle size and strength. These drugs can cause high blood pressure, heart and kidney disease, and liver cancer. Heroin is a drug that is used to relieve pain. It is illegal in the United States. Heroin is addictive and deadly. Other pain-killing drugs that are not illegal are still dangerous if not used properly. They can produce physical and mental dependence quickly. Hallucinogens are drugs that confuse the brain and nervous system. They change the way the brain processes sight, sound, smell, and touch information. A person may feel, hear, or see things that are not there. This might cause people to injure others or themselves. Hallucinogens increase the heart rate and blood pressure. Hallucinogens can cause permanent brain damage.

Making healthy lifestyle choices is not always easy. You may end up making a decision based on what others are doing instead of making a decision that is good for you. Even if you make a poor decision at an early age, long-term success is possible. However, it may be more difficult to achieve. People who abuse drugs or alcohol will likely have fewer chances for success in a career and in relationships with others. They may need to work harder to overcome some obstacles before they can reach their goals. Making healthy decisions now will help you reach your goals for the future.

Lesson 3 Review Write your answers to these questions on a sheet of paper.

1. How can an unhealthy diet and lack of exercise affect your work life?

2. A common saying is that "prevention is the best cure." Explain how that is true in relation to such diseases as Type II diabetes, heart disease, and sexually transmitted diseases.

3. What are some common effects of drug and alcohol use?

Get Involved

If there is something you enjoy doing, it is very likely that there are local organizations that can put your interests and talents to work. Do you like to play basketball? Volunteer your time helping coach an after-school program. Do you like computers? Find an organization that repairs old computers and gives them to not-for-profit organizations. Do you enjoy painting? Help work on a home with Habitat for Humanity. You don't have to use "job" skills to be of service. Anything that you like to spend your time on can benefit other people. Contact a local community center, library, YMCA, or park district office to find out about volunteer opportunities in your area.

Ethics

Rules for behavior

Dilemma

A situation that requires a choice between two or more values

Your ability to get and keep a job can be affected by the things you consider important in life. This lesson is about what some employers consider most important when hiring someone. For example, employers will want to know if you are a responsible person. They will want to know if you are dependable and respectful. Employers evaluate a good employee as someone who values time and can be counted on. This lesson shows how you can develop these behaviors.

What Does It Mean to Live Ethically?

Ethics are rules for behavior. Living ethically means making choices or doing things that follow these rules. Ethics are similar to but not the same as values. Values are what you think is important or good. For example, you may think that making a lot of money is important. Someone else may value having more leisure time and may be willing to work for less money. Neither choice is right or wrong. Each choice is based on what a person values.

Both ethics and values guide your behavior. For example, suppose you see a friend cheating on a test in school. Should you report the friend to your teacher? The right, or ethical, decision would be to tell the teacher. You may also value hard work. Suppose that you studied hard for the test. You report your friend to the teacher because you value hard work. Suppose you need to decide whether to spend time with your family or go out with your friends one evening. You value both your family and your friends. You need to choose between two values. A situation in which you must choose between two or more values is called a **dilemma**. Many times, the decisions you face are difficult. Think about your experiences. What are some times you have had to make decisions based on ethics or values?

Group values

The beliefs that a specific group of people considers to be important

You have learned that values are beliefs that people consider to be very important. If you believe that being at home for the family's evening meal is very important, then that is one of your values. Everybody has values. They are what help to determine how people act or behave. Remember that personal values are different from work values. Work values are the things you want to get out of your job. Personal values are the beliefs that are important to you but may not be considered important by others, even your friends. For example, personal values may include the importance of family, socializing with friends, maintaining friendships, and having time for yourself.

What Are Group Values?

Another kind of values are **group values.** Group values are the beliefs that a group of people considers to be important. These groups may include your family, neighborhood friends, or the members of the sports team to which you belong. Some of the values that groups may consider to be important are loyalty to the group, sticking to group decisions, or some other belief that sets them apart from others. There may even be a group at your school that places a lot of importance on getting good grades. They may meet regularly to encourage each other in that goal. Employers may be more likely to hire someone who shares the group values of the company.

Suppose you have a busy evening planned. You have to review for a test that you need to score well on tomorrow, watch a video with your friends, and then go to bed early. However, on the evening you arranged to get together, you realize that reviewing for the test is taking longer than you thought it would. What do you do? Do you cancel the invitation to see the video and spend the evening studying instead? Or do you have your friends over anyway and give up the opportunity to prepare better for the test and get the amount of sleep you want?

Universal values

The beliefs that most people in many societies all over the world consider important

Keeping a promise or sticking to a plan made by the group may be an important value to you. Getting good grades may also be important. Then you may view your dilemma as making a decision between personal success and loyalty or commitment to a group decision.

What Are Universal Values?

Universal values are the beliefs that most people in many societies all over the world consider important. They include being trustworthy, truthful, fair, and kind or helpful to others. Following these values means you act in a way that causes people to trust you with their secrets, money, and other property.

Let's look more closely at the idea of living ethically. You have learned about personal and group values. Generally, your personal values affect other people only when they clash with group values. For example, suppose you have to decide whether to study for a test or spend the time watching a video instead. This decision does not affect others. However, choosing between watching the video with friends and spending the time studying for the test is different. If you choose to spend the time studying, your choice of personal success instead of group loyalty may not sit well with your group of friends.

However, their judgment may not affect you very much. Their judgment may not affect you because there may be other groups that judge your action differently. For example, if your parents or guardians hear about your decision, they may think very highly of you. You may be living up to a value that they consider important. Because you earned the respect of your parents or guardians, what your friends think doesn't bother you as much.

Because most members of many groups consider universal values to be important, criticism for disregarding universal values is stronger than criticism concerning personal and group values. The choice of preparing for the test instead of watching a video with a group of friends shows how personal success may be more important than group loyalty in some situations. However, honesty may be always more important than personal success. Therefore, friends and teachers very likely will not think highly of anyone cheating on a test to get the highest grade in the class.

From time to time in your career, you will be asked to make decisions that go against personal, group, or even universal values. Remember that *you* are the one that will have to live with the choices. If you are asked to go against what you believe, don't be afraid to stand up and say so. Even if it costs you a job, you will know you've done what is right for you.

What Are Some Guidelines for Making Ethical Decisions?

Living ethically is not always easy. Some people might say that it is never easy. Living ethically can be very difficult because of the dilemmas involved. But with practice, you can learn to make ethical decisions more easily. When you are faced with a difficult decision, you can ask yourself these three questions:

1. **What is the right thing to do?**

   Do what your conscience tells you is the right thing to do. This guideline says that there are some values most people share. These will include the universal values you read about in the earlier sections of this lesson.

2. **Would I like anyone to do to me what I am going to do to this person?**

   Do to others what you would like others to do to you. This guideline calls on you to imagine yourself as the person who will benefit or suffer from the action you are about to take. Some people refer to it as putting yourself in the other person's shoes. How you imagine yourself feeling in the other person's situation should determine the action you take.

3. **Would my action result in what is good for the greatest number of people?**

   Think of how the consequences of your action will affect the greatest number of people in the best way. With this guideline, you consider the outcome or results of your actions. Your decision will be based on what will create the greatest benefit for the greatest number of people. The consequences and benefits that you think about should not relate to you alone, but to all the people who might be affected.

You may find it easiest to try to answer these three questions in order when you are trying to make a decision. Call on your sense of right and wrong to decide what is the right thing to do. If there is no clear answer, or if taking two actions seem right, the next step is to check to see what values are in conflict. Identify the values involved and decide which is more important to you. If you find that the values are equally important, then think of the person who will be affected by your action. Put yourself in the person's position and ask yourself if you would like anyone to do to you what you are going to do to the person. This question will give you an answer that is either yes or no. If the answer does not make the decision clear for you, think of how the consequences may affect other people. Try to determine to the best of your knowledge how your action might result in what is best for the greatest number of people.

Each dilemma you face is different. The place, the people, and other details involved will vary. As a result, going through every step to reach a decision in each situation may not be necessary. Also, you may go through this sequence of steps without arriving at a very clear decision to act on. In living ethically, the important thing is often to make every effort to find the best ethical decision according to the situation you are dealing with.

Gender and Careers

In the past, women were excluded from certain careers because people believed they weren't physically qualified. For example, women were not admitted to jet-pilot training in the U.S. military until 1973. This is partly because it was assumed that they could not withstand G-forces as well as men. Women have challenged these assumptions. The result has been that women are finding more opportunities in physically demanding fields that have traditionally been male-dominated. These fields include the military, law enforcement, emergency services, and construction. The first women who took steps to enter these fields often had to prove their abilities. They had to do much more than their male coworkers in order to gain acceptance. This challenge to physical stereotypes has opened many doors for women.

Lesson 4 Review Write your answers to these questions on a sheet of paper.

1. Give three examples each of personal values, group values, and universal values.

2. Is it possible for personal, group, and universal values to overlap? Explain.

3. What are some guidelines for making ethical decisions?

Your Hobbies

You have learned in this chapter that how you live your life *outside* of work and school has a big impact on how well you do *in* work and school. People develop hobbies and interests for different reasons. Consider the benefits of hobbies in your life. Think about how you would answer each question in the form below. Then, on your own paper, answer the questions on page 273. Use complete sentences. Add the activity to your portfolio.

Which column best represents your answer to each question?

Questions About Your Hobbies	Yes	Somewhat	No
Do you have a variety of hobbies?			
Do you participate in your hobby activities regularly?			
Do you feel that you spend the right amount of time on your hobbies?			
Are most of your hobbies active (requiring physical activity) rather than passive (TV, video games)?			
Do your hobbies help to relieve your stress?			
Do your hobbies involve socializing with other people?			
Do your hobbies involve skills and knowledge that you use at school or work?			

1. Name one activity you do for each of these reasons: to relieve stress, to be competitive, to meet other people, to stay physically fit, to practice or develop a skill, and to be quiet or reflective.

2. Which of the needs noted in question 1 (stress relief, competition, social outlets, physical fitness, skill development, and quiet time) do you consider most important in your life? Which do you consider least important? Why?

3. Consider the activities you identified in question 1. Do any of these activities meet more than one need? Which ones?

4. Which of the activities do you enjoy the most? How often do you do that activity?

5. Write a brief plan for how you can ensure that you fit in a healthy amount of time to pursue hobbies and interests. If a need that you consider important is not being met, is there a new hobby you would like to try that could meet that need?

Your hobbies can help you stay physically fit.

Chapter 9 REVIEW

Word Bank

addictive

alcoholism

diabetes

diet ✓

dilemma

drug ✓

ethics

group values ✓

~~hobby~~ ✓

leisure time ✓

nicotine ✓

nutrient

obligation

physical fitness ✓

sexually
  transmitted
  disease

stress ✓

symptom

time management ✓

universal values ✓

Vocabulary Review

Choose the word or phrase from the Word Bank that best completes each sentence. Write the answer on your paper.

1. Free time away from work or school is also called _____.

2. The body's ability to meet the demands of living is _____.

3. A(n) _____ changes the way your mind or body works.

4. Using your time well to achieve your goals is known as _____.

5. Beliefs important to a specific group are called _____.

6. One addictive chemical found in tobacco is _____.

7. Your _____ is the food that you regularly eat and drink.

8. A(n) _____ is an activity done for enjoyment.

9. The rules for behavior in a society are _____.

10. Beliefs considered important by most societies in the world are _____.

11. A substance found in food and that your body needs to work properly is a(n) _____.

12. A state of physical or emotional pressure is _____.

13. A disease in which a person is dependent on alcohol is _____.

14. If you are in a situation where you must choose between two values, you are facing a(n) _____.

15. An activity that is required is a(n) _____.

16. Any disease spread through sexual activity is called a(n) _____.

17. A high fever is a(n) _____, or physical sign, of an illness.

18. If a substance is _____, it is habit forming.

19. When the body is not able to use sugar from food, a disease called _____ may be to blame.

Concept Review

Choose the word or phrase that best completes each sentence.
Write the letter of the answer on your paper.

20. People pursue hobbies for all of these reasons EXCEPT _____.
  A to fulfill an obligation **C** to stay physically fit
  B to relieve stress   **D** to meet people

21. A good schedule will include _____.
  A no non-scheduled time
  B time to get from one activity to the next
  C only the most important activities
  D time-wasting activities

22. People who use drugs or alcohol when they are young _____.
  A usually do not become addicted
  B risk their health, their future, and the safety of others
  C are hurting only themselves
  D are better at decision making

23. Ethical decisions are made in all of these ways EXCEPT _____.
  A thinking about how other people will be affected
  B considering what is best for the most people
  C following your conscience
  D doing what feels good to you at the moment

Critical Thinking

Write the answer to each question on your paper.

24. Is physical fitness and a healthy lifestyle the same for
everyone? Explain. Give examples to support your answer.

25. Think about the four areas discussed in the chapter: hobbies,
time, health, and ethics. What is one area you want to work
on? How will improvements in that area help you pursue
your career goals?

Test-Taking Tip

Be sure you understand what a test question is asking. Read
it twice if necessary.

10

Looking Ahead

Throughout this book you have identified your strengths and skills. You have set career goals and learned more about your options. These are the first steps down a lifelong road. As you take this journey, you will continue to learn, grow, and change. Your experiences and choices along the way may take you down paths you never dreamed of. You can make the most of the trip by knowing yourself, responding to feedback, and making good decisions about your life and your career. Good decisions are true to who you are. They match your talents, strengths, and values. As you read this chapter, you will learn to adapt your career goals and map out the path to achieving them.

Goals for Learning

◆ To learn to get and respond to feedback

◆ To develop a career action plan to meet career goals

Communication Connection

Feedback can be a very helpful tool. The key: Be open to it. No one wants to give feedback to someone who doesn't listen or who takes criticism badly. So listen politely and try to see the other person's point of view when you receive feedback, whether it is positive or negative.

You have now learned a lot about work and which work options you want to consider. If you practice the skills that you have learned in this book, you will manage your career well, now and in your future. This lesson will review some of the key steps in career planning. It will also show you how to respond to feedback from others.

Work, Careers, and Self-Assessment

Remember that you first learned about the nature of work and what a career is. Then, you practiced self-assessment to understand your abilities, interests, and values. Understanding yourself is the most important part of your career development. You can use the information you have learned about yourself to guide your career decisions. If you do this, you will be on your way to putting an effective career plan into action.

Using Self-Assessment

The information that you learn about yourself is useful as you consider which occupations you would like to explore. In Chapter 3, you learned how to use self-information to make career decisions. When you follow the five decision-making steps, you pull together information about yourself and occupations. As you learn about different occupations, you should also use what you have learned about yourself. This will help you understand which career clusters will contain the occupations that you should investigate further.

For example, suppose you enjoy social studies and get good grades in your social studies classes. You also enjoy helping others and have good communication skills. Considering these things, occupations in Education and Training as well as Human Services are likely good matches for you. You can explore these career clusters to learn more about them.

Most employers have regular evaluations for all employees. The purpose is to provide feedback and to set new goals. Many employees dread evaluations because they are afraid of criticism. Instead of fearing them, view evaluations as opportunities for growth. Work with your employer to identify areas of growth. Set new goals that you want to accomplish.

Perhaps you are good in science. You enjoy researching and reading about health. You also value helping others, especially when they are sick or hurt. Occupations within the Health Science cluster are good choices for you to explore. By focusing on occupations within career clusters that make sense for you, you take part in effective career planning and exploration.

Gathering Additional Information

Besides exploring careers you have interest in, you can gather additional information about the options you are exploring. For instance, you can learn about jobs by networking or visiting a workplace. You can also learn about possible careers by visiting postsecondary schools or colleges. As you gather more information, you are taking an important step—you are "testing out" whether certain actions make sense for you. For example, you might decide whether attending a college to study business administration is a good choice for you. You make these decisions based on what you know about yourself and the options you are exploring.

Taking Action

Throughout this book, you have been asked to take action. You have gathered information about yourself and about occupations. You have made a career plan. You have written your résumé and collected references. Taking action in these ways helps you to manage your career effectively. When you take action, you learn things about yourself and about career options. You receive feedback about the career planning you have done so far. Another important step in your career planning is using feedback effectively.

Receiving Feedback

You receive feedback at all stages in your career planning. When you take a test in school, your grade gives you feedback about your performance in a subject area. When you try out for a school sports team, you receive feedback about your skills in that sport. When you apply for a job, you receive feedback about your job skills and about how prepared you were for the job interview. When you apply to attend a postsecondary school, you receive feedback about your education and career preparation. As you make plans and set goals, you are receiving different kinds of feedback along the way.

Listening to feedback from others can help you set and reach your career goals.

Using Feedback

How can you use the feedback you receive? It can sometimes be a challenge to sort through the feedback you receive. Sometimes you might get different feedback from different people. For example, you may be trying to get a short story published in a magazine. You will likely get different responses from each magazine you send your story to. Getting a mix of positive and negative feedback might not be very helpful to you. Examples like this are not very common, however. Most of the feedback you receive from teachers, employers, parents, guardians, coaches, and school counselors is very useful. This is especially true when the feedback you receive from several sources is the same. For example, you might think you are not very good at drawing. Your art teacher and your parents think that you are good at drawing, however. In this case, you are receiving important feedback that you may be a better artist than you think you are.

Career Tip

Your résumé should change as your career goals change. If you decide to take a different career path, you may need to change your résumé to reflect different experiences and skills. When you revise your goal statement, take a minute to make sure your résumé is still on target.

How Feedback Affects Your Goals

It is risky if you do not pay attention to the feedback you receive. It can be helpful to talk with someone you trust, such as a school counselor or parent. These people can help you understand feedback and to make decisions about your career and educational planning. As you think about feedback you receive from your teachers, coaches, advisors, school counselors, parents, guardians, and employers, think about your personal goal statement. (You made a personal goal statement in Chapter 7, Lesson 2.) Does the feedback fit your goals? Does the feedback suggest you are on the right path or does it suggest that you should revise your goals? If your feedback matches the direction you need to take to reach a goal, that is great! If the feedback does not match or is not so positive, don't be discouraged. This does not always mean that you need to change your plans. You may just need to strengthen your skills in a particular area. For example, suppose you are not getting good grades in a math class. You want to improve your grades because math is a class you need to do well in for your career goals. Talking with a counselor, teacher, parent, or guardian can help you answer questions like these:

- Are you working as hard as you can?
- Are you using good study skills?
- Could some extra help from a tutor help you improve your skills?

It is important to think about whether you are doing what you need to do in order to achieve your goals. If you think you are doing everything you can, then it may be the right time to discuss whether you need to change your goals.

Writing Practice

Consider a time recently when you have received feedback. Was it positive or negative? How did it make you feel? What action did you take or do you plan to take? What would have made the feedback more constructive or helpful? Write a journal entry describing the feedback and your response to it.

Revising Your Goals

You may also decide to revise your goals if they do not focus on activities that you enjoy. You are not likely to achieve your goals in the long run if you don't enjoy the activities you need to do along the way. If you try an activity and find that you do not enjoy it, think about why that is. What is it that you do not like about the activity? To figure this out, you can talk with a teacher, school counselor, parent, or guardian. In your discussion, be sure that it is the activity itself that you do not like. For example, it is possible to like playing basketball but not like the basketball coach. When this occurs, it often makes sense to continue with the activity. If you decide that you really do not like the activity, then discuss what you have learned about yourself from your participation in the activity. Try to identify other interests that may be important to include in your revised goal statement.

Career Profile

Financial Advisor

 Most people have some idea of how to make money. However, they might not be certain how to invest their money to provide more financial gain. Personal financial advisors provide analysis and guidance to individuals to help them with their investment decisions. They gather financial information, analyze it, and make recommendations to their clients.

Personal financial advisors are also called *financial planners.* They use their knowledge of investments, tax laws, and insurance to recommend financial options to their clients. Some of the issues that planners address are retirement and estate planning, funding for college, and general investment options. An advisor develops a financial plan that identifies problem areas, makes recommendations for improvement, and selects appropriate investments for the client.

Because investment by businesses and individuals is expected to continue to increase, this field is seeing employment growth that is faster than the average. Good candidates must have excellent math skills and good business knowledge, and most employers require a college degree.

Lesson 1 Review Write your answers to these questions on a sheet of paper.

1. What are some sources of feedback that you can consider?

2. Is feedback always true? Explain.

3. What is a possible result of ignoring feedback?

Career Tip

One common question interviewers ask is "What is a mistake you have made and what did you learn from it?" The interviewer wants to know that you are flexible and willing to learn and grow. Be prepared with an exact answer that shows you aren't afraid of change.

A career action plan is related to your personal goal statement. But it is not the same thing. Your personal goal statement identifies where you would like to go in your career. Your career action plan describes how you can get from where you are in your career to where you would like to go. In other words, your career action plan is a description of how you plan to achieve your goal. Here is a simple example:

Goal Statement: "I would like to visit Orlando, Florida."

Action Plan: "In order for me to visit Orlando, I need to save enough money for an airplane ticket to Florida. I will need to make travel plans and hotel reservations. I will need to get directions to Orlando once I am in Florida."

Your goal statement is your destination and your career action plan is your road map for getting there.

The Economy

When a region is heavily dependent on one industry or type of workforce, the local economy can be affected. Many communities that are hit hard by unemployment because of declines in a local industry see a desperate cycle begin. As people are less able to afford goods and services because of job loss and decreased wages, local business owners have to increase prices to maintain profits. Spending more on basic needs, people are less able to save. They have more debt. The effect on communities when this cycle continues can make economic recovery difficult.

It is for this reason that researchers are now looking at ways to improve economic opportunities at the community level. If there were more job opportunities locally, a community might be less hurt by a weak national economy. Providing low-cost loans and tax incentives to small business owners can increase the availability of local jobs. It can also encourage local spending. The hope is that it will create economic advantages and opportunities that improve the overall health of the economy.

Revising Your Career Action Plan

When the feedback you receive leads you to revise your personal goal statement, then you will also need to revise your career action plan. For example, suppose that you cannot save enough money to go to Orlando. You would need to identify another place to visit. You would not follow the same plans you had for your trip to Orlando. You would need to identify a new destination that is less expensive. Revising your travel plans would probably require you to do additional research. The same is true when you revise your career action plan. You may need to do new research on specific occupations, college majors, or other training programs that relate to your new goal. You may need to get new experiences in new activities. For example, if you revised your personal goal statement related to your choice of college major from English to engineering, you may find out that you need to take additional science and math courses. You would then probably talk to your school counselor about which courses would be most helpful to you in achieving your new goal.

Gender and Careers

Both women and men can face the problem of sexual harassment in the workplace. Sexual harassment is defined as any unwelcome sexual advances, requests for sexual favors, and other verbal abuse or physical contact of a sexual nature. All sexual harassment is considered a form of gender discrimination that violates the Civil Rights Act of 1964. It is important that people who feel they have been victims of sexual harassment be vocal about their experiences. If someone is making you uncomfortable, you need to tell the offender and/or your supervisor. Use any employee complaint system your company has in place. If the problem continues, the U.S. Equal Employment Opportunity Commission can investigate. Your refusal to give in to sexual pressure in the workplace *cannot* be used as grounds for dismissal. It is up to you to stand up for your rights.

Revising a personal goal statement and career action plan is not a negative thing. In fact, it can be a very good sign of the ways in which you are learning more about yourself and the world of work!

Putting Your Plan Into Action

As you put your plan into action, remember to use the feedback you get to review whether your personal goal statement still works for you. As you plan for your future, you will continue to network. You will also seek out opportunities to learn more about your goal. Never consider your goal to be "written in stone." Rather, consider your goal statement and career action plan a "snapshot" of how things stand today in your life. Because you will receive feedback every day, your plan may be different tomorrow, next week, next month, or next year. You will continue to learn more about yourself and about the workplace. Using the new information you receive as you plan your future will help you to become productive and successful. The more you use the strategies in this book, the more skilled you will become at managing your career planning.

Get Involved

You might have heard the phrase "pay it forward." This is an idea that many not-for-profit organizations count on. The idea is that when you have personally benefited from the service of someone, you turn around and do something to help someone else. Gus Samuel, Jr., a high school student in Greenville, S.C., did just that. After benefiting from the work of the Salvation Army Boys and Girls Club of Greenville, he turned around and became a volunteer there. He served for four years as a junior staff member, coach, recreation aide, and mentor. His decision to "pay it forward" helped other kids grow and learn as he had. You can do the same. Think of people and organizations that have made a difference to you and your family. Remember that people have taken time to invest in your life and your future. Then pay that involvement forward. You can make a difference, too.

Lesson 2 Review Write your answers to these questions on a sheet of paper.

1. How is a career action plan different from a career goal statement?

2. How might a career action plan for a goal of becoming a nurse practitioner be different from a career action plan for becoming an interior designer?

3. Why is it important that you never consider a career action plan as "set in stone"?

Technology Note

Many career fields require certification, or proof of your qualifications through testing and other methods. This certification, if it is not done directly through a government agency, is usually offered through a national or international professional organization. If you need to prepare for certification, this step should be part of your career action plan. Do research to find out certification requirements. This will give you clues about subjects to pursue and skills that you may have overlooked.

Many professional organizations provide online study tools, discussion groups, and testing for certification. Contact an organization that includes professionals in your chosen field. Find out about certification requirements and programs that may be available online.

Career Action Plan

You have learned in this chapter that getting feedback and using it to revise your career goals is an important part of finding a career and making a living. You use these goals to create a career action plan, or specific steps for getting where you want to be in your career. Write answers to each question to develop a career action plan based on your current career goal statement. Then add the activity to your career portfolio. Use the format on page 289 as a way to organize your answers.

1. Summarize your current career goals.

2. What skills and abilities do you need to have to pursue that career?

3. What classes or activities are you involved in now to develop those abilities?

4. What classes or activities will you need to be involved in during and after high school to develop those abilities?

5. What subjects will you need to learn more about in a post-secondary setting?

6. What are some specific steps you need to take in the coming year to pursue this career?

7. What are some specific steps you need to take in the next five years to pursue this career?

My Career Action Plan

1. My Current Career Goals

Goal 1: _____

Goal 2: _____

2. Skills Needed

_____

_____

Abilities Needed

_____

_____

3. Current Classes and Activities

_____

_____

4. Classes and Activities Needed

_____

_____

5. Postsecondary Subjects

_____

_____

6. This Year's Steps

Step 1: _____

Step 2: _____

Step 3: _____

7. Future Steps

Step 1: _____

Step 2: _____

Step 3: _____

Concept Review

Choose the word or phrase that best answers each question or completes each sentence. Write the letter of the answer on your paper.

1. Feedback is _____.
   A always positive and constructive
   B information you receive about how you are doing at something
   C information about college admissions and financial aid
   D rarely useful

2. If you are receiving feedback that consistently and over a long period of time suggests that you aren't really on the right track, you should _____.
   A look at your career goal and use the feedback to revise it
   B have a discussion with your parents and teachers to get them to change their views
   C ignore the feedback and keep going down the same path
   D assume that everyone is out to get you

3. A career action plan should _____.
   A be vague so that you won't be disappointed
   B change as your career goals change
   C be "set in stone" to be effective
   D take into account many possible scenarios

4. A career action plan includes all of the following EXCEPT _____.
   A abilities and skills you will need to develop
   B school subjects or degree programs you will need to pursue
   C school or community activities that will help to prepare you
   D names of companies you expect to work for

5. Career goal statements and career action plans can be considered "snapshots" because they _____.

   A never change

   B are good reminders of what your dreams are when you are young

   C tell who you are and what your dreams are at a particular point in time

   D are done on a whim and without much thought

Critical Thinking

Write the answer to each question on your paper.

6. How can getting and responding to feedback be considered a skill?

7. You have a friend who wants to be an engineer. She enters a project in the school science fair but does not win. Now she is considering changing her career goal. What is some advice you can give her about dealing with this kind of feedback?

8. Why is it important to evaluate why your attitude about a particular activity has changed before you change your career plans?

9. Imagine you are an author whose novel was turned down repeatedly before becoming a bestseller. What kinds of encouragement or motivation might have contributed to your persistence?

10. How specific do you think a career action plan should be? Explain.

Test-Taking Tip

To answer a multiple-choice question, read every choice before you answer the question. Cross out the choices you know are wrong. Then choose the best answer from the remaining choices.

Appendix: Definitions of Occupational Titles

A

accountant studies financial information, keeps track of money spent and money earned, and prepares financial reports for a business or organization (Ch. 1–2, 4, 6)

actor/actress Performs in plays, television shows, radio shows, videos, or movies to entertain, inform, or instruct (Ch. 2, 4)

administrative assistant provides support to workers by doing research, writing reports, writing letters and e-mails, scheduling meetings, and other clerical tasks (Ch. 2, 4) *See also* executive secretary (Ch. 2)

administration services manager plans and directs recordkeeping, mail delivery, telephone, and other office support services; may also be in charge of building operations planning and maintenance (Ch. 4) *See also* office manager (Ch. 2, 4)

advertising and promotion representative sells advertising such as graphic art, advertising space in publications, custom made signs, or television and radio advertising time; gets retailers to display items in their stores (Ch. 4)

advertising manager plans and directs advertising for products; oversees creation of posters, coupons, or give-away materials (Ch. 2)

agricultural inspector makes sure food products; equipment; and food production, fishing, and logging operations meet laws and standards for health, quality, and safety (Ch. 2)

aircraft structure assembler puts together a section of aircraft such as the tail, wing, or fuselage; installs functional equipment such as landing gear, doors, and floorboards (Ch. 4)

airplane pilot flies aircraft to transport passengers and cargo; must have Federal Air Transport rating and certification (Ch. 2, 4)

air traffic controller monitors air traffic near an airport, keeps track of flight movement between locations, makes sure commercial airline flights follow government and safety rules (Ch. 2)

animal caretaker feeds, waters, herds, brands, weighs, or provides other care for animals on farms, ranches, or other facilities (Ch. 2, 4)

animal scientist researches the genetics, nutrition, reproduction, growth, and development of animals (Ch. 4)

announcer talks on radio, television, or in front of an audience; may conduct interviews, read news, or introduce music (Ch. 4) *See also* radio/TV announcer (Ch. 2)

anthropologist studies the beginnings and behavior of humans and cultures (Ch. 4)

architect plans and designs homes, office buildings, theaters, factories, and other structures (Ch. 1–2, 4)

architectural drafter creates drawings of building designs and plans based on plans from an architect (Ch. 4)

art director designs and creates art for products such as books, magazines, newspapers, packaging, television and Internet ads, etc.; is in charge of workers who work on these products (Ch. 2)

artist creates art by drawing, painting, taking photographs, or sculpting (Ch. 2)

art teacher teaches art classes about painting, drawing, photography, sculpture, and design (Ch. 2)

athletic trainer helps athletes stay physically fit, avoid being hurt, and recover from injuries (Ch. 2, 4) *See also* personal trainer (Ch. 9)

auditor studies financial records and prepares reports about the financial status of a business or organization; makes sure a business or organization is following rules and regulations related to accounting (Ch. 2)

auto mechanic repairs cars, trucks, buses, and other vehicles (Ch. 2)

automotive master mechanic repairs any part on cars, trucks, buses, and other vehicles; often specializes in the transmission system (Ch. 2)

auto salesperson sells cars, trucks, buses, and other vehicles (Ch. 2)

auto technician repairs only one system or part of a vehicle, such as brakes, steering, or alternator (Ch. 2)

B

baker, manufacturing bakes products such as breads and pastries in large amounts to be sold at grocery stores and other retailers (Ch. 4)

bank manager oversees activities of tellers, loan officers, and other workers at a bank; may also be responsible for bank policies and rules, managing the budget, and hiring bank employees (Ch. 2, 6)

bank teller handles the exchange of money with customers at a bank (Ch. 2) *See also* teller (Ch. 2, 6)

barber cuts, trims, shampoos, styles hair; trims beards and gives shaves (Ch. 6)

bill collector finds and notifies customers of late bills, receives payments from customers, and keeps records of customer accounts (Ch. 4)

biologist studies plant and animal life (Ch. 2, 4)

boilermaker builds, maintains, and repairs steam boilers; inspects and repairs safety valves and control systems of boilers (Ch. 4)

bookkeeping clerk keeps track of data to maintain financial records for a business or organization; may also verify other workers' calculations for accuracy (Ch. 2)

brickmason and blockmason lays brick, tile, concrete block, glass block, and other block; binds block with mortar to build or repair walls and other structures (Ch. 4)

brokerage clerk writes orders for stock purchases and sales; figures taxes; keeps records of stock transactions and prices (Ch. 4)

building inspector makes sure buildings are structurally sound and are built according to safety codes and regulations (Ch. 4)

bus driver drives a city, charter, private, or school bus; may enforce safety rules, help riders get on and off the bus, or collect bus fares (Ch. 2, 6)

business executive oversees operation of a business; supervises and oversees employees; handles budget, sales, and other financial plans (Ch. 2)

buyer purchases equipment, supplies, or services needed to operate a business or organization; or purchases farm products to resell (Ch. 2, 4) *See also* purchasing agent (Ch. 4), retail merchandise buyer (Ch. 8)

C

cabinetmaker cuts and puts together wooden parts for wood products; sets up and operates power saws and other woodworking tools (Ch. 4) *See also* carpenter (Ch. 2, 4, 6)

camera operator uses a camera and darkroom equipment to take and develop pictures to be printed; uses a television, video, or movie camera to capture images for television news, advertisements, or film (Ch. 4)

cargo and freight agent plans and oversees movement of cargo and freight on plans, trains, trucks, and ships; takes customer orders; calculates shipping charges and taxes (Ch. 4)

carpenter cuts and puts together wooden parts for wood products; sets up and operates power saws and other woodworking tools (Ch. 2, 4, 6) *See also* cabinetmaker (Ch. 2)

cartoonist creates cartoon art by drawing, painting, sculpting, or other technique (Ch. 2, 4)

cashier handles exchange of money with customers at businesses or organizations other than banks (Ch. 2–4)

cement mason finishes or patches poured concrete floors, sidewalks, roads, or curbs (Ch. 4)

chef prepares and directs the preparation of food; may plan menus, order supplies, and keep records (Ch. 4, 6)

chemical engineer designs equipment for chemical plants; creates ways to manufacture chemicals and products such as gasoline, plastics, cement, and paper (Ch. 4)

chemist conducts studies and chemical experiments to help develop new products or knowledge (Ch. 2, 4)

child care provider dresses, feeds, bathes, and supervises children at schools, homes, or child care centers (Ch. 6) *See also* child care worker (Ch. 2, 4)

child care worker dresses, feeds, bathes, and supervises children at schools, homes, or child care centers (Ch. 2, 4) *See also* child care provider (Ch. 6)

chiropractor helps patients with back pain by adjusting the spine (Ch. 2, 4)

choral director directs performances of a choir; selects music to perform; conducts practice sessions with singers (Ch. 2)

choreographer creates and teaches dances; may also direct performances on stage (Ch. 2)

civil drafter makes drawings and maps for projects such as highways, bridges, pipelines, and water control systems (Ch. 4)

civil engineer plans, designs, and oversees construction and maintenance of buildings, roads, airports, bridges, dams, pipelines, power plants, and water and sewage systems (Ch. 4)

clergy lead religious worship and ceremonies; provide support and guidance to members (Ch. 2, 4, 6)

clinical psychologist diagnoses and treats mental and emotional disorders; observes, interviews, and tests patients (Ch. 2, 4)

coach teaches people individual or team sports, including techniques and rules (Ch. 2)

college administrator plans and oversees teaching, student life, research, and other educational services and activities at postsecondary institutions, including universities, colleges, and junior and community colleges (Ch. 2) *See also* educational administrator (Ch. 2), school administrator (Ch. 2, 4, 6)

college professor teaches classes at a college or postsecondary school (Ch. 2) *See also* postsecondary teacher (Ch. 4)

columnist writes stories or opinion pieces for newspapers, news magazines, or Web sites (Ch. 4)

comedian tells jokes in front of an audience; writes and performs material for comedy shows (Ch. 2)

commercial designer designs and create products such as cars, appliances, and toys (Ch. 2, 4)

composer writes music for an instrument, singer, instrumental group, or choral group (Ch. 2, 4)

computer hardware engineer studies, tests, and designs computers or computer equipment; may oversee the manufacturing and installation of computers or computer equipment (Ch. 4)

computer operator use computer and electronic equipment to keep records of data; may enter commands, set computer controls, and track error messages (Ch. 2)

computer programmer writes programs using various computer languages that tell a computer what to do; may write programs for Web sites (Ch. 2, 4)

computer scientist studies, tests, and designs computers, computer equipment, or computer software (Ch. 2)

computer service technician helps computer users with technical problems, answer users' questions regarding use of computer hardware and software (Ch. 2) *See also* computer support specialist (Ch. 2, 4)

computer software engineer studies, designs, develops, and tests computer software and programs; may design and study databases (Ch 2, 4)

computer support specialist helps computer users with technical problems, answer users' questions regarding use of computer hardware and software (Ch. 2, 4) *See also* computer service technician (Ch. 2)

computer systems analyst studies and solves problems related to computer systems and software; finds ways to use computer systems better (Ch. 2, 4)

computer systems manager oversees the study of computer systems and software to solve problems and find ways to use computer systems better (Ch. 4)

conductor directs performances of a instrumental group or choir and conducts practice sessions with musicians (Ch. 2)

construction equipment operator operates machines used in construction such as excavators, dump trucks, crushers, boring machines, and cranes (Ch. 2, 4)

construction laborer provides physical labor for the construction of buildings, roads, and other projects; may operate tools, clean up building sites, and transport construction materials (Ch. 4)

construction manager plans and oversees the construction and maintenance of buildings and other structures (Ch. 2)

continuous mining machine operator operates machines that remove coal, metal, ores, rock, stone from the earth and load it for transport in a continuous operation (Ch. 4)

contractor arranges for an individual or business to perform work involved with building houses, roads, or other structures (Ch. 4)

cook prepares food in restaurants, fast-food restaurants, schools, hospitals, or cafeterias; may order supplies, plan menus, and keep records (Ch. 2, 6)

copywriter writes advertising copy that will promote a product or service in newspapers, magazines, Web sites, television, or radio (Ch. 4)

corporate trainer trains and educates workers at businesses or organizations (Ch. 4) *See also* training and development specialist (Ch. 4)

corrections officer guards prisoners in jails or other correctional institutions (Ch. 4)

counseling psychologist interviews and observes patients to help them with personal, social, educational, or work-related problems (Ch. 4)

counselor helps people with their problems by talking with them (Ch. 2, 6) *See also* educational counselor (Ch. 2), school counselor (Ch. 2, 4), vocational counselor (Ch. 2)

court reporter takes word-for-word reports of speeches, meetings, conversations, and other legal proceedings (Ch. 2)

credit analyst studies financial data of people or businesses to find out how risky it would be to lend them money (Ch. 4)

customer service representative handles questions and complaints from customers, usually by answering phones at a business or organization; may place customer orders (Ch. 2, 4)

customs inspector makes sure goods and merchandise arriving in or leaving from another country or state does not violate customs laws and regulations (Ch. 2) *See also* immigrations and customs inspector (Ch. 4)

D

dancer performs dances; may also sing or act (Ch. 2, 4)

data entry keyer operates a keyboard or other data entry device to verify data and prepare materials for printing (Ch. 2)

database administrator oversees, tests, and coordinates changes to computer databases (Ch. 2, 4)

dental assistant helps dentist, sets up equipment, and keeps records (Ch. 2)

dental hygienist cleans teeth and looks for signs of oral disease; may teach patients about oral hygiene, take X-rays, or administer fluoride treatments (Ch. 2)

dentist diagnoses and treats oral diseases and injuries (Ch. 2, 4)

derrick operator, oil and gas sets ups derrick equipment and operate pumps to circulate mud through a drill hole (Ch. 4)

desktop publisher prepares documents using computer software to produce material for publication (Ch. 4) *See also* desktop publishing specialist (Ch. 2)

desktop publishing specialist prepares documents using computer software to produce material for publication (Ch. 2) *See also* desktop publisher (Ch. 4)

detective investigates crimes to find criminals, prevent further crime, and solve cases (Ch. 4) *See also* police detective (Ch. 2)

diagnostic medical sonographer takes X-rays of patients to determine broken bones or other internal injuries (Ch. 2)

dietician plans food and nutritional programs to keep people healthy, supervises food service programs, gives nutritional advice, and conducts nutritional research (Ch. 2, 4)

dispatcher schedules and sends construction, repair, and installation workers or equipment to a site (Ch. 4) *See also* police dispatcher (Ch. 2)

doctor diagnoses, treats, and helps prevent diseases and injuries; may specialize in one of various medical fields (Ch. 6) *See also* physician (Ch. 2, 4)

drafter prepares detailed drawings of buildings, structures, or machinery based on an architect's or engineer's plans (Ch. 2) *See also* mechanical drafter (Ch. 2)

drama teacher teaches courses in drama and acting (Ch. 2)

drywall installer applies plasterboard or other wallboard to ceilings and walls inside of buildings (Ch. 4)

E

economist studies economic problems dealing with the production and distribution of good and services; conducts research and prepares economic reports (Ch. 2, 4)

editor performs editorial duties such as laying out, indexing, and revising content of written materials to prepare them for publication (Ch. 2)

educational administrator plans and oversees teaching, student life, research, and other educational services and activities at elementary, secondary, or postsecondary schools (Ch. 2) *See also* college administrator (Ch. 2), school administrator (Ch. 2, 4, 6)

educational counselor helps individuals with education and career planning (Ch. 2) *See also* counselor (Ch. 2, 6), school counselor (Ch. 2, 4), vocational counselor (Ch. 2)

electrical engineer designs, develops, and tests electrical equipment (Ch. 2, 4)

electrician installs, maintains, and repairs electrical wiring and equipment according to proper codes (Ch. 2, 4, 6)

electronic assembler puts together electronic equipment, such as computers and electric motors (Ch. 4)

electronic equipment installer and repairer installs and repairs communications, sound, security, or navigation equipment in motor vehicles, home entertainment, and other electronic products (Ch. 2)

electronics repairer repairs communications, sound, security, or navigation equipment in motor vehicles, home entertainment, and other electronic products (Ch. 2)

elementary school teacher teaches students basic academic and social skills in public or private schools at the elementary level (Ch. 2, 4)

elevator installer puts together and installs repair electric or hydraulic elevators and escalators (Ch. 4)

emergency medical technician (EMT) provides emergency medical care by assessing injuries, freeing trapped individuals, and transporting patients to medical facilities (Ch. 2, 4)

engineer designs and plans activities and projects in architectural, civil, electrical, mechanical, or other engineering fields (Ch. 2)

engraver engraves designs or lettering onto objects (Ch. 2)

environmental scientist studies sources of pollutants and hazards that affect the air, food, soil, and water (Ch. 4)

executive secretary provides support to workers by doing research, writing reports, writing letters and e-mails, scheduling meetings, and other clerical tasks (Ch. 2, 4) *See also* administrative assistant (Ch. 2, 4)

explosive worker and blaster places and set off explosives to tear down structures or to remove rock or other materials (Ch. 4)

F

faller cuts down trees using axes and chainsaws and controls the direction in which trees fall when they are cut down (Ch. 4)

farmer owns and operates a farm that produces crops and/or livestock; plants, cultivates, harvests, and markets crops and livestock; maintains and operates farm machinery (Ch. 2)

farm and ranch manager oversees the activities of farm or ranch workers engaged in crop or livestock production for farm or ranch owners (Ch. 2, 3)

farmworkers, farm and ranch animals feed, water, herd, brand, weigh, and provide other care for animals on farms or ranches (Ch. 4)

fashion designer designs clothing and accessories (Ch. 2)

FBI agent government worker who investigates crimes, gathers evidence, and interviews witnesses to capture criminals (Ch. 2, 4)

film and video editor edits movie soundtracks, film, and video (Ch. 4)

finance manager oversees the financial activities of workers in a bank, brokerage firm, insurance agency, or credit department (Ch. 4)

financial advisor counsels individuals or businesses on ways to best spend, save, or invest their money; helps individuals plan for retirement (Ch. 10) *See also* financial planner (Ch. 2)

financial analyst studies information regarding how a business or organization investments its money (Ch. 2, 4)

financial planner counsels individuals or businesses on ways to best spend, save, or invest their money; helps individuals plan for retirement (Ch. 2) *See also* financial advisor (Ch. 10)

firefighter responds to emergency calls of fires; puts out fires; may conduct investigations to determine causes of fires and explosions (Ch. 2, 4)

fisher catches fish or other aquatic animals by using nets, fishing rods, traps, or other equipment (Ch. 2)

flight attendant greets passengers, verifies tickets, explains safety equipment, and serves food or beverages to airline passengers during flight (Ch. 2)

floral designer cuts and arranges flowers and other plants (Ch. 2, 4)

food preparation worker prepares food, but does not cook; may prepare cold foods, slice meat, or brew coffee (Ch. 2)

food server serves food to restaurant customers, or to customers in hotels, hospital rooms, or cars (Ch. 6)

food service manager plans and oversees workers in a business or organization that serves food and beverages (Ch. 2, 4)

food services manager *See* food service manager (Ch. 2, 4)

forest and conservation worker transports tree seedlings, fights insects and pests, inspects soil, and plants trees to develop, maintain, and protect forests (Ch. 2, 4)

forester manages forested lands for economic, recreational, and conservation purposes; keeps track of number and types of trees, conserves wildlife habitats, and makes plans to plant new trees (Ch. 2, 4)

funeral director arranges and directs funeral services such as transportation and embalming of the body, interviewing family members, finding religious officials, and providing transportation for mourners (Ch. 6)

G

geologist studies the earth's crust, rocks, minerals, and fossils (Ch. 4)

glazier installs glass for windows, skylights, store fronts, display cases, interior walls, ceilings, and tabletops (Ch. 4)

government administrator plans, directs, and coordinates activities related to the operation of a government department or office (Ch. 4, 6)

graphic designer designs or creates graphics for product packaging, displays, or logos (Ch. 2, 4)

H

hairdresser, hairstylist, and cosmetologist shampoos, cuts, colors, and styles hair; massages and treats scalp; applies makeup; provides nail and skin care (Ch. 4, 6)

hair stylist shampoos, cuts, colors, and styles hair (Ch. 2)

heating and air-conditioning mechanic installs, maintains, and repairs heating and air-conditioning systems (Ch. 2, 6)

helper, construction and trades helps construction workers by performing duties such as holding materials or tools and cleaning the work area and equipment (Ch. 4)

highway maintenance worker keeps highways and roads in safe condition by patching broken pavement, repairing guard rails and signs, and clearing brush or plowing snow from road (Ch. 2, 6)

home health aide bathes, dresses, and cares for elderly, injured, or disabled people in their homes or in care centers (Ch. 2)

hotel/motel clerk registers guests, hands out room keys, answers phones, takes messages, takes reservations, and collects payments at a hotel or motel front desk (Ch. 2–4, 6)

hotel/motel manager oversees the activities of workers at a hotel or motel; directs and coordinates record keeping and billing, as well as housekeeping and maintenance activities (Ch. 2) *See also* lodging manager (Ch. 4)

housekeeper makes beds, cleans rooms, vacuums, and performs other cleaning duties in homes or other businesses such as hotels and hospitals (Ch. 6) *See also* maid/housekeeper (Ch. 4, 6)

human resources assistant keeps records of employee addresses, paychecks, and attendance; updates employee files and gives information to other human resources workers (Ch. 2, 4)

I

immigration and customs inspector makes sure people, goods, or merchandise arriving in or leaving from another country or state does not violate immigration and customs laws and regulations (Ch. 4) *See also* customs inspector (Ch. 2)

industrial designer designs, models, creates, and tests new products or finds ways to improve old products (Ch. 2)

information systems manager plans and oversees workers who are involved in data processing, information and computer systems analysis, and computer programming (Ch. 2)

insulation worker installs insulation materials in structures such as homes, offices, and other buildings; applies insulation materials to pipes, ducts and other temperature-control systems (Ch. 4)

insurance agent sells life, automobile, homeowner's, and other kinds of insurance (Ch. 2) *See also* insurance sales agent (Ch. 4)

insurance claim and policy processing clerk gets information from people filing or otherwise involved in insurance claims; takes applications for and keeps records of insurance policies (Ch. 4)

insurance claims adjuster determines how much an insurance company will pay to a claimant by investigating losses and damages and interviewing witnesses and claimants (Ch. 2)

insurance sales agent sells life, automobile, homeowner's, and other kinds of insurance (Ch. 4) *See also* insurance agent (Ch. 2)

insurance underwriter determines whether an insurance company will cover an applicant and how much risk is involved in doing so (Ch. 4)

interior designer plans and designs the decoration and layout of rooms inside homes or businesses (Ch. 2–4)

interpreter translates one language to another in writing, words, or sign language (Ch. 4) *See also* translator (Ch. 2, 4)

J

janitor cleans floors, rugs, walls, and windows of buildings; may also remove garbage, clean snow from sidewalks, and keep track of needed repairs (Ch. 1)

jeweler designs, creates, cleans, and repairs various pieces of jewelry (Ch. 4)

judge oversees cases in a court of law, advises participants, sentences defendants; may also issue licenses for marriages (Ch. 2)

L

landscaper plans, designs, and completes projects to beautify land at homes, parks, or businesses (Ch. 2)

landscaping and groundskeeping worker lays sod; mows, trims, plants, and waters grass; installs trees, shrubbery, sprinklers, rock, and retaining walls (Ch. 2, 4)

law enforcement officer enforces laws, directs and monitors traffic, controls crowds, provides security, arrests criminals, and responds to emergencies (Ch. 6) *See also* police officer (Ch. 2, 4)

lawyer represents, manages, and advises clients in legal cases or transactions (Ch. 2, 4)

legal assistant helps lawyers by doing legal research and preparing documents (Ch. 2) *See also* paralegal (Ch. 2, 4)

legal secretary prepares legal documents, writes letters, takes messages, and assists with legal research (Ch. 4)

librarian selects books for libraries and provides library services such as cataloguing and circulating books and other library materials; may conduct research and set up computer databases to manage library information (Ch. 4)

licensed nurse practitioner provides care for patients in hospitals, health care centers, private and group homes, and other institutions; gives medication, prepares equipment, and assists doctors; license required (Ch. 2) *See also* licensed practical nurse (Ch. 4), nurse (Ch. 2, 6), nurse practitioner (Ch. 2), registered nurse (Ch. 4)

licensed practical nurse provides care for patients in hospitals, health care centers, private and group homes, and other institutions; gives medication, prepares equipment, and assists doctors; license required (Ch. 4) *See also* licensed nurse practitioner (Ch. 2), nurse (Ch. 2, 6), nurse practitioner (Ch. 2), registered nurse (Ch. 4)

loan officer determines whether a bank, credit union, or other financial institution should give a loan to a customer, advises customers on loan accounts (Ch. 4)

locomotive engineer drives passenger or freight trains according to railroad signals, rules, and regulations (Ch. 4)

lodging manager oversees the activities of workers at a hotel, motel or other lodging facility or department; directs and coordinates record keeping and billing, as well as housekeeping and maintenance activities (Ch. 4) *See also* hotel/motel manager (Ch. 2)

log grader and scaler inspects and measures logs to determine their volume and market value (Ch. 4)

logger cuts down trees using axes and chainsaws and controls the direction in which trees fall when they are cut down (Ch. 4) *See also* faller (Ch. 4)

M

machine operator sets up and operates various machines used to manufacture, produce, or assemble products (Ch. 2)

machinist sets up and operates various machines to make parts and tools; may also make parts to build, maintain, or repair machines (Ch. 4)

maid/housekeeper makes beds, cleans rooms, vacuums, and performs other cleaning duties in homes or other businesses such as hotels and hospitals (Ch. 4, 6) *See also* housekeeper (Ch. 6)

mail carrier sorts and delivers mail (Ch. 4)

management analyst studies organizations to see how they operate and recommends ways to simply or improve work procedures (Ch. 4)

manufacturer's representative sells products from the manufacturer to a business or individual; acts as a product expert for the manufacturer (Ch. 4) *See also* wholesale sales representative (Ch. 4)

manufacturing optician produce lenses and frames for glasses according to prescription; may grind lenses and set them in frame (Ch. 4)

marketing manager studies the market to see what products or services are in demand, studies competitor offerings, sets prices, and oversees the development of new products and services (Ch. 2, 4)

mathematician studies mathematics and does mathematical research to solve problems related to business, science, management, and other fields (Ch. 2, 4)

mechanic tests, repairs, and maintains mechanical equipment such as automobiles, aircraft, farm equipment, engines, and industrial machinery (Ch. 4, 6)

mechanical drafter prepares detailed drawings of machinery based on an engineer's plans (Ch. 2) *See also* drafter (Ch. 2)

mechanical engineer plans and designs tools, engines, and machines; oversees the installation, maintenance, and repair of mechanical equipment and systems (Ch. 2, 4)

mechanical inspector inspects and tests motors, vehicles, and other machines and mechanical systems to make sure they are in good working order (Ch. 4)

medical and clinical laboratory technician does regular medical laboratory tests to diagnose and treat diseases (Ch. 4) *See also* medical lab technician (Ch. 2)

medical and clinical laboratory technologist does complicated medical laboratory tests to diagnose and treat diseases; may supervise and train medical and clinical laboratory technicians (Ch. 4)

medical and health services manager plans and oversees health service activities and employees at hospitals, clinics, health care centers, and other health care organizations (Ch. 2, 4)

medical assistant schedules appointments, maintains records, tracks billing; takes vital signs and medical histories, draws blood, administers medications under the direction of a doctor (Ch. 2, 4)

medical lab technician does regular medical laboratory tests to diagnose and treat diseases (Ch. 2) *See also* medical and clinical laboratory technician (Ch. 4)

medical records and health information technician gathers and maintains medical records; processes and maintains patient information (Ch. 4) *See also* medical records technician (Ch. 2)

medical records technician gathers and maintains medical records (Ch. 2) *See also* medical records and health information technician (Ch. 4)

medical technician does regular medical laboratory tests to diagnose and treat diseases (Ch. 2) *See also* medical and clinical laboratory technician (Ch. 4), medical lab technician (Ch. 2)

medical transcriptionist uses medical terminology to compile and maintain medical records, charts, reports, and letters (Ch. 4)

meeting and convention planner plans and oversees arrangements and travel for group meetings and conventions (Ch. 4)

mental health counselor talks with people about addiction, substance abuse, family problems, stress management, self-esteem and other mental health issues (Ch. 4)

metal-refining furnace operator operates gas, oil, coal, electric, or oxygen furnaces that melt and refine metal (Ch. 4)

military office member of the Armed Forces who supervises and manages other military personnel (Ch. 4)

mining and geological engineer locates coal and ores to be extracted, makes geological maps, finds ways to extract deposits, and supervises mining workers (Ch. 4)

mobile heavy equipment mechanic inspects and repairs mechanical equipment such as cranes, bulldozers, and conveyors used in construction, logging, and mining (Ch. 4)

model wears clothing for display at fashion shows, stores, or for photographers; may pose for paintings, sculptures or other kinds of art (Ch. 2)

molding and casting worker mixes materials, puts together mold parts, and fills and stacks molds to create a variety of products (Ch. 4)

music arranger writes musical notes and arranges musical parts for music to be performed by an individual or group (Ch. 2)

musician plays a musical instrument or instruments in a solo performance or as a member of a musical group (Ch. 2, 4)

music teacher teaches music classes such as note-reading, performance, music theory, or individual singing or instrumental lessons (Ch. 2)

N

network systems and data communications analyst designs and tests network systems or groups of computers working together; recommends ways to use hardware and software better; finds ways for computer systems to work together with telephone and other communications systems (Ch. 4)

new accounts clerk helps customers open new bank accounts by explaining bank services and preparing application forms (Ch. 4)

novelist writes original books for publication (Ch. 2, 4)

nurse provides care for patients in hospitals, health care centers, private and group homes, and other institutions; gives medication, prepares equipment, and assists doctors (Ch. 2, 6) *See also* licensed nurse practitioner (Ch. 2), licensed practical nurse (Ch. 4), nurse practitioner (Ch. 2)

nurse practitioner provides care for patients in hospitals, health care centers, private and group homes, and other institutions; gives medication, prepares equipment, and assists doctors (Ch. 2) *See also* licensed nurse practitioner (Ch. 2), licensed practical nurse (Ch. 4), nurse (Ch. 2, 6)

O

oceanographer studies ocean and sea life (Ch. 1)

office clerk performs clerical duties such as answering phones, keeping records, typing, taking messages, operating office machines, and filing (Ch. 4)

office manager plans and directs recordkeeping, mail delivery, telephone, and other office support services; May also be in charge of building operations planning and maintenance (Ch. 2, 4) *See also* administration services manager (Ch. 4)

operations research analyst studies see how an organization operates by looking at management, use of time, costs, and logistics; uses mathematical models to suggest solutions for a business or organization; may develop software and products to collect and study data and model solutions (Ch. 2, 4)

optometrist examines the eyes, treats eye and visual system diseases, prescribes glasses or contact lenses (Ch. 2, 4)

P

painter paints original artwork using watercolors, oils, acrylics, tempera, or other kinds of paint (Ch. 2, 4)

painter, construction and maintenance paints surfaces such of walls, buildings, bridges, and equipment; may remove old paint and mix new paint (Ch. 4)

painting, coating, and decorating worker applies paint or decoration to products such as furniture, glass, dishes, pottery, jewelry, toys, and books (Ch. 4)

paralegal helps lawyers by doing legal research and preparing (Ch. 2, 4) *See also* legal assistant (Ch. 2)

park ranger patrols national, state, or local parks to ensure visitors are following rules; provides maintenance for parks; may plan or conduct informational programs about the history and natural features of a park (Ch. 1)

paving, surfacing, and tamping equipment operator operates equipment used to build and maintain roads, parking lots, and other surfaces (Ch. 4) *See also* road paving and surfacing operator (Ch. 4)

payroll clerk keeps track of hours worked and pay rates for employees; may prepare paychecks (Ch. 2)

personal and home care aide helps the elderly or disabled with daily tasks at the person's home; may make beds, wash clothes, wash dishes, and prepare meals (Ch. 4)

personal trainer helps people stay physically fit, avoid being hurt, and recover from injuries; may suggest exercise and nutritional programs (Ch. 9) *See also* athletic trainer (Ch. 2, 4)

personnel recruiter searches for applicants for job opportunities at a business or organization; may interview and screen applicants (Ch. 4)

personnel specialist finds, interviews, and screens job applicants for a business or organization (Ch. 7)

petroleum engineer studies the drilling of oil and gas, and finds ways to improve drilling processes and tools; oversees drilling operations (Ch. 4)

pharmacist prepares and gives out medications according to prescriptions from medical professionals (Ch. 2, 4)

pharmacy technician measures, mixes, counts, and labels medications according to directions from a pharmacist (Ch. 4)

photographer takes photographs of various subjects for artwork, advertising, magazines, newspapers, Web sites, or scientific purposes (Ch. 2, 4) *See also* professional photographer (Ch. 2)

photographic developer produces prints of images by putting film into chemical and water baths (Ch. 2)

photographic processing machine operator uses machines to develop film and produce print of images (Ch. 4)

physical therapist helps patients recover from disease or injury by creating programs to help with movement, pain relief, and strength (Ch. 2, 4)

physician diagnoses, treats, and helps prevent diseases and injuries; may specialize in one of various medical fields (Ch. 2, 4) *See also* doctor (Ch. 6)

physicist studies matter and energy, including mechanics, heat, light, sound, electricity, magnetism, and atomic energy (Ch. 2)

pipefitter puts together and installs pipes and pipe systems for air-conditioning, heating, water, and other systems (Ch. 4)

plant scientist studies plants, including how to produce crops and control pests (Ch. 4)

plasterer applies plaster, cement, or stucco to building interiors or exteriors (Ch. 4)

playwright writes original plays or dramas to be performed on stage (Ch. 2)

plumber puts together, installs, and repairs pipes and fixtures for heating, water, and drainage systems (Ch. 4, 6)

poet writes original poems to be published or performed (Ch. 2)

police chief oversees the activities of workers of a police force, including detectives, officers, and dispatchers (Ch. 4)

police detective investigates crimes to find criminals, prevent further crime, and solve cases (Ch. 2) *See also* detective (Ch. 4)

police dispatcher operates radio, telephone, and computer equipment to receive reports of crimes or emergencies; relays information to proper officials (Ch. 2) *See also* dispatcher (Ch. 4)

police officer enforces laws, directs and monitors traffic, controls crowds, provides security, arrests criminals, and responds to emergencies (Ch. 2, 4) *See also* law enforcement officer (Ch. 6)

post office clerk receives letter and packages, sells stamps and postcards, examines mail for proper postage (Ch. 4) *See also* postal service clerk (Ch. 2)

postal service clerk receives letter and packages, sells stamps and postcards, examines mail for proper postage (Ch. 2) *See also* post office clerk (Ch. 4)

postsecondary teacher teaches classes at a college or postsecondary school (Ch. 2) *See also* postsecondary teacher (Ch. 4), college professor (Ch. 2)

preschool teacher teaches young children social skills and school readiness skills at a preschool, child care center, or other facility; certification required in certain states (Ch. 2, 4)

printing press machine operator runs printing machines that print on paper, plastic, cloth, or other materials (Ch. 4)

private investigator gathers information for a customer; determines whether people or businesses have been breaking laws (Ch. 2)

producer plans and oversees activities involved in making a radio, television, or stage show, or a movie; may choose scripts, oversee writing and directing, and arrange ways to pay for the production (Ch. 2) *See also* radio/TV/movie producer (Ch. 2, 4), television news producer (Ch. 5)

product assembler puts together parts of a product or products (Ch. 2)

professional photographer takes photographs of people, events, and other subjects to be sold to customers or media outlets (Ch. 2) *See also* photographer (Ch. 2, 4)

property or real estate manager plans and oversees the sale or leasing of various properties including businesses, apartments, and homes (Ch. 2)

psychiatric aide helps patients who are mentally or emotionally impaired, under supervision of nursing or medical professionals (Ch. 2)

psychiatrist examines and treats patients with disorders of the mind (Ch. 2)

public relations specialist helps people or organizations create a positive public image; may write publicity material, prepare displays, and give speeches (Ch. 4)

pump operator controls or operates gas, oil, water, and other pumps (Ch. 4)

purchasing agent purchases equipment, supplies, or services needed to operate a business or organization; or purchases farm products to resell (Ch. 4) *See also* buyer (Ch. 2, 4), retail merchandise buyer (Ch. 8)

R

radio/TV announcer interviews guests, reads news, acts as host or hostess, announces music on radio or television (Ch. 2) *See also* announcer (Ch. 4)

radio/TV/movie producer plans and oversees activities involved in making a radio or television show, or a movie; may choose scripts, oversee writing and directing, and arrange ways to pay for the production (Ch. 2, 4) *See also* producer (Ch. 2), television news producer (Ch. 5)

radio/TV program assistant assists a program director with tasks involved in preparing radio or television schedules and shows (Ch. 2)

radio/TV program director plans and oversees workers involved in preparing radio or television schedules and shows (Ch. 4)

railroad conductor oversees passenger and freight train workers and coordinates railroad activities such as train makeup, yard switching, and scheduling (Ch. 4)

real estate appraiser inspects property or land to determine how much it is worth (Ch. 2)

real estate agent represents a customer who is buying or selling property; creates property listings, interviews customers, and prepares real estate documents (Ch. 2) *See also* real estate sales agent (Ch. 4)

real estate sales agent represents a customer who is selling property; creates property listings, interviews customers, and prepares real estate documents (Ch. 4) *See also* real estate agent (Ch. 2)

receptionist answers phone calls to a business from the public and from customers; gives information about the business or organization including department or office locations, phone numbers, and employees (Ch. 2, 4)

recreation leader plans and oversees activities such as arts and crafts, sports, games, music, trips, and hobbies for groups in public or private organizations; considers individual members' needs and interests when planning activities (Ch. 2)

recreational worker conducts activities such as arts and crafts, sports, games, music, trips, and hobbies with groups in public or private organizations (Ch. 2, 4)

registered nurse helps determine patients' health needs and problems; maintains medical records; cares for ill, injured or disabled patients; licensing or registration required (Ch. 4) *See also* licensed nurse practitioner (Ch. 2), licensed practical nurse (Ch. 4)

reporter gathers facts for news stories; writes news stories for newspapers, magazines, Web sites, radio, or television (Ch. 2, 4)

reservation and transportation ticket agent makes airline, bus, railroad, and ship reservations for passengers; sells tickets; may check luggage and give passengers directions (Ch. 4)

restaurant host/hostess welcomes and seats customers at a restaurant; may provide menus and take beverage orders (Ch. 4)

restaurant manager supervises employees who prepare and serve food at a restaurant; oversees business activities such as ordering food and supplies, setting prices, planning menus, and paying bills (Ch. 2)

retail merchandise buyer purchases equipment, supplies, or services needed to operate a business or organization; or purchases farm products to resell (Ch. 8) *See also* buyer (Ch. 2, 4), purchasing agent (Ch. 4)

retail salesperson sells products or merchandise in a furniture, appliance, clothing, or other retail store (Ch. 2, 4) *See also* retail sales worker (Ch. 2) salesperson (Ch. 2, 6)

retail sales worker sells products or merchandise in a furniture, appliance, clothing, or other retail store (Ch. 2) *See also* retail salesperson (Ch. 2, 4) salesperson (Ch. 2, 6)

road paving and surfacing operator operates equipment used to build and maintain roads, parking lots, and other surfaces (Ch. 4) *See also* road paving and surfacing operator (Ch. 4)

roofer covers roofs with shingles, slate, asphalt, aluminum, wood, and other roofing materials (Ch. 4, 6)

rotary drill operator, small oil and gas sets up and operates mining and extraction drills (Ch. 4)

roustabout, oil and gas puts together or repairs equipment used in oil and gas mining and extraction (Ch. 4)

S

sailor performs various duties aboard a ship such as navigating, standing watch, measuring water depth, and working with rigging (Ch. 4)

sales agent: securities and commodities buys and sells bond or stock certificates; develops financial plans for businesses and organizations (Ch. 4)

sales manager oversees sales workers; may be in charge of purchasing, budgeting, and accounting (Ch. 2, 4)

salesperson sells products or services for retail or wholesale stores, or as an individual (Ch. 2, 6) *See also* retail salesperson (Ch. 2, 4) retail sales worker (Ch. 2)

school administrator plans and oversees teaching, student life, research, and other educational services and activities at elementary, secondary, or postsecondary schools (Ch. 2, 4, 6) *See also* college administrator (Ch. 2), educational administrator (Ch. 2)

school counselor helps individuals with education and career planning (Ch. 2, 4) *See also* counselor (Ch. 2, 6), educational counselor (Ch. 2), vocational counselor (Ch. 2)

school psychologist studies ways people learn and teach in schools; uses psychology to solve educational problems related to learning and teaching (Ch. 4)

science teacher teaches science courses such as biology, chemistry, and physics (Ch. 4)

script editor prepares and makes changes to scripts of movies, plays, or radio and television programs for performance (Ch. 4)

secondary school teacher teaches students in secondary public or private schools; may teach one or more subjects such as English, mathematics, or science (Ch. 2, 4)

secretary writes letters, schedules appointments, organized files, gives information to callers, and performs other clerical duties (Ch. 2, 4)

security guard watches a building, buildings, or other area to prevent trespassing, violence, or crime (Ch. 2, 4)

service station attendant pumps fuel, changes oil, replaces tires, and provides other service for automobiles and other vehicles (Ch. 6)

sheet metal worker makes, puts together, and installs products and equipment made from sheet metal such as ducts, pipes, and furnace casings (Ch. 4)

sheriff enforces laws in rural areas or towns and responds to emergencies; may guard courthouses and provide escorts (Ch. 2)

ship and boat captain is in charge of all operations on a ship or boat in an ocean, bay, lake, river, or coastal waters (Ch. 4)

ship's engineer oversees the operation and maintenance of a ship's boilers, electrical and refrigeration equipment, and deck machinery (Ch. 4)

shipping, receiving, and traffic clerk keeps records of shipments coming in and leaving a business and arranges for the transportation of products (Ch. 4)

short order cook cooks and prepares foods that need only a short amount of preparation time; may take customer orders (Ch. 4)

singer performs vocal music as an individual or part of a group (Ch. 2, 4)

ski instructor teaches people to ski at a resort, ski school, or other recreational area (Ch. 1)

sketch artist creates drawings of people involved in legal cases or suspects in criminal cases (Ch. 2)

social and human services assistant helps psychologists or social workers provide services to clients; may develop, organize, and conduct programs to resolve substance abuse, relationship, or other problems (Ch. 4)

social worker provides services to clients to help them solve substance abuse, relationship, or other social problems (Ch. 2, 4, 6)

sociologist studies human society and behavior, including group behavior (Ch. 2)

special education teacher teaches students who have educational, emotional, mental, or physical needs (Ch. 2, 4)

speech-language pathologist diagnoses and treats people who have speech, language, voice, and fluency disorders (Ch. 4)

stage director plans and oversees movement of people and props on stage in a play, television show, or movie (Ch. 2)

stationary engineer runs and maintains industrial engines and mechanical equipment such as steam engines, generators, motors, and steam boilers (Ch. 4)

statistician studies and develops mathematical theories to gather and summarize numbers and data (Ch. 4)

store manager supervises employees at a retail store; oversees business activities such as ordering products and supplies, setting prices, arranging store displays, and paying bills (Ch. 2, 6)

structural iron and steel worker builds structures out of iron or steel such as buildings, building framework, and metal storage tanks (Ch. 4)

structural metal fabricator makes and puts together metal framework for machinery, ovens, tanks, and metal parts for buildings and bridges (Ch. 4)

surgeon performs medical surgery to treat diseases and injuries (Ch. 2)

surveyor measures land boundaries; collects data to create maps of land for mining, construction, and other purposes (Ch. 2, 4)

T

tax collector collects taxes from people or businesses in accordance with laws and regulations (Ch. 6)

tax preparer gets tax returns ready to send to people or businesses (Ch. 2, 6)

taxi driver transports passengers in automobiles or vans and collects fares from passengers (Ch. 2, 4)

teacher teaches students in a variety of settings from child care centers to colleges; may teach basic social and academic skills or higher educational courses such as mathematics, science, and social studies (Ch. 1–2, 6)

teacher assistant helps teachers instruct students and provide educational programs and services to students and parents; may prepare and grade assignments and talk with parents about students (Ch. 4)

technical illustrator creates technical drawings and diagrams for owner guides, operating and maintenance manuals, and repair instructions (Ch. 2)

technical writer writes materials for technical manuals such as owner guides, operating and maintenance manuals, and repair instructions (Ch. 2, 4)

telecommunications line installer strings telephone, television, and fiber optic cables for communication and television programming (Ch. 4)

telephone, power line, and cable repairer finds problems with and repairs telephone lines, power lines, and cable lines (Ch. 6)

television news producer plans and oversees activities involved in making television news program; may select news stories, oversee writing and directing, and arrange ways to pay for the production (Ch. 5) *See also* producer (Ch. 2), radio/TV/movie producer (Ch. 2, 4)

teller handles the exchange of money with customers; keeps records of money for a financial institution such as a bank or credit union (Ch. 2, 6) *See also* bank teller (Ch. 2)

therapist provides treatment of physical or emotional problems, diseases, or disorders (Ch. 6)

tile and marble setter installs wood, marble, and other hard tiles to walls, floors, ceilings, and roofs (Ch. 4)

tool and die maker creates and puts together parts to fix dies, cutting tools, jigs, and other hand tools used by machinists (Ch. 4)

tour guide takes people or groups of people to various tourist attractions and places of interest; provides background or historical information to tourists and visitors (Ch. 4)

tractor-trailer truck driver drives tractor-trailer trucks to transport products, livestock, mail, or other materials from one location to another (Ch. 4)

training and development specialist trains and educates workers at businesses or organizations (Ch. 4) *See also* corporate trainer (Ch. 4)

translator translates one language to another in writing, words, or sign language (Ch. 2, 4) *See also* interpreter (Ch. 4)

transportation attendant takes tickets, greets passengers, answers questions, and provides other services to make passengers aboard ships, buses, and trains feel safe and comfortable (Ch. 4)

travel agent organizes trips and vacations; sells transportation and lodging to customers (Ch. 2, 4)

truck driver drives trucks to transport products, livestock, mail, or other materials from one location to another (Ch. 2, 6)

truck driver, light or delivery services drives trucks or vans with a gross vehicle weight under 26,000 tons to deliver products or packages (Ch. 4)

V

veterinarian diagnoses and treats diseases or injuries in animals (Ch. 2, 5)

veterinarian technologist and technician cares for animals and assists veterinarian in treatment of animal diseases or injuries; may administer medications to animals and conduct laboratory tests (Ch. 4)

vocational counselor helps individuals with education and career planning (Ch. 2) *See also* counselor (Ch. 2, 6), educational counselor (Ch. 2), school counselor (Ch. 2, 4)

vocational education teacher teaches students vocational and occupational subjects such as woodworking, auto mechanics, and metal working (Ch. 4) *See also* vocational teacher (Ch. 2)

vocational teacher teaches students vocational and occupational subjects such as woodworking, auto mechanics, and metal working (Ch. 2) *See also* vocational education teacher (Ch. 4)

W

waiter/waitress takes customer orders and serves food and beverages at a bar, restaurant, cafeteria, or other dining establishment (Ch. 2, 4)

water treatment plant operator oversees the controls for a system that treats or transports water or liquid waste (Ch. 6)

Web site developer creates Web sites for individuals, businesses, or organizations by using computer programming languages or software (Ch. 2)

welders, production put together metal parts on a production line using welding equipment (Ch. 4)

well and core drill operator operates machines that drill wells or take rock samples from the earth (Ch. 4)

wholesale sales representative sells products and materials to businesses or people; acts as the wholesaler's or manufacturer's expert on material sold (Ch. 4) *See also* manufacturer's representative (Ch. 4)

word processor/typist uses a computer or typewriter to prepare final copies letters, reports, forms, and other written materials (Ch. 2, 4)

Z

zookeeper cares for and trains animals in zoos; may also supervise zoo workers and oversee activities such as accounting, marketing, and zoo management (Ch. 1)

Glossary

A

ability (ə bil′ ə tē) a talent; something a person is able to do well (p. 24)

achievement (ə chēv′ mənt) something you earn based on performance or something you do with success (p. 23)

action verb (ak shən vėrb) a word that shows action (p. 200)

addictive (ə dik′ tiv) habit forming (p. 262)

agriculture (ag′ rə kul chər) farming; producing crops and raising livestock (p. 80)

alcoholism (al′ kə hȯ liz əm) a disease in which a person is dependent on alcohol (p. 263)

apprenticeship (ə pren′ tis ship) on-the-job training to learn the skills required for a job (p. 78)

architecture (är′ kə tek chər) planning and designing buildings or other structures (p. 92)

assemble (ə sem′ bəl) to put together (p. 85)

attitude (at′ ə tüd) how someone thinks, feels, and acts (p. 177)

authority (ə thȯr′ ə tē) the power to enforce rules (p. 179)

automation (ȯ tə mā′ shən) the use of machines to do jobs that used to be done by people (p. 87)

B

business cycle (biz′ nis sī′ kəl) the pattern of ups and downs in production and need, supply and demand, in the economy (p. 11)

C

career (kə rir′) a job path one prepares for and follows for a lifetime (p. 7)

career group (kə rir′ grüp) occupations with related abilities, interests, and education requirements (p. 32)

chronological résumé (kron ə loj′ ə kəl rez ə mā′) a résumé that focuses on the history of an applicant's education and work experience (p. 201)

clergy (klėr′ jē) people who do religious work, such as priests, rabbis, ministers, nuns, or pastors (p. 113)

commodity (kə mod′ ə tē) something that is bought or sold (p. 123)

competency (kom′ pə tən sē) being able to do something well (p. 20)

construction (kən struk′ shən) the act of building (p. 92)

core services (kȯr ser′ vis iz) the 11 industries a community needs in order to function (p. 162)

corrections (kə rek′ shənz) field that involves the treatment and rehabilitation of prisoners in jails (p. 119)

cover letter (kuv′ər let′ ər) a one-page letter that you send with your résumé to introduce yourself to employers (p. 208)

D

database (dā′ tə bās) stored information (p. 102)

decision (di sizh′ ən) a choice to take action (p. 64)

developer (di vel′ ə pər) person who plans for putting up buildings on open land (p. 93)

diabetes (dī ə bē′ tēz) a disease in which the body is not able to use sugar from food (p. 260)

a	hat	e	let	ī	ice	ȯ	order	u̇	put	sh	she	ə	a	in about
ā	age	ē	equal	o	hot	oi	oil	ü	rule	th	thin		e	in taken
ä	far	ėr	term	ō	open	ou	out	ch	child	ᵺ	then		i	in pencil
â	care	i	it	ȯ	saw	u	cup	ng	long	zh	measure		o	in lemon
													u	in circus

diet (dī′ ət) the food that you regularly eat and drink (p. 258)

dilemma (də lem′ ə) a situation that requires a choice between two or more values (p. 266)

distribute (dis trib′ yüt) to move or give out goods and products to buyers or customers (p. 88)

drug (drug) any substance, other than food, that changes the way your mind and body work (p. 262)

E

economy (i kon′ ə mē) state of business of an area or country, including how resources are used for goods and services (p. 11)

engineering (en jə nir′ ing) the science of planning and building machines, tools, and transportation systems (p. 98)

ethics (eth′ iks) rules for behavior (p. 266)

extraction (ek strak′ shən) the pumping of oil and natural gas from underground (p. 82)

F

finance (fī′ nans) management of money (p. 123)

financial aid (fī nan′ shəl ād) money available to students to help pay for postsecondary education (p. 154)

freight (frāt) goods or products transported by truck, train, boat, or airplane (p. 88)

functional résumé (fungk′ shə nəl rez ə mā′) a résumé that focuses on the job tasks or skills that the applicant can perform (p. 201)

G

goal (gōl) a plan, an intention, or aim; something that a person want to get or reach (p. 64)

group values (grüp val′ yüz) the beliefs that a specific group of people considers to be important (p. 267)

H

hobby (hob′ ē) an activity done for enjoyment (p. 244)

hospitality (hos pə tal′ ə tē) taking care of guests or customers (p. 116)

I

industry (in′ də strē) a large-scale business or service area that provides a product or service (p. 76)

information technology (in fər mā′ shən tek nol′ ə jē) the way information is stored and used in a computer or computer system (p. 102)

informational interview (in fər mā′ shən əl in′ tər vjü) an opportunity to talk with someone at a business to gather information (p. 168)

interest (in′ tər ist) something you like, want to know more about, or want to see or do (p. 32)

interest rate (in′ tər ist rāt) a percentage of money charged for borrowing money (p. 11)

internship (in′ tèrn ship) doing work for an employer for a specified period of time to learn about an industry or occupation (p. 167)

investment (in vest′ mənt) time, effort, or money spent to get something in the future (p. 151)

J

job (job) a specific activity done for pay; employment (p. 3)

job security (job si kyür′ ə tē) an understanding that workers will not lose their jobs (p. 11)

L

leisure time (lē′ zhər tīm) free time away from work or school (p. 245)

logistics (lō jis′ tiks) planning and operations involved in moving people and products (p. 88)

a	hat	e	let	ī	ice	ȯ	order	ú	put	sh	she		a	in about
ā	age	ē	equal	o	hot	oi	oil	ü	rule	th	thin		e	in taken
ä	far	ėr	term	ō	open	ou	out	ch	child	ᵺ	then	ə	i	in pencil
â	care	i	it	ȯ	saw	u	cup	ng	long	zh	measure		o	in lemon
													u	in circus

M

manufacturing (man yə fak´ chə ring) turning raw material into products people use every day (p. 85)

manufacturing plant (man yə fak´ chə ring plant) a group of buildings where manufacturing happens (p. 85)

mining (mī´ ning) removing minerals from the earth (p. 82)

motivation (mō tə vā shən) an inner drive or encouragement from others for a person to act on or seek a goal (p. 68)

N

natural resources (nach´ ər əl rē´ sôr səz) minerals and other things found in nature (p. 80)

network (net´ wèrk) a group of computers linked together (p. 102)

networking (net´ wèr king) the exchange of information or services among individuals, groups, or institutions (p. 167)

nicotine (nik´ ə tēn) a chemical in tobacco to which people become addicted (p. 262)

nutrient (nü´ trē ənt) a substance in food that your body needs to work properly (p. 258)

O

obligation (ob lə gā´ shən) something that is required or must be done (p. 244)

occupation (ok yə pā´ shən) a group of similar or related jobs or job skills (p. 4)

offshore outsourcing (ȯf´ shȯr out´ sȯr sing) giving jobs to workers in countries outside the United States (p. 87)

option (op´ shən) a choice (p. 66)

P

personal goal statement (pėr´ sə nəl gōl stāt´ mənt) a description of a career goal along with the knowledge, abilities, skills, and personal values that are related to the goal (p. 194)

personal resources (pėr´ sə nəl rē´ sôr səz) the knowledge, skills, abilities, and personal values a person can use to be successful (p. 197)

physical fitness (fiz´ ə kəl fit´ nis) the body's ability to meet the demands of everyday living (p. 259)

portfolio (pôrt fō´ lē ō) a collection of evidence of planning, skills, competencies, achievements, letters of recommendation, résumés, references, jobs held, activities performed, and writing samples (p. 49)

postsecondary (pōst´ sek ən der ē) after high school (p. 148)

prestige (pre stēzh´) how important or valuable people believe something is (p. 5)

priority (prī ôr´ ə tē) something that is more important than something else (p. 65)

probability (prob ə bil´ ə tē) the likelihood that an event will happen (p. 66)

production worker (prə duk´ shən wèr kər) person who manufactures products (p. 85)

psychological (sī kə loj´ ə kəl) having to do with the mind or brain (p. 112)

psychologist (sī kol´ ə jist) someone who studies the mind and human behavior (p. 112)

R

recruitment (ri krüt´ mənt) getting a number of applications from which to choose new employees (p. 188)

reference (ref´ ər əns) someone who can share your skills, personal qualities, and job qualifications with an employer (p. 211)

a	hat	e	let	ī	ice	ȯ	order	u̇ put	sh she	a in about
ā	age	ē	equal	o	hot	oi	oil	ü rule	th thin	e in taken
ä	far	ėr	term	ō	open	ou	out	ch child	ᴛʜ then	ə { i in pencil
â	care	i	it	ȯ	saw	u	cup	ng long	zh measure	o in lemon
										u in circus

résumé (rez ə mā´) a summary of knowledge, abilities, and experience that shows how a person is qualified for a particular occupation (p. 188)

risk (risk) a chance of danger or loss (p. 40)

S

screening (skrē´ ning) going through a number of applications to pick out the most suitable people for a job opening (p. 188)

selection (si lek´ shən) choosing a person for a job opening (p. 188)

self-advocacy (self ad´ və kə sē) supporting, defending, or speaking up for yourself (p. 234)

self-assessment (self ə ses´ mənt) finding out your strengths and weaknesses (p. 20)

self-confidence (self kon´ fə dəns) feeling good about oneself (p. 24)

sexually transmitted disease (sek´ shü ə lē tranz mit´ təd də zēz´) any disease that is spread through sexual activity (p. 261)

skill (skil) something you can do that comes from training or practice (p. 20)

software (sȯft´ wâr) program that tells a computer what to do (p. 104)

stereotype (ster´ ē ə tīp) general belief about a person or group of people that is not necessarily true (p. 6)

stress (stress) a state of physical or emotional pressure (p. 244)

symptom (simp´ təm) a physical sign or indication that you have an illness (p. 259)

T

technology (tek nol´ ə jē) the use of science to create new products or make old ones better (p. 98)

time management (tīm man´ ij mənt) the best use of your time to achieve your goals (p. 252)

tourism (tùr´ iz əm) business of providing services to visitors and travelers (p. 116)

U

unemployed (un em ploid´) to be without a job (p. 12)

universal values (yü nə vėr´ səl val´ yüz) the beliefs that most people in many societies all over the world consider important (p. 268)

V

value (val´ yü) what is important to a person (p. 38)

W

wage (wāj) a set amount of money earned per hour of work (p. 56)

wage equity (wāj ek´ wə tē) men and women earn the same amount of money for doing the same job (p. 57)

work (wėrk) what people do or how they spend their time to earn a living (p. 2)

workplace (wėrk plās) where work is done (p. 8)

work value (wėrk val´ yü) something people want to get our of a job or that brings them job satisfaction (p. 39)

a	hat	e	let	ī	ice	ȯ	order	ù	put	sh	she	ə {	a	in about
ā	age	ē	equal	o	hot	oi	oil	ü	rule	th	thin		e	in taken
ä	far	ėr	term	ō	open	ou	out			ᵺ	then		i	in pencil
â	care	i	it	ȯ	saw	u	cup	ng	long	zh	measure		o	in lemon
													u	in circus

Index

C

P

T

U

Photo Credits

Cover images: (inset and background center) © Royalty-Free CORBIS, (background lower left) © Lawrence Lawry/PhotoDisc/Getty Images; p. xxvi, © Ron Chapple/Thinkstock/Alamy Images; p. 2, © Syracuse Newspapers/Suzanne Dunn/The Image Works, Inc.; p. 3 (left), © Natalie Fobes/CORBIS; p. 3 (center), © Spencer Grant/PhotoEdit; p. 3 (right), © Mitch Wojnarowicz/The Image Works, Inc.; p. 5, © Wayne Eardley/Masterfile; p. 8, © Paul A. Souders/CORBIS; p. 10, © Mark Richards/PhotoEdit; p. 14, © Jeff Greenberg/PhotoEdit; p. 18, © JIStock/Masterfile; p. 22, © Tom Stewart/CORBIS; p. 24, © Noel Hendrickson/Masterfile; pp. 26, 30, © AP/Wide World Photos; p. 28, © Lester Lefkowitz/CORBIS; p. 34, © Kathy McLaughlin/The Image Works, Inc.; p. 38, © Peter Beck/CORBIS; p. 43, © Rob Gage Photography/ImageState; pp. 47, 138, 231, 255, © David Young-Wolff/PhotoEdit; p. 54, © Eureka Slide/SuperStock, Inc.; p. 56, © Jose Luis Pelaez, Inc./CORBIS; p. 61, © Eric K. K. Yu/CORBIS; p. 62, © Getty Images; p. 65, © CORBIS; p. 68, © Dick Young/Unicorn Stock Photos; p. 74, © Maximilian Stock Ltd./Photo Researchers, Inc.; p. 92, © XINHUA/CORBIS; pp. 118, 182, © Michael Newman/PhotoEdit; p. 142, © Richard T. Nowitz/CORBIS; p. 144, © Rainbow; p. 150, © Lawrence Sawyer/Index Stock Imagery; p. 157, © Thinkstock; p. 160, © Jonathan Nourok/PhotoEdit/PictureQuest; p. 169, © Bruce Forster/Stone/Getty Images; p. 179, © Stewart Cohen/Getty Images; p. 180, © Stone/Getty Images; p. 186, © James Leynse/CORBIS SABA; p. 190, © Bob Daemmrich/PhotoEdit; p. 194, © Brad Wrobleski/Masterfile; p. 204, © Tony Freeman/PhotoEdit; p. 218, © Martin Barraud/Image Bank/Getty Images; p. 223, © Matthew Wiley/Masterfile; p. 239, © Bob Daemmrich/The Image Works, Inc.; p. 242, © Rolf Bruderer/Masterfile; p. 246, © Tony Savino/The Image Works, Inc.; page 251, © Myrleen Ferguson Cate/PhotoEdit; page 273, © Peter Griffith/Masterfile; p. 276, © Richard Berenholtz/CORBIS; p. 280, © Image Bank/Getty Images; p. 282, © Elyse Lewin/Image Bank/Getty Images